The Migration of Peoples from the Caribbean to the Bahamas

UNIVERSITY PRESS OF FLORIDA

Florida A&M University, Tallahassee
Florida Atlantic University, Boca Raton
Florida Gulf Coast University, Ft. Myers
Florida International University, Miami
Florida State University, Tallahassee
New College of Florida, Sarasota
University of Central Florida, Orlando
University of Florida, Gainesville
University of North Florida, Jacksonville
University of South Florida, Tampa
University of West Florida, Pensacola

The

Migration of Peoples from the Caribbean to the Bahamas

Keith L. Tinker

University Press of Florida

Gainesville · Tallahassee · Tampa · Boca Raton

Pensacola · Orlando · Miami · Jacksonville · Ft. Myers · Sarasota

16 15 14 13 12 11   6 5 4 3 2 1

Library of Congress Cataloging-in-Publication Data
Tinker, Keith L.
The migration of peoples from the Caribbean to the Bahamas / Keith L. Tinker.
p. cm.
Includes bibliographical references and index.
ISBN 978-0-8130-3531-4 (alk. paper)
1. Bahamas—Emigration and immigration—Social aspects.
2. West Indians—Bahamas. I. Title.
JV7329.3.T56 2010
304.8'72960729—dc22
2010023262

The University Press of Florida is the scholarly publishing agency for the State
University System of Florida, comprising Florida A&M University, Florida Atlantic
University, Florida Gulf Coast University, Florida International University, Florida
State University, New College of Florida, University of Central Florida, University
of Florida, University of North Florida, University of South Florida, and University
of West Florida.

University Press of Florida
15 Northwest 15th Street
Gainesville, FL 32611-2079
http://www.upf.com

Contents

Illustrations

Figures

Tables

Preface and Acknowledgments

One of the most rewarding experiences for any Caribbean historian is to participate in the revelation of the story of the demographic history of Caribbean peoples. This experience becomes especially emphatic when it is revealed that the history of the region is based on a dramatic series of continuous migrations and immigrations. And so it becomes particularly rewarding for this Bahamian historian to be the first to systematically trace the story of the migration of groups of Caribbean peoples to the island nation he calls home.

I first became interested in this subject of Caribbean migration to the Bahamas in the early 1990s, after becoming acquainted with the works of Franklin Knight, Gordon K. Lewis, and Bonham Richardson. In the late 1970s into the early 1980s, I was primarily tutored by Jamaicans, whose significant numerical presence in the public school system in the Bahamas—along with Trinidadian prison overseers, Haitian tailors, and Guyanese surveyors—I questioned, but did not understand until I read the works of Knight and Richardson, and discovered that the presence of these people was but one physical expression of the traditional history of Caribbean peoples constantly moving between metropoles in search of economic opportunity and political asylum.

Today, the population of the Bahamas is widely represented by peoples of Caribbean descent in every sphere of society: civics, religion, arts, and politics. For example, the first prime minister of the independent Bahamas was the son of a Jamaican immigrant; the first president of the national College of the Bahamas was Guyanese; and the first attorney general of the independent Bahamas was the son of St. Lucian immigrants.

This work was made easy by the support of my colleagues Ruth Adderley-Forbes, Grace Turner, and Kim Outten Stubbs of the National Museum of the Bahamas, who served as sounding boards for my initial discussion on this subject. My inspiration, however, came from my family, including my wife and sons, who were especially supportive and patient with my frequent distraction from familial obligations and experiences.

Introduction

Generally, scholarship has neglected the role of West Indian migration to the Bahamas. In fact, few scholars have deemed it important to include the Bahamas in their research of West Indian history, except to briefly mention the islands as the site of Columbus's first landfall in the Americas or its economic position as a popular tourist destination and an international financial center. One result of the limited scholarship is that today few people are aware that the Bahamas has a history of migration that saw it oscillate between the positions of a predominantly "sending society" and of a "receiving society" (albeit on a comparatively small scale). Bahamians must bear some of the blame for this exclusion, since traditionally most dislike being identified as West Indian. As early as 1812, William Wylly, the Bahamian attorney general, stated that "the People of this Colony do not consider themselves to be West Indians" [GB/COR, The Bahamas, *Colonial Secretary's Office Papers*, No. 23, item 63. "William Wylly to Zachary Macaulay, April 15, 1812." Enclosure in "Charles Cameron to Earl Bathhurst, January 24, 1816." (Nassau: Public Records Office, 1971)]. The perception persisted into the twentieth century, causing Sir Alan Burns to comment that, despite the geographical fact that the Bahamas is a part of the West Indies, Bahamians persistently reject that identity (Burns 1948:93).

The Bahamas, even with its history of colonization and African slavery, did not experience the wider effects of a predominantly agro-culture that continues to define societies and economics throughout the region (Lewis 1968). Instead, the Bahamian economy and culture has historically featured a system of extractive commercialism in which the labor force (primarily, but not exclusively black) was effectively controlled by a white mercantile elite which monopolized employment, land, mechanisms of production, access to capital, and state power (Johnson 1991:vi). The elite used its political control to implement a system of immigration designed to protect its socioeconomic interests. Under the system, groups of professional and unskilled West Indians were recruited mainly from Barbados, Jamaica, the Turks and Caicos Islands, and Haiti to supplement the local labor force.

One of the primary objectives of this volume is to examine the history of West Indian migration to the Bahamas. The evidence examined demonstrates the need for a revision of some of the generalizations scholars have made concerning the Bahamas, Bahamians have made of West Indians in general, and Bahamians have made of themselves in particular. Another objective is to examine the "Bahamian identity" and the geographical, political, economic, and social position of the islands within the region. The final objective is to fit the Bahamian migration experience into the broader historical, cultural, and geographic framework of traditional West Indian migration. Reaching these objectives will establish a foundation upon which further research on Bahamian labor migration and identity is based, one of the least known, often understated, yet important aspects of the history of West Indian migration.

The first chapter presents a brief historical review of emigration from the West Indies since Emancipation. It demonstrates how Emancipation provided the ex-slaves with the limited freedom of mobility to choose employers and places of employment. The chapter does not examine migration from all West Indian countries such as the non-English speaking countries. For example, it does not mention the movements from Puerto Rico to Santo Domingo, Cuba, Venezuela, and Guatemala that began in the 1870s (Palmer 1990:13–43). Instead, in keeping with the thesis of the research, it focuses exclusively on migration from the English-speaking Caribbean and Haiti. Haiti is included because Haitians represent the single largest migrant group in the Bahamas.

Chapter 2 explores the influence of Spanish and British imperialism on the population of the Bahamas from the 1490s to the 1770s and from the American Revolution onward. It discusses the role of the United States in sending settlers to and receiving settlers from the Bahamas. The chapter begins with a study of the indigenous population of the Bahamas, and their annihilation within thirty years of "discovery" by Spanish marauders seeking slaves for labor, primarily in Cuba and Española. The islands remained virtually unpopulated until they became an English possession in 1629, and were subsequently colonized in 1647 by a group of religious dissidents from Bermuda. Other groups from Bermuda and the Carolinas followed and established cotton and tobacco plantations, so that by 1670 the population of the islands had increased to over one thousand. More than 80 percent of the population resided on New Providence. During the remainder of the seventeenth and early eighteenth centuries, lax colonial administration and geographical location along the shipping lanes resulted in the transformation of Nassau into a haven for pirate activity.

The aftermath of the American Revolution significantly affected the demographic, social, and economic life of the Bahamas. Between 1783 and 1789, over 2,000 Loyalists and their slaves migrated to the islands from destinations in New York, the Carolinas, Georgia, and Florida. The influx trebled the population and increased the proportion of blacks from 50 to 75 percent. The Loyalists, with enthusiasm and vigor, established the city of Nassau and substantially increased commercial and social activities in the islands. The émigrés used generous Crown land grants to re-create American plantation lifestyles on New Providence and the outlying islands. By the early 1800s, however, a combination of factors that included insect infestation and infertile soil combined to destroy the plantation systems. Some Loyalists migrated to other destinations, while those remaining adopted the subsistence lifestyle of the earlier settlers, including small-scale farming, fishing, and wrecking.

The post-Emancipation period witnessed a search for a more secure economic base. Thousands of slaves were virtually free to chart their own destinies. Shanty communities were established just beyond the city limits to accommodate first the liberated Africans and later the new citizens. The economically depressed post-Emancipation years, however, produced an atmosphere of uncertainty among the general population. Some Bahamians produced agricultural and marine products, such as pineapples, salt, and sponges for export primarily to Europe and the United States. Others, however, including many young black men, migrated to Florida, Central, and South America in search of improved employment opportunities. The Bahamian outward migration was simultaneous with a larger West Indian labor migration, which sent waves of workers to similar destinations including (to a lesser degree) the Bahamas.

Chapter 3 explores the migration of small groups of Barbadians to the Bahamas. Beginning in the 1890s, there were three small waves of Barbadian migration to the Bahamas, and in 1892, systematic migration began when forty-two Barbadians were recruited as constables to replace the

West Indian Regiment troops stationed in the colony. The constables, generally encouraged by the Bahamian white minority, quickly demonstrated prejudices against the less-educated local police and black Bahamian majority. Consequently, the Barbadians became the objects of distrust and occasional aggression by black Bahamians. The simmering animosity began to fade after the police and constabulary forces were equitably amalgamated by the Police Act of 1908. The recruitment of Barbadian men, mostly as police and later as prison officers, continued until the 1930s, when systematic migration was interrupted by the events of World War II.

During the 1920s, groups of Barbadian skilled artisans responded to job opportunities created by the development of public and private projects in New Providence. The artisans, mostly carpenters and masons, worked on the construction of new hotels, public projects, and private homes throughout the island. The Barbadians contributed substantially to the revival of the apprenticeship system, under which many young Bahamian artisans were trained. From the 1940s into the 1960s, many apprentices eventually became the leading artisans in the country. Some Barbadian artisans migrated to North America and England after the construction boom ended in the early 1930s. Those who remained became absorbed into Bahamian society.

The third group of Barbadians, mainly recruits for the police and prison services, immigrated to the Bahamas during the 1950s and 1960s. They differed from former groups in several respects. First, they were older than the earlier groups with an average age of twenty-four. Second, most were previously employed in Barbados as low to mid-level professionals; most resolved to use employment in the Bahamas as a steppingstone to North America and England. Third, the majority of the latter immigrants remained in the Bahamas. Some married local women or "imported" wives from Barbados and either transferred to other sectors of the public service or resigned to work in the private sector. Barbadians contributed significantly to the development of society, politics, and economics in the Bahamas. Generally, the Barbadian experience in the Bahamas exemplified an unassuming modesty in the face of obviously significant contributions to the social, economic, and political development of their adopted country.

Chapter 4 traces the history of Jamaican migration to the Bahamas from the 1920s to Bahamian Independence in 1973. It demonstrates how illegal Jamaican migration into the colony created serious labor imbalances, motivated public resentment against Jamaicans, and forced colonial officials to implement restrictive immigration laws. The nearly xenophobic Bahamian reaction to the Jamaican-led West Indian migration of the early decades of this century demonstrated a carefully considered Bahamian immigration policy of "open doors" when convenient for Bahamians and "closed doors" when they perceived a threat to employment and the social status quo.

Small numbers of Jamaicans illegally migrated to the Bahamas during the 1920s and 1930s. Many came as skilled artisans and educators. Some, however, engaged in a variety of criminal activities. Evidence suggests some paid relatively large sums of money to be smuggled into the colony. Others, recruited for employment in one specific area, absconded to more lucrative jobs. Some illegal Jamaican women engaged in prostitution and became the concubines and wives of Bahamian men and skilled artisans. Some Jamaicans relocated to the outer islands, where they assumed new identities.

Despite their small numbers, Jamaicans significantly affected economics, society, and politics in the colony. During the 1920s, immigrant skilled artisans introduced black Bahamians to innovations in modern construction. The artisans provided a supply of skilled labor that resolved an existing labor shortage and facilitated economic development in New Providence. More importantly, their professionalism provided a model for aspiring black Bahamians. Most Jamaican artisans remained in the colony for an average of five years, and then departed to other countries in search of employment opportunity.

In the late 1920s, Bahamian colonial officials introduced immigration restrictions that appeared to especially target Jamaicans. The new immigration laws responded to growing public protest over competition from West Indians for limited jobs. Despite protests from the Jamaican press and others, the restrictions eventually prohibited the entry of most skilled artisans into the colony. Thereafter, Jamaican immigration was reduced to a small number of professionals recruited primarily for the government service. Many others, however, came as visitors, gained illegal employment, and overstayed the time allotted for their visits.

Perhaps the most significant Jamaican contribution was made to the development of politics and society. Evidence suggests that the early artisans—primarily through the establishment of trade unions—encouraged black Bahamians to resist white political and social domination (Saunders 1991:78–85). In the 1920s, Jamaican artisans collaborated with black Bahamians to facilitate Marcus Garvey's appearance at a predominantly black political rally. According to one report, Garvey addressed what was reportedly the largest crowd ever assembled for an event in Bahamian history, galvanizing black Bahamians to address the social, economic, and political barriers that separated them from the white elite (Saunders 1991:78–85).

A small number of Jamaicans were recruited to develop a new approach to agriculture in the Bahamas. The horticulture and agriculture teachers introduced a variety of new plants to the colony. The agriculture teachers, in particular, were recruited by the colonial authorities and Bahamian elite for the (controversial) purpose of encouraging out-island youth to remain in the rural islands and become self-employed in agricultural production. Consequently, agricultural education had the long-term effect of discouraging educational initiatives as it served to curb mass migration from the outer islands to New Providence.

Chapter 5 examines early Haitian migration to the Bahamas. Historically, since the first group of aborigines migrated northward from northwestern Española, the Bahamas and Haiti have been linked by centuries of mutual trade and migration. The Bahamian-Haitian linkage was heightened during the Haitian Revolution, when hundreds of white St. Domingans and their slaves were forcibly migrated to the Bahamas aboard privateers. The new immigrants significantly influenced politics and economics in the colony. Many became wards of the state. Others, in rebellion against confinement aboard prison ships and forced exile in the Bahamas, staged many attempts to escape. Invariably, the escape methods devised, together with the presence of a large number of non-white foreigners in the colony, created discontent and fear among the white Bahamians. The Haitian refugees were mostly resettled in islands in the southern Bahamas away from Nassau.

During the post-Emancipation period and into the nineteenth century, Haitian sloops laden with agricultural produce and rum traded for a variety of European and U.S. manufactured goods at southern Bahamian ports. Merchants and traders from the southern Bahamas engaged in reciprocal trade with Haiti. Before the 1950s, few Haitians attempted to settle in the Bahamas and few Bahamians settled in Haiti. Beginning in the late 1950s, however, the balance of the relationship began to shift, as the Bahamas became economically prosperous, while Haiti became increasingly economically depressed under the Duvalier dictatorships. The patterns of Haitian trade shifted from the southern to the northern Bahamas, and primarily to the islands of New Providence, Grand Bahama, and Abaco. Additionally, an influx of illegal immigrants arrived aboard trading sloops. Bahamian officials initiated a series of restrictive immigration policies to control Haitian migration.

Chapter 6 explores later Haitian migration to the Bahamas after the 1950s. It discusses the restrictive immigration policies aimed at Haitians initiated during the 1950s and early 1960s by the predominantly white United Bahamian Party government and later during the late 1960s and early 1970s by the predominantly black government of the Progressive Liberal Party (PLP). In the Bahamas, illegal Haitian immigration has become a perennial problem that defies simple remedial action. A major, often ignored, factor in the immigration equation is Bahamian ambivalence and complicity. Steve Dodge aptly characterized the history of the "illegal, officially unwanted, but apparently necessary" Haitian laborer in the Bahamas. Dodge noted that "the Haitians perform useful work disdained by most Bahamians. They provide low-cost, agricultural labor, collect garbage, scrape boat bottoms, and do other heavy and menial chores" (Dodge 1983 [1968]). Many Bahamians demand increased Haitian repatriation exercises, yet continue to hire the illegal aliens to perform menial tasks at low wages. The chapter concludes that as long as the Bahamas remains politically and economically stable, and Haiti continues to experience economic and political maladies, the "Haitian Problem" will persist.

Chapter 7 discusses the migration of Turks and Caicos islanders to the Bahamas. It attempts to explain why Turks and Caicos islanders were able to more successfully assimilate into Bahamian society than other West Indian immigrants. Attracted by jobs in the lumber industry in the north and in the shipping industry in the southern islands, hundreds of Turks and Caicos islanders migrated to the Bahamas, beginning in the 1890s. Official records and interviews with immigrants and their descendents provide details. However, contributions by Turks and Caicos islanders to the broader patterns of Bahamian society, economy, and politics are not fully known.

The Turks and Caicos Islands were settled in the 1500s by the combined efforts of "salt rakers" from Bermuda and Loyalists from Georgia. In 1799, after invasions by Spanish and French forces, the English claimed the islands and placed them under the political supervision of the Bahamas. In 1848, in response to repeated requests from the inhabitants, the islands were separated from the Bahamas and allowed self-government. Efforts at self-government, however, failed and in 1873 the Turks and Caicos Islands became a dependency of Jamaica. The political dependency lasted until 1962, when Jamaica became an independent country. The islands renewed political affiliation with Jamaica. Later negotiations between the governments of Great Britain and the Bahamas to politically annex the Turks and Caicos as a part of the Bahamas were rejected by the latter. Today, the Turks and Caicos continue as a British colony.

In the 1890s, Turks and Caicos islanders began a steady migration to the Bahamas. Initially, the migration was to islands in the southern Bahamas, where immigrants sought employment as deck hands and stevedores on ships transporting cargo between ports on the eastern coast of the United States and destinations in the Caribbean, Central, and South America. During the early 1900s, immigrants sought employment in the salt industry at Inagua. Some immigrants returned to their home islands after employment opportunities failed, but most remained and settled in the southern Bahamas. By 1920, scores of immigrants began to migrate to Nassau where construction was booming and employment as laborers was available. Beginning in 1906 and continuing into the 1970s, hundreds of Turks and Caicos islanders were recruited to work in the lumber industries in the northern Bahamian islands of Andros, Abaco, and Grand Bahama. Some immigrants used the Bahamas as a migration conduit to the United States, while many others settled in New Providence. Some settled in Grand Bahama, where they eventually established permanent communities such as Pine Ridge and Seagrape.

Chapter 8 explores aspects of West Indian immigration to the Bahamas after Independence in 1973. It focuses specifically on the Guyanese, who were the last major group to immigrate, and Haitians, who continue to comprise the largest and most significant group of West Indian immigrants in the Bahamas. In the aftermath of Independence, an official immigration program of "Bahamianization" influenced migration to the Bahamas. Essentially, Bahamianization was attempted by the government to control the recruitment of non-Bahamian labor into the country. Specifically targeted under this program were white foreigners recruited by the Grand Bahama Port Authority, Haitians, and Jamaicans.

During the 1980s, hundreds of Guyanese were recruited to teach in the Bahamas. In 1946, Guyanese were first recruited for employment in the colony as policemen. The recruits, ex-servicemen from the last world war, displayed antipathy toward the social values of the local white elite. Perhaps because of this antipathy, no other Guyanese policemen were recruited. Later, in the 1960s and 1970s, Guyanese were recruited to work as surveyors and in public legal agencies. The early surveyors were largely responsible for charting much of the islands. Many used employment in the Bahamas as an avenue for re-migration to North America. Those remaining established private real estate and surveying practices that are among the most prestigious in the Bahamas today. The Guyanese professionals recruited included draftsmen and judges, and notably, a former chief justice of the Bahamas. Teachers represented the largest category of Guyanese immigrants to the Bahamas. Most were recruited during the 1980s when the Guyanese economy was unstable and the government of the Bahamas was involved in a protracted dispute with public school teachers. Many Bahamian and Jamaican public school teachers left the public service for employment in other professions or at other schools. The resignation of large numbers of Bahamian and foreign teachers from the public service created a vacuum, which the recruitment of Guyanese teachers was designed to fill. Simultaneously, the new recruits formed a buffer between the government and the disgruntled teachers.

After Independence, large numbers of illegal Haitians continued to migrate to the Bahamas. By 1974, it was estimated that more than 40,000 Haitians lived in the country, which had a population of just over 200,000. Generally, most Haitian immigrants lived in communities on the islands of New Providence, Grand Bahama, Abaco, and Eleuthera. The immigrants were subjected to different experiences on each island. In New Providence, for example, many Haitians lived in communities isolated from the center of town, where they built shanties and existed at substandard levels. Others rented miserable accommodations in predominantly poor black communities, where they were forced to constantly avoid official detection, but where they had easier access to employment as laborers in the service industries and gardeners on private properties.

Generally, Haitians on Grand Bahama were able to assimilate into the local society more rapidly than Haitians living on other islands, including New Providence. This phenomenon is partially explained by the fact that Haitian migration to Grand Bahama was simultaneous with that of their Bahamian and non-Bahamian neighbors. Many Haitians in Grand Bahama, who have married Bahamians, raised children, and live in low-income communities, are generally accepted as social equals by their neighbors. Some have established businesses and relocated to more affluent neighborhoods. Second and third generation Haitian-Bahamians have anglicized their names to become virtually undistinguishable from other Bahamians.

Haitians in Abaco are mostly agricultural laborers employed on large farms. Most live in squalid shanty communities, such as the Mud and Pigeon Peas located on the fringes of the city of Marsh Harbour. The communities are not equipped with basic amenities such as water, electricity, and proper sanitation facilities. The immigrants are relegated to a subservient social role and constantly reminded of their place in society. Some live in the woods in small makeshift communities and subsist largely on the sale and use of produce grown on small farms. Their mostly white employers protect the Abaconian Haitians from raids by immigration authorities.

Most Haitians in Eleuthera live on Russell Island, a small cay located at the northern end of the island. They are employed primarily by their white "neighbors" on Spanish Wells, for whom most work and, perhaps, all are indebted. Their physical environment is considerably more improved than in other Haitian enclaves throughout the archipelago. Generally, their houses are neatly maintained and equipped with basic amenities such as water, electricity, and indoor plumbing. Haitians living on the mainland of Eleuthera, in contrast, squat in unauthorized shanties built on public and private lands. Their existence is uncertain, largely because they are compelled to eke out an existence among predominantly hostile neighbors who generally resent their presence.

The Afterword examines perceptions of Bahamian and West Indian identity. It affirms the belief that migration is essentially a widely accepted aspect of the West Indian experience in which all West Indians, including Bahamians, are descendants of immigrants and *dramatis personae* in an essentially dynamic historic-social experience. The section summarizes aspects of the history of West Indian migration from the pre-Columbian era, through European colonization and Emancipation and into the twentieth century. It places migration to the Bahamas within the wider historical context of West Indian migration, explaining the causes and effects of migration from the English-speaking West Indies and Haiti to the Bahamas within the context of Bahamian self-perception. To achieve this goal, it examines the influence of geographical proximity and historical linkages to the United States and the resultant "Americanization" of the islands. It argues that a number of factors—including the process of Americanization—have combined to influence traditional discrimination against West Indians and argues that the anti-West Indian sentiment is a reaction based on the fear that continued West Indian (especially Haitian) migration could eventually adulterate Bahamian culture and possibly supplant its identity. Recognizing failure of the deterrence traditionally used by Bahamian authorities, it concludes that an official process of social acceptance and systematic assimilation could begin to solve the Haitian problem in the Bahamas and re-create a more socioculturally realistic and acceptable Bahamian identity.

1

British West Indian Migration

Interterritorial Migration in the Post-Emancipation Era, 1835–1880

Caribbean history includes a continuous flood of people into and out of the region resulting in a patchwork of races and cultures. European occupation, forced African migration, slavery, indentured servitude, and modern outward migrations to metropoles have combined to create a legacy of a region constantly in flux. This chapter will present a brief historical overview of migration from the Anglophone Caribbean since Emancipation in the 1830s granted the newly freed the mobility to leave plantations—a right they exercised frequently during the succeeding 150 years. Occasional comparisons will demonstrate how most of the non-English speaking Caribbean societies have had similar experiences.

The English-speaking, or Commonwealth, Caribbean (Figure 1.1) (comprising former British colonies) is comparatively small by global standards. Guyana (the former British Guiana) on the mainland is the largest country, covering a total land area of 83,000 square miles (population 734,000). Next in listed size are Jamaica (population 2.5 million) and the two-island country of Trinidad and Tobago (population 1.3 million), with areas of 4,411 and 1,980 square miles respectively. The sizes of the other countries range from Dominica, covering 305 square miles (population 86,500), to Montserrat with just 33 square miles (population 12,600) (*Goode's World Atlas* 1996). More than one half of the populations—55 percent in 1996—live in urban areas. However, some countries have large rural populations and limited lands for non-agricultural use. Urban populations range from highs of 70 to 80 percent in the Bahamas, Cuba, and Martinique to lows of 20 to 30 percent in Haiti and St. Vincent

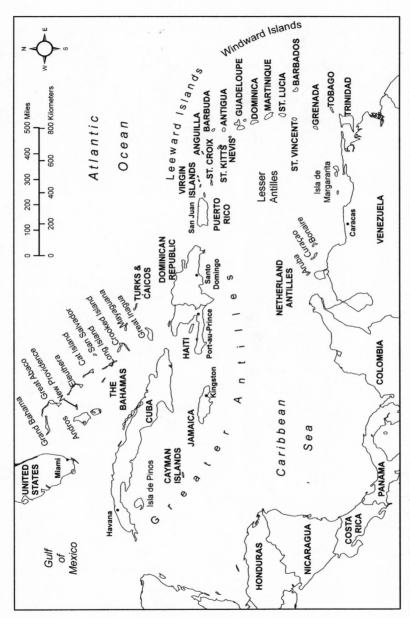

Figure 1.1. The West Indies.

and the Grenadines (*Goode's World Atlas* 1996). Limited resources and opportunity in the region combine to make the impact of migration on the development of these countries significant.

Historically, the first emigration after Emancipation proved to be the precedent for the continuous movements that followed. Initially, many former slaves moved away from the plantations, first to small communities on the periphery of the towns and plantations and eventually to other islands. Statistics for most islands demonstrate significant decreases in the sizes of plantation labor forces in the post-Emancipation period. For example, of the estimated 22,359 slaves living and working on plantations in Trinidad and Tobago, only 8,000 remained after Emancipation (Hall 1978:7–22). Although most ex-slaves found it necessary to continue working on plantations in the post-Emancipation period, many decided to exercise their new freedom of mobility and seek employment on plantations other than those operated by their former masters (Richardson 1983).

In 1835, the "newer" British colonies of Trinidad and Tobago and British Guiana offered opportunity for thousands of laborers, primarily to clear virgin lands for the cultivation of sugarcane. Spain held Trinidad and Tobago from 1498, when Columbus claimed the islands for Spain, until 1797 when Britain captured the territory. Trinidad and Tobago was formally ceded to Britain under the terms of the Treaty of Amiens in 1802. In the seventeenth century the Dutch developed a swampy strip of seacoast in what is today Guyana by establishing trading posts at Essequibo, Demerara, and Berbice. After continued dispute, the Netherlands ceded the territory to Great Britain in 1814 under the terms of the Treaty of London. In 1831 Great Britain unified the three territories as the colony of British Guiana, with Stabroek renamed Georgetown as the capital. The name "Guyana" was officially adopted after independence in 1966 (Dunn 1973:15–23). Planters in both territories employed agents to recruit labor from the neighboring "older" British islands, luring laborers to the territories with the offer of attractive wages. Trinidadian planters reportedly "adopted a bounty system in which they paid captains of sailing vessels for each laborer imported, and in addition fringe benefits such as free passage and land for cultivation were also offered" (Marshall 1982:17). Immigrants to the new territories generally came from the eastern Caribbean islands, with most immigrants to British Guiana coming from Barbados.

Initially, planters and colonial authorities in the sending societies protested the interterritorial migration, and in 1838 the Barbadian authorities passed two laws to restrict emigration in hopes of controlling migration from the island. The colonial authorities voiced concern for the welfare of the "inexperienced" and "disadvantaged" ex-slaves, many of whom were allegedly vulnerable to the fraudulent practices of some recruiting agents. Marshall may be correct in her assessment of the paternalistic attitude some post-Emancipation British colonial officials may have exhibited toward their charges. However, she may have overlooked the fact that by 1838, many freedmen had already experienced fraudulent employment practices by former and new employers wishing to retain or obtain their services (Levy 1980). It is reasonable to suspect that these authorities were more concerned about the adverse effect emigration must have had on their own labor markets than the fortunes of the newly freed (Marshall 1982:17). However, for the most part, the efforts to curb emigration failed.

The post-Emancipation years were difficult for the newly emancipated. Occurrences during the period helped encourage many of the newly freed to emigrate. The initial euphoria of freedom began to dissipate as the harsh realities of subsistence in a wage-earning environment began to dawn. Most planters opposed emancipation and continued to treat their employees as chattel property. Much of the arable land was controlled by the planters, leaving very little for the newly freed to use.

Conditions worsened when the Sugar Duties Act of 1846 removed the protection of West Indian sugar on the British market. Wages on plantations plummeted as a result. In the 1860s, extensive droughts plagued the eastern Caribbean and worsened already economically depressed conditions. The adverse economic conditions caused many planters and island officials to accept emigration as a reaction to local economic malaise (Marshall 1986:6–14). In 1871, the colonial government in Barbados began to encourage migration as a viable response to the economic depression afflicting that island. In 1873, legislation was enacted to assist the migration of the poorer classes (Marshall 1986:8–9). Active discouragement of emigration gave way to a policy of active encouragement.

Emigrants were generally young, adult males with experience working on sugar plantations, as such workers were the most actively recruited by both sending and receiving societies. They were required to sign and honor annual contracts to assure a labor force throughout the year, but many workers deliberately reneged on contracts and arrived in the territories after June when the cane harvest season in their home-islands had passed and employment had become scarce. Traditionally, they returned to their homes to enjoy Christmas with family and friends (Marshall 1986:8–9).

Migration to Non-British Destinations, 1880s–1919

Movements to non-British territories became significant in the mid-1880s. Destinations included Cuba and the Dominican Republic for work on the expanding sugar plantations; Central America for employment on banana plantations and railroads; and the United States in search of the "Yankee dollar." In all cases, the movements were in direct response to a demand for labor created by expansion in U.S. foreign investments, and an escape from economic depression at home. The nexus between human migration and capital migration was becoming inextricable in Caribbean migration.

European and North American beet sugar entered the world market during the 1880s and 1890s in direct competition with West Indian sugarcane. Beet sugar, heavily subsidized by European governments, subsequently sold more cheaply than cane sugar. In 1884, Britain imported large quantities of German beet sugar, thus creating a drastic fall in the value of West Indian sugar from 30 to 20 shillings per ton. Although cane sugar continued to be important in the United States, in the 1890s the U.S. government gave preferential sugar duties to Brazil, Cuba, the Dominican Republic, and Puerto Rico, and discontinued the purchase of West Indian sugar. Perez noted that the terms of the 1891 Foster-Canovas agreement, which granted reciprocal trade arrangements between Cuba and the United States, resulted in the expansion of sugar production from 623,000 tons in 1890 to one million tons in 1894 (Perez 1988:149). These arrangements were intensified during the imperial expansion of the United States in the Caribbean in the early twentieth century.

A combination of natural disasters and the outbreak of cane disease also affected sugarcane production in the islands. Hurricanes devastated Barbados in 1898 and Montserrat and Nevis in 1899. In 1902, the Soufriere volcano on St. Vincent erupted, claiming 2,000 lives and destroying large amounts of arable land. Between 1911 and 1919 a spate of hurricanes devastated Jamaica and forced the closure of many plantations (Stephens and Stephens 1986:33–34). Thousands of unemployed and underemployed workers chose emigration as the most viable alternative to poverty. Most laborers turned to Central America in search of employment in agriculture or in the construction of the Panama Canal.

Migration to Panama occurred in three distinct waves, beginning with the construction of the railroad across the isthmus (1850–1855); initial work on the canal by the French (1880–1889) and completion by the Americans (1914); and the relocation of the railroad (1904–1914). The first wave involved from 2,000 to 3,000 Jamaicans. Other West Indians did not participate until 1880 when the French firm, Universal Inter-Oceanic Company, began construction of the canal. Migration subsided temporarily in 1889 when the French venture failed. Between 1894 and 1904 the Panama Canal Company was incorporated and recruitment resumed but was restricted primarily to those migrants who remained in Panama. Another, larger movement began in 1906 when American investors assumed control of the project. This last wave continued almost unabated for at least six years after the completion of the project in 1914 (Conniff 1985; Knox 1985:23–26).

West Indian out-migration expanded to other Central American countries, including Nicaragua, Honduras, Guatemala, Costa Rica, and Mexico, where most participants cultivated bananas. Immigrants moved between various countries and their home islands in response to the availability of jobs (Petras 1988:26–35). Although patterns of recruitment varied as in the eastern Caribbean, it continued to rely upon immigration agents, while in Jamaica migration was generally based on individual efforts.

From the 1880s to the first decade of the twentieth century, migration resulted in significant demographic shifts in the populations of most sending societies. For instance, more than 70,000 mostly young Jamaican men reportedly migrated to Cuba during the first two decades of the twentieth century to work in the sugarcane fields and on coffee plantations. An additional 40,000 sought employment in the United States. Roberts noted that the population of Jamaica increased from less than 400,000 in 1855 to over one million in 1920, despite the loss of population to migration (1975:140–146).

Perez confirmed that most of the approximately 84,000 Caribbean immigrants to Cuba between 1915 and 1919 represented "cheap contract labor" from Jamaica and Haiti. The movement lasted until the 1930s, when it came to an abrupt end with the 1933 "Cuba for Cubans" injunction that, inter alia, resulted in the "cancellation of existing contract labor arrangements with Haiti and Jamaica" (Perez 1988:204, 268). Barbados, with a smaller population of approximately 150,000 (in 1900), experienced proportionally greater population decreases between 1904 and 1914 when more than 60,000 Barbadians immigrated to Panama. Newton noted that during the "Panama phase," fertility rates in Barbados declined to as low as thirty-four per thousand. She attributed this dramatic decline to "massive male migration" to the Canal Zone (Newton 1977:22).

Most West Indian immigrants in Panama worked under unfavorable conditions as manual laborers in the excavation of the canal and the construction of support facilities. Some sources note that both the American authorities (especially the Isthmian Canal Commission) and many Panamanians discriminated against English-speaking West Indian immigrants. According to one report, the Isthmian Canal Commission allegedly underpaid West Indian immigrants and classified most as common laborers, disregarding the administrative experience and technical skills some possessed. In an interview with the author on September 6, 1996, Harold, the son of a laborer in Manchester, Jamaica, recalled some of the stories his father recounted of his experiences working in Panama during the 1920s. According to Harold, his father and other West Indians were segregated from Spanish-speaking laborers (presumably on the basis of language differences), confined in deplorable living conditions, and denied services in many food and entertainment facilities. Velma Newton stated that many Central American governments enacted restrictive immigration laws in the late 1920s and early 1930s to curtail the entry of black West Indians (Newton 1977). Generally, Central American elites welcomed the investment of U.S. dollars into their economies, but unilaterally resented the Yankee introduction of black, anglophone, protestants into their predominantly mestizo, Spanish-speaking, Roman Catholic societies. This became a major issue in Central American nationalism and anti-imperialism directed at the United States. Between 1906 and 1920 an estimated 20,000 West Indians in Central America succumbed to debilitating diseases, malnutrition, and isolated cases of violence (Cronon 1969:17).

Between World Wars, 1919–1939

Between the wars, smaller West Indian migrations focused on the oil fields of Venezuela and the oil refinery in Curaçao. Between 1919 and 1929, only 10,000 West Indians, mostly from Trinidad and Tobago, Barbados, and Curaçao migrated to Venezuela in search of employment. The move-ment ended when the Venezuelan government "restricted the entry of foreign-born black people" (Van Soest 1977:5–6). In 1915, the Shell Oil Company constructed a refinery in Curaçao, which it expanded in 1923. Almost overnight, Curaçao was transformed from a predominantly send-ing society to a receiving society, so that by 1945, immigrants from Hol-land, the Dutch Caribbean, Venezuela, and the British Caribbean repre-sented 20 percent of the population of Curaçao (Van Soest 1977). In 1930, the Shell Oil Company (Caribbean) work force numbered some 8,500, of which 3,000 were reportedly British West Indians. However, as a result of the devastating economic effects of the Great Depression, this number of mostly skilled workers was drastically reduced by almost 70 percent the following year. By 1931, the Shell Oil Company was forced by worsening economic conditions to dismiss or repatriate much of its work force. It was not until 1942 that Shell resumed the contract of some 2,200 workers from the eastern Caribbean (Van Soest 1977).

Most West Indians repatriated from receiving societies returned to de-pressed economies that could not compete with the quality of life and level of wages many had experienced in places like the United States. Between 1935 and 1938 a series of labor protests occurred throughout the British Caribbean. The disturbances began in St. Kitts when sugar workers staged a massive demonstration for higher wages and ended in Jamaica in 1938 with a strike at the West Indies Sugar Company. Elsewhere, spontaneous demonstrations in Barbados, Trinidad, St. Vincent, and St. Lucia ended in bloodshed and widespread property damage. The Depression, diminish-ing agricultural markets and prices, closing migration outlets, and signifi-cantly increasing local populations had worsened economic conditions in the region (Lewis 1977:54–68 [1938]).

Some discontented returnees become prominent anticolonial protago-nists. Sir Eric Gairy, a Grenadian who worked at an oil refinery in Aruba, used the widespread discontent of the period to spur the people of his island to action against the British colonial authorities and foreign-owned businesses (Singham 1968). Two nationalist leaders, Robert Bradshaw in St. Kitts and Vere Bird in Antigua, both worked in Panama before return-ing to the West Indies during the 1930s to assume positions of prominence as champions of the labor class. In the years that followed they became the architects of self-government in their respective islands. Sir Alexander Bustamante returned to Jamaica in the 1930s from work in Cuba, Panama, and the United States to become a dominant agitator for Jamaican labor reform. In 1962 he became the first prime minister of an independent Jamaica (Eaton 1975).

Concerned by the disturbances in the West Indies, the British colonial office dispatched a royal commission headed by Lord Moyne in 1937 to inquire into the state of the colonies. The Moyne Commission reported on the need for migration opportunity: "extreme difficulty of movement . . . creates a sense of being shut in, of being denied opportunity and choice, and of subsequent frustration in the minds of young men. [Limiting migration] may be a more important element than appears at first in the psychology of discontent" (Moyne 1945:10–11). It concluded that solutions to the problems lay both outside the region in increased foreign investment and new avenues for migration, and inside the region in the reduction of birth rates.

Movements to Metropoles, 1940–1977

During World War II, the mobilization of workers in the armed forces and other war efforts created a shortage of labor in many industries throughout the United States. Immigrants recruited from Mexico, Canada, and the British Caribbean worked in agriculture, on railroads, in logging, and in other industries where primarily unskilled labor was required. Between 1942 and 1945, over 400,000 migrants were recruited under the Bracero program. Approximately 73 percent of the total 400,000 were Mexicans, followed by 17 percent West Indians, and 10 percent Canadians (Henderson 1945:22–26). Recruitment from the British Caribbean began in the Bahamas and Jamaica. The eastern Caribbean was generally excluded because of the distance and cost of transportation involved. Henderson said a limited number of Barbadians were included after 1944 because of the insistence of the Barbadian colonial administration (1945).

The recruitment of West Indians continued after the Bracero program ended and eventually included workers from St. Vincent, the Grenadines, and St. Lucia. Bahamian participation in the program gradually declined until it came to an end in the 1960s, when a period of tourism-related prosperity began to transform the colony from a predominantly sending society to a receiving society. In 1952, the Immigration and Nationality Act (McCarran-Walter Act) restricted migration to the United States from the British Caribbean, and served to redirect movements toward the United Kingdom (Peach 1990:34–47). According to Peach, Caribbean migration to Britain had its origins in World War II, when many West Indians migrated to the motherland.

Large-scale West Indian migration to Britain started as a result of labor shortages caused by World War II. Some West Indians had settled there during the war as members of the armed forces. Others arrived during the period 1955–1960 (Rumbold 1991:52). British citizens generally opposed the influx of colonials and demanded that their government curtail migration. Between 1960 and 1962, almost 170,000 West Indians recognized the inevitability of controlled migration and flocked to the "Mother Country" before the impending legislation was enacted. Ironically, in 1962—the same year the British government granted independence to Jamaica and Trinidad and Tobago—the Commonwealth Emigration Act to control immigration to the United Kingdom was passed. The *White Paper on Immigration from the Commonwealth*, issued by the British government in 1965, established specific criteria for future legislation aimed at restricting black immigrants. Ceri Peach argued that the principle was quite simple: that black people were, in themselves "a problem and that the fewer of them in the United Kingdom, the better it would be" (1990:38).

In sum, the history of migration to, from, and within the Commonwealth Caribbean is a complex phenomenon, which began more than five centuries ago with Amerindian movements north from Central and South America. It continued with the Columbian voyages, subsequent European colonization, the introduction of African slavery and indentured servitude, and outward migration to metropoles. Shaped by continuously evolving historical conditions, Commonwealth Caribbean migration demonstrates the many variants that both sending and receiving societies exhibit. The effects of this phenomenon are perhaps best appreciated through the careful study of its politics, economics, and social causes (Kelly and Portes 1992:248–257).

The Commonwealth (British) Caribbean evolved as a direct result of five centuries of European imperialism in the region. Over the centuries, the indigenous population was violently displaced by a minority class of European migrants and a majority class of subjugated Africans. The Africans and their descendants were subsequently subjected to gross economic, social, and political exploitation by the Europeans, whose primary interest was the advancement of their own economic and political interests through the plantation system.

According to Bonham C. Richardson, much of the human movement into and through the Caribbean can be directly attributed to the plantation, the metropolitan-focused institution that has dominated the region for centuries. The plantation system effectively focused on the use of forced labor to produce and process crops for export to external, metropolitan markets. The system gained the dubious distinction of producing persistent economic inequities, skewed land-tenure policies, environmental destruction, dependency on foreign markets and consumers to the neglect of national development, and overpopulation (Richardson 1983:3).

Summary

During the post-Emancipation era, migration became the most important choice for the Afro-Caribbean majority seeking to escape the legacy of plantation life. In the mid-nineteenth century, many newly emancipated British Caribbean inhabitants migrated between British colonies such as Jamaica, Barbados, Trinidad and Tobago, and British Guiana in search of employment opportunities. Migration movements extended to South and Central America, Cuba, and the United States in the late nineteenth and early twentieth centuries primarily in response to the flow of predominantly U.S. capital investments. Successive movement from the British (later Commonwealth) Caribbean occurred during and after the World Wars to meet labor demands in war-torn Great Britain and in North America. In all cases, the movements continued almost unabated until emergency developments were completed and migrant labor became unnecessary. Receiving societies then enacted restrictive immigration laws to remove supposedly undesirable migrants and deter unsolicited migration.

The effects of external stimuli on the Commonwealth Caribbean over the past five hundred years have encouraged continuous migration, and we have seen the irony of how hundreds of thousands of Commonwealth Caribbean peoples have progressively migrated to most colonial and neocolonial societies, which historically created the conditions that traditionally encouraged migration. There remain the wider issues of the methods in which Commonwealth Caribbean peoples have reciprocated by affecting the internal character of the dominant metropoles themselves, through the introduction of exotic foods, clothing, festivals, and religious and cultural practices.

The next chapter will explore the influence of Spanish and British imperialism on the population of the Bahamas from the 1490s to the 1770s, and from the American Revolution onward, focusing on the role of the United States in sending settlers to and receiving migrants from the Bahamas.

2

Migration to the Bahamas

Pre-Columbian to 1888

Pre-Columbian Peoples

Beginning in 1492, Spanish and British imperialism significantly influenced the demography of the Bahamas (Figure 2.1) by first exterminating the existing population and replacing it with European and African peoples and their customs and institutions, including slavery. This influence continued unchallenged until the events of the American Revolution in the 1770s resulted in the migration of large groups of "Loyalists" from the United States to the Bahamas. In time, the American settlers became the dominant class, and were largely responsible for transforming the colony through the institution of a plantation economy fueled by African slavery. After Emancipation, they introduced the pre-capitalist "truck" labor system in which the dominant class maintained control of production and consumption loans. In 1888, this white elite class attempted to protect its monopoly on state and economic power by ensuring social control through the introduction of a predominantly Barbadian police force. The distinctive ethnic groups that emerged during the period examined helped to shape modern Bahamian history and influence present-day Bahamian class structure.

Christopher Columbus is historically credited with the discovery of the people on the island of San Salvador in what later became the Bahamas during his epoch-making voyages to the Americas beginning in 1492. Columbus offered an eyewitness account of these early Bahamians:

They go about naked as they were born . . . everyone appeared to be under thirty years of age, well proportioned and good looking. The hair of some was thick and long like the tail of a horse, in some it was short and brought forward over the eyebrows, some wearing it long and never cutting it. Some, again, are painted, and the hue of their skin is similar in colour to the peoples of the Canaries, neither black nor white. (Granberry 1973:22–30)

Columbus believed he had sailed to the East Indies and presumed the natives he first met to be East Indians. The people, however, called themselves *Lukku-cari,* which is traditionally interpreted as "island people." Europeans later translated this as "Lucayans." Archaeologists Charles Hoffman Jr., James MacLaury, and Julian Granberry used this term interchangeably with "Arawak" to identify the pre-Columbian Bahamians. Dr. Granberry, one of the earliest archaeologists to excavate pre-Columbian sites in the Bahamas, recognized the distinctive pottery of the Lucayans, which he named "Palmetto Ware" and which was found in sites throughout the Bahamas (Granberry 1973:31).

Archaeologists, in the absence of written records, speculate on the origin, social organization, subsistence technology, and population of these early Bahamians on the basis of surveys of the central and southern islands (Keegan 1992:72–76). Recent discoveries of a possible aceramic people who already inhabited the northern islands are provoking a reevaluation of the prehistory of the Bahamas. The evidence collected from excavations on Grand Bahama, the Berry Islands, New Providence, Long Island, Conception Island, Samana Cay, and San Salvador led Keegan (1992) to suggest pre-Columbian populations of between 20,000 and 40,000, but Hoffman and Granberry both estimate the number closer to 20,000. This supports Columbus' claim that he found "innumerable small villages and a numberless population" in the islands in 1492 (Granberry 1973:33).

The pre-Columbian natives reportedly "sailed or drifted to the Greater Antilles following large sea mammals from the Yucatan and Central America possibly as early as 5,000 B.C." (Cash 1992 [1978]). Cash also suggested that the early Bahamians were "chased by the Caribs, a very warlike people," and so were forced to migrate north to the Bahama Islands (1992 [1978]). However, archaeological evidence suggests that the Lukku-cari reached the Bahamas, probably via Hispaniola or the Virgin

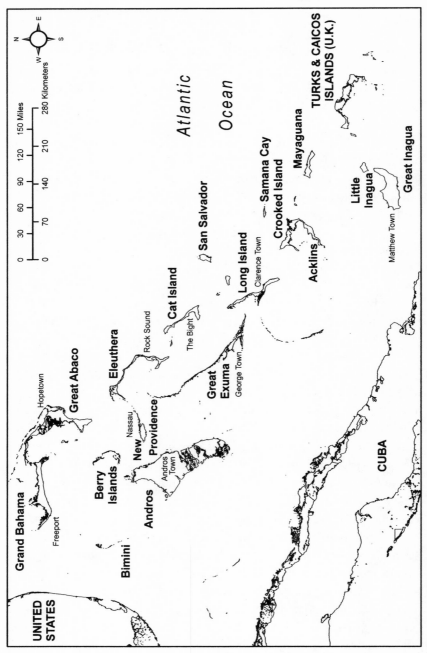

Figure 2.1. The Bahamas.

Islands, around 800 to 900 A.D. Granberry says Palmetto Ware pottery demonstrates a close similarity to the "Ostiones" pottery found in the Virgin Islands. Two other pottery styles, namely "Meillac" and "Carrier," were found in the Bahamas, "but are known to have originated in northern Haiti, Meillac around 900 A.D. and Carrier around 1,000 to 1,100 A.D." (Granberry 1973:31–33). They were a seafaring people, "traders who originally came from various sections of the West Indies to the south of the Bahamas, but who maintained contact with the lands of their origins" (Keegan 1992:74). The northerly migration of the Lukku-cari to the Bahamas was halted and traumatically reversed in the years following their historic encounter with the Spaniards.

Between 1509 and 1613, the Lukku-cari population of the Bahamas was compelled to migrate southward as slaves by the Spaniards they had earlier welcomed. The Bahama Islands were virtually ignored until 1509 when Governor Ovando of Española dispatched a raiding force to the archipelago to capture slaves for labor on Cubagua, the famed pearl island off the coast of Venezuela. According to Granberry (1973:34), Alonso de Hojed, who led an initial slave raid into the Bahamas, had in 1499 found the pearl fisheries off Cubagua, and presumably requested that Governor Ovando authorize him to capture laborers from the islands to exploit the resource. The Spanish cleric and Indian-rights activist Bartolomé de Las Casas described the situation: "the Spanish began to send the Lucayan Indians to gather pearls [on Cubagua], because they are in general excellent swimmers. . . . In that arduous and pernicious work . . . they finally killed and finished them off in a few years; and in that way the entire population of those islands which we called Lucayos perished" (Iglesias 1969:8–10). Ponce de León passed through the Bahamas in 1513 and reportedly found just one elderly native woman on a cay north of Grand Bahama. Less than twenty years after Spanish "discovery," the indigenous population of the Bahamas was exterminated (Cash 1992:18 [1978]).

Eleutheran Adventurers, Buccaneers, and Pirates

According to most accounts, the name "Bahamas" is probably a corruption of *baja mar* (shallow sea), which appeared on Spanish maps dating from 1523. Smith (1986:5–6) noted that other Spanish places seem to indicate the initial impression sailors had of the areas in question. For instance, Honduras means "depths," Costa Rica is "rich coast," and Trinidad ("trinity") may have referred to the three mountains that Columbus saw upon approaching the island. According to Mary Moseley (1926:7–8), "the earliest reference to the present name found in any book is in a narrative of John Hawkins' voyage in 1567 in which the chanell and gulfe of Bahama which is between the Cape of Florida and the Ilandes of Lucayo is mentioned." The Spanish made no serious attempts to colonize the islands, choosing instead to exploit the more profitable Spanish Main.

The Bahamas remained a Spanish possession, virtually unpopulated for over 100 years after the forced expatriation of the natives. It is not certain when the islands came under English dominion. However, one historian suggests that the presumption of King Charles I of England to grant the islands to Sir Robert Heath indicates that by 1629 the English considered the Bahamas to be a possession of their crown (Albury 1976). However, it was not until almost twenty years later that the first permanent European settlers came from Bermuda.

Religion was perhaps the primary motive for the migration from Bermuda to the Bahamas. In 1640 a major religious conflict, which mirrored the dissension that engulfed England in a bloody civil war, seriously divided Bermudans into camps of Anglicans and Puritans. Anglicans systematically persecuted the Puritans and denied them freedom of religion to the point where, as the Pilgrim Fathers left England for Massachusetts in the 1620s, so in Bermuda a group of Puritans sought the Bahamas as a home where they could enjoy religious freedom. The group, called the Company of Adventurers for the Plantation of the Islands of Eleutheria, was led by Captain William Sayle, a former governor of Bermuda. According to Albury, the company replaced the name Bahamas with the Greek word "Eleutheria," meaning freedom, to demonstrate its intention to allow freedom of religion and justice for all citizens of the new republic (Albury 1976:38). The company of about seventy persons, including twenty-eight slaves, sailed to the Bahamas in 1648 aboard the 100-ton *William*. The settlers organized themselves into a republic, with a governor, a Council of twelve, and a Senate of 100 members, respectively.

Albury states that the government in Eleutheria constituted the first republic established in the New World (1976:41). Over the next decade many criminals, free slaves, and troublesome slaves from Bermuda and New England were sent into exile in Eleutheria (Albury 1976:45). In 1684 the colony was attacked and destroyed by a Spanish force dispatched from Havana. The slaves were captured and the settlement, located near Preacher's Cave and Governor's Harbour "was plundered and burnt, never to rise again from the ashes," and the settlers were reportedly so devastated by and fearful of Spanish military incursions that they deserted the island and migrated to other English colonies (Albury 1976:45).

In the mid-seventeenth century a group of buccaneers-turned-pirates migrated to the Bahamas, where they proceeded to dominate trade and politics in the islands. Buccaneers were European (mostly French, Dutch, and English) robbers, shipwrecked seamen, and runaway slaves who inhabited the islands of Española and Tortuga, whence they attacked Spanish ships and settlements. The buccaneers cooked large quantities of meat on wooden grates over a slow fire. The grate was called a *boucan,* and from this word buccaneer is reportedly derived. In 1689, when England went to war with France and Spain, many English buccaneers separated from their French cohorts in Tortuga and migrated to the Bahamas. There, the buccaneers-turned-pirates, who were formerly authorized by the English authorities to attack Spanish treasure fleets, illegally preyed upon unsuspecting ships of any nationality (Miller 1945:33–46). In 1692, other English pirates came to the Bahamas from Jamaica, after the governor there, Sir Thomas Lynch, introduced harsh laws against them, and after the pirate base at Port Royal was destroyed by an earthquake.

Nassau, the main center of pirate activity in the late seventeenth century, became an arena for Spanish, French, and English imperialist conflicts. From 1703 to 1715, the town was invaded thirty-four times by Spanish and French forces seeking to end attacks on their shipping and colonies (Miller 1945:42–43). Pirate infestation of the Bahamas continued until 1718, when Woodes Rogers was appointed the first royal governor of the colony, and a concerted effort was made by the colonial government to expel the pirates and legitimize commerce (Cash et al. 1992:17–18). These authors noted that although some 600 of the estimated 1,000 pirates who terrorized the islands surrendered to Governor Rogers, many disregarded their "oaths of allegiance . . . to their sovereign [and] plot [ted] . . . to mutiny and feloniously and piratically steal [from the] islands" (1992:17–18). The Bahamas, with the demise of piracy, became sparsely populated and grossly impoverished until the arrival of the Loyalists in 1783.

The Loyalists

Between 1783 and 1785, a new wave of emigrants from the newly independent United States of America doubled the population of the Bahamas and initiated a program of economic development heretofore unprecedented in the islands. The Loyalists, so-called because they chose to remain loyal British subjects, came with their slaves from the southern states of Georgia and the Carolinas, and from New York and states along the eastern seaboard (Peters 1960:62–63). The first group came to Abaco Island from New York, via St. Augustine, Florida, in September 1783. One month later, they were joined by over 3,000 others. In the two years that followed, other Loyalists settled on New Providence, Long Island, the Exumas, Cat Island, Crooked Island, and San Salvador. After 1785, no significant numbers of Loyalists immigrated to the islands (Peters 1960:87).

The Loyalists, many of whom had lost most of their possessions in the United States, were determined to re-create their colonial lifestyles in the Bahamas primarily through the cultivation of cotton and the perpetuation of slavery. They used their superior numbers, education, and will to succeed to eventually dominate social, economic, and political life in the colony. By 1787, they had established over 120 plantations and exported an estimated 219 tons of cotton. They displayed disdain for the "old inhabitants" and "derisively called them 'conchs' after the lowly mollusks which formed an important part of their diet" (Albury 1976:117). By 1800, however, the system of plantations in the Bahamas ended after insects and severely depleted soil combined to devastate the sea-island cotton industry. Some Loyalists became discouraged and left the islands (Cash 1992:37). Others remained and developed a system of "controlled commercialism" that allowed them to monopolize politics and economics in the colony (Johnson 1992: vii). Many remaining Loyalists engaged in the production of salt, wrecking, boat-building, and livestock raising to stave off economic disaster. The *Bahamas Gazette*, January 11, 1786, reported that some Loyalist merchants maintained a "lucrative trade with Spaniards from Cuba and Hispaniola."

The Loyalist migration significantly shaped society and culture in the Bahamas. The population grew from just under 4,000 in 1783 to over 11,300 in 1789. Loyalists introduced agricultural innovations, boat-building skills, and new architectural styles patterned after those of the places they left (Ferguson 1966:17–25). Anglicanism, which became the religion of choice for the majority, was reflected in the construction of imposing edifices. John Wells established the *Bahama Gazette* in 1784 as the first newspaper in the colony. The Loyalists built new streets, schools, a jail, established a police force in Nassau, and extended parliamentary representation to other islands. Perhaps, the Loyalist legacy is best perpetuated in their names, which most Bahamians bear today. A review of the local telephone book shows that most Bahamians share the common Loyalist names of Adderley, Bethel, Bowe, Carey, Cartwright, Culmer, Dean, Dorsett, Ferguson, Forbes, Fox, Ingraham, Johnson, Kelly, Kemp, Knowles, Lowe, Newbold, Pinder, Rolle, Russell, Sands, and Sawyer.

Afro-Bahamian Migration

Most Afro-Bahamians were brought to the Bahamas as slaves. The earliest record of Africans in the islands referred to the slaves of the Eleutheran Adventurers. Arguably, blacks probably came to the Bahamas prior to the arrival of the Eleutheran Adventurers first in the company of Spanish conquistadors and later with pirates either as slaves, members of gangs, personal servants, or as part of the plundered loot destined for sale. In 1773, there were 2,241 blacks in a total Bahamian population of just over 4,000 [GT/COP, Bahamas Annual Report for 1773 (Bahamas/PRP, 1971), 32]. By 1831, the influx of the Loyalist's slaves significantly increased the number of blacks in the colony to 12,259 (Cash 1992:38). The slaves, widely distributed throughout most of the islands, were generally provided with a subsistence plot of land, allowed freedom from work on most Sundays and holidays, and given a significant degree of mobility uncommon in most New World communities (Higman 1976:46).

Some blacks were brought to the Bahamas aboard slavers and sold at public auctions. The September 17, 1785, *Bahama Gazette* advertised the sale of a group of "newly-arrived" slaves that included several valuable young carpenters, a cooper, "house wenches" and "several Boys, who have been accustomed to boats and fishing." Other blacks were imported from the southern Caribbean in response to demands from cotton planters. On May 12, 1789, the *Bahama Gazette* announced the arrival of "seventy-two Windward Coast Slaves" from Barbados and "between fifty and sixty Windward Coast Negroes . . . imported in the sloop *William* from

Grenada." In 1807 the British government abolished the slave trade and utilized its navy to enforce the Act. Blacks continued to arrive in the Bahamas, not as slaves but as liberated wards of the crown.

From 1807 to 1860, British naval patrols "liberated" an estimated 6,000 Africans from slave ships, mostly Portuguese-owned, bound for Cuba and resettled them in the Bahamas (Wood 1974:16). Many of the liberated blacks came directly from Africa and did not share a common language. Subsequently, they were "delivered or tendered to the Collector or Chief Officer of the Customs . . . to provide in a proper manner for their support and maintenance . . . until such Negroes [could] be entered, enlisted, apprenticed or disposed of according to the terms, intent, and meaning of the said Act [abolition of the slave trade]" (Malcolm 1910).

Special communities were established to accommodate the liberated Africans. In 1832, over 500 were resettled near the Carmichael estate, six miles southwest of Nassau, and 134 at Adelaide, west of the town. The collector of customs was instructed to insure that "the husband and wife, parent and child [were] in no case separated" (Malcolm 1910). General compliance with this directive kept most liberated African families united and relatively independent. Subsequently, many of these families combined the advantages of relative freedom from the impediments of slavery with their wage-earning potential to purchase land, engage in small-scale businesses, and thus gain a degree of upward-mobility heretofore denied Afro-Bahamians. The attempts made to establish free-slave communities on other islands, however, failed when cotton ceased to be an economically viable crop. In some cases the liberated blacks were virtually abandoned by both authorities and colonists, and left to survive by subsistence farming and fishing (Albury 1976; Craton 1962; Saunders 1994).

The liberated Africans were apprenticed in a variety of indentured services, including agriculture and salt raking. In 1811, the Legislative Council reported that of 450 Africans liberated that year, ninety were employed as public servants and the remaining 360 were indentured among the local citizenry [BR/COR, Bahamas. Joint Petition of Legislative Council and House of Assembly [microfilm edition] folio 13, no.176, 6 June 1812 (Bahamas/ PRO, 1971), 17]. Those apprenticed for work in the rural islands were reportedly "an orderly, quiet and industrious set of people" [BR/COR, Bahamas, Collector of Customs to Colonial Office, 1816. 27 September 1817. folio 2 (Bahamas/PRO, 1971)]. Those apprenticed in New Providence, however, were described as generally undisciplined, untrustworthy, and of "a more worthless race than will be seldom met anywhere." In New Providence, the Africans were frequently encouraged by "free coloreds" and runaway slaves to rebel against white authority (Eneas 1976:5).

No apprentices were released from service until 1823, apart from the few women allowed to emigrate to Jamaica in 1816 with their husbands and masters. The collector of customs, in a report to the governor, noted that masters were reluctant to release their apprentices early because some, "although they certify their capacity and good conduct, are not disposed to voluntarily forego their valuable services. [Others] from inveterate prejudice against this race . . . or from a sordid desire to perpetuate their servitude for their own emolument, will not admit them to be capable or fit to be liberated" [BR/COR, Bahamas. Collector Of Customs to Governor, 1827. [microfilm edition], folio 15. no. 18, 23 March 1828 (Bahamas: PRO, 1971), 7]. Some unscrupulous masters reportedly overworked their apprentices to the point of ill-health. The collector of customs complained that such masters would subsequently "cast [the apprentices] back on the care of the Government when worn out and really incapable of providing for themselves."

The resettlement of liberated Africans in the Bahamas and the decline of the cotton industry combined to reduce reliance on slave labor and spark protest by some whites against the further immigration of blacks into the colony. The editor of the *Royal Gazette,* N. McQueen, complained on August 23, 1828, that "there are more Negroes in these islands than can be employed to advantage in them." Some white Bahamians protested in this same newspaper on September 12, 1828, of the decrease in the value of their slaves which resulted partially from the supply of relatively inexpensive labor the apprentice program provided. Others on October 4th of that same year expressed concern for security, noting that "the liberation of large numbers of Africans, who have been brought . . . as prize and apprenticed out, [can serve] to instill in the minds of the slaves a spirit of insubordination by creating the expectancy that their emancipation is at hand." Most Africans remained under civil authority, which indentured them until 1838, the official year of full emancipation.

From Emancipation to 1888

Beginning in the mid-nineteenth century, a reverse migration between the Bahamas and the United States took effect. The Slavery Abolition Act of 1833, which abolished slavery in the British colonies as of August 1, 1834, motivated many Bahamians to migrate, initially to Key West, Florida, and Demerara, British Guiana. The high level of migration became a cause for alarm in some quarters. The district chairman of the Wesleyan Methodist Missionary Society reported that the district of Nassau was "likely [to be] greatly affected by the active and extensive system of emigration [then] being carried on between this colony and Demerara and other emigrations to Key West and other parts of the American possessions" [District Chairman to Wesleyan Methodist Missionary Society. 12 May 1838. Nassau Quarterly Mission Papers. vol. II. no. 2, (Bahamas/PRO, 14 June, 1978)].

Many Bahamians emigrated in search of employment at higher wages and trade opportunity. The post-Emancipation economy of the Bahamas was depressed and offered limited employment prospects. Traditionally, plantation agriculture was never very successful or profitable in the islands. In the 1830s, most Bahamians eked out a meager subsistence from the sea and small-scale farming. Many were, therefore, lured by the geographical proximity of Florida and the prospect of cash wages. Additionally, Florida presented a lucrative market for the sale of marine products. Some whites left because they "preferred the protection of the Stars and Stripes, with the Negro's degradation, to that of the British Lion, with his [the Afro-Bahamian's] acknowledged right as a free denizen of the world" [Archdeacon Trew to Society for the Propagation of the Gospel, 12 January 1849, Bahamas: Annual Report. no. 13, (Bahamas/PRO, January 1976), 11].

In 1852, Bahamas governor Rawson W. Rawson proposed a bill in the House of Assembly to encourage the emigration of African Americans to the Bahamas. The bill was intended to counter the growing number of Afro-Bahamians migrating to the United States and other destinations in search of employment opportunities. The House of Assembly, however, rejected the proposal because, among other things, "Her Majesty's free black and Coloured subjects [were] not admitted to the enjoyment within the Southern States of the Union in full and free participation in the privileges and civil rights enjoyed by Her Majesty's white subjects" [BR/COR. Bahamas Blue Books, 1853–1854 (Bahamas/PRO, 1971), 3]. The House concluded "until these disabilities are ameliorated, it would be inconsistent with the enlightened legislation for this colony to hold out inducements for the encouragement of emigration from those states to the Bahamas."

Up to 1885, the United States had traditionally provided the primary markets for most Bahamian agricultural and marine produce, including pineapples, sponges, and salt. United States expansion into the Pacific Ocean and Caribbean Sea, however, seriously affected its trade relationship with the Bahamas. For example, the *Royal Gazette* reported in 1885, "American vessels brought specie for purchase of Pine-apples to the amount of $47,320." By 1888, however, "a heavy duty in the United States operate[d] to the disadvantage of Bahamian exports, which [had] to compete with those from Cuba [and Hawaii], which are admitted free, and are of a larger and more marketable size" [BR/COR, Bahamas Blue Book, 1887–1888 (Bahamas/PRO, 1971), 6].

The Bahamian salt and sponge industries were equally affected by shifts in United States trade policies. In 1888, it was reported that the once lucrative salt export to New York, the Carolinas, Georgia, and Florida was "of little account, extensive shipments to the United States being no longer profitable under a duty of twenty-five cents per bushel." The *Nassau Guardian* reported on September 16, 1888, that a small quantity of salt continued to be exported to Jamaica, Cuba, and Belize as late as 1890. During the 1880s, the sponge industry suffered because "a duty of twenty-five cents [was imposed] on all sponges imported into the Unites States . . . to protect the Florida sponge industry" (Stark 1891:76–77). Ironically, the Bahamas benefited from the restrictive trade legislation. Cash-paying jobs enabled many Bahamians to send remittances home to improve the economic lot of relatives and friends and to purchase land. After Emancipation, the dominant white Bahamian elite sought to control access to land and political suffrage (only male landowners were eligible to vote) by increasing the financial requirements for potential buyers of land (Stark 1891:76–77).

Summary

The indigenous population of the Bahamas was annihilated within thirty years of "discovery" by Spanish marauders seeking slaves for labor, primarily in Cuba and Española. The islands remained virtually unpopulated until they became an English possession in 1629, and were subsequently colonized in 1647 by a group of religious dissidents from Bermuda. Other groups from Bermuda and the Carolinas followed and established cotton and tobacco plantations, so that by 1670 the population of the islands had increased to over one thousand. More than 80 percent of the population resided on New Providence. During the remainder of the seventeenth and early eighteenth centuries, lax colonial administration and geographical location along the shipping lanes transformed Nassau into a haven for piracy.

The aftermath of the American Revolution significantly affected the demographic, social, and economic life of the Bahamas. Between 1783 and 1789, over 2,000 Loyalists and their slaves migrated to the islands from destinations in New York, the Carolinas, Georgia, and Florida. The influx trebled the population and increased the proportion of blacks from 50 to 75 percent. The Loyalists, with enthusiasm and vigor, established the modern city of Nassau and substantially increased commercial and social activities in the islands. The émigrés used generous crown land grants to re-create American plantation lifestyles on New Providence and the outlying islands. By the early 1800s, however, insect infestation and infertile soil combined to destroy the plantation systems. Some Loyalists migrated to other destinations, while those remaining adopted the subsistence lifestyle of small-scale farming, fishing, and wrecking of the earlier settlers.

The post-Emancipation period witnessed a search for a more secure economic base. Thousands of former slaves were virtually free to chart their own destinies. Shanty communities were established just beyond the city limits to accommodate first the liberated Africans and later the new citizens. The economically depressed post-Emancipation years, however, produced an atmosphere of uncertainty among the general population. Some Bahamians produced agricultural and marine products, such as pineapples, salt, and sponges for export primarily to Europe and the United States. Others, however, including many young black men, migrated to Florida, Central, and South America in search of improved employment opportunities. Simultaneous with the Bahamian outward migration was a larger West Indian labor migration, which sent waves of workers to similar destinations including (to a lesser degree) the Bahamas. The following chapters will trace the history of West Indian migration to the Bahamas.

3

Barbadian Migration
to the Bahamas

Country Profile

Barbados, the most easterly and one of the smallest of the Caribbean islands, measuring just 166 square miles, nonetheless presents one of the most significant cases of migration in the region. Between 1904 and 1914, an estimated 60,000 Barbadians, or about 25 percent of the island's total population, migrated to Panama (Newton 1977:22). Essentially, the history of Barbados is tied to England and sugar. In the early 1500s, Spanish sailors captured Carib Indians on the island and transferred them as slaves for the fields and mines of larger Spanish possessions. The first English group, which arrived in 1620, reported the island to be uninhabited. Subsequently, between 1627 and 1650, some 25,000 English settlers arrived in a mass migration comparable to that of Europeans to New England (Newton 1977:22).

The early settlers were mostly small landowners in a peasant economy, cultivating tobacco, cotton, and food crops for export. Sugarcane, introduced from Brazil in 1641, produced a major agricultural revolution that resulted in the demise of small holdings and tropical environment at less cost. Between 1645 and 1680, the slave population increased from 5,680 to over 60,000 (Holmes 1988:211). With the growing importance of sugar, small owners were gradually squeezed off their lands. Many migrated to the Carolinas and other British territories. Within forty years after the introduction of sugar, an estimated 30,000 white settlers had gone, leaving Barbados with a predominantly black population (Patterson 1965:38). The island became a classic colonial monocultural society, where a great majority of African slaves produced sugar, molasses, and rum for sale in the metropolitan markets of Europe, while political, social, and economic power was concentrated in the hands of a minority white plantocracy (Patterson 1965:38).

In 1838, an estimated 70,000 Barbadians of African descent were emancipated. The white planters opposed Emancipation, fearing that, once liberated, the ex-slaves would refuse to work on the plantations, and as a result, the sugar industry would collapse. The sugar industry, nonetheless, survived Emancipation and whites retained their social and economic dominance (Hope 1982:21–39). Most Barbadian blacks were on the sugar estates. Others, however, felt the need to leave the island for destinations where they could test the bounds of Emancipation and assert their individual freedom. One source noted that these first black migrants "stretched their kin networks to other islands, establishing migration avenues for future generations of Barbadians to follow" (Gmelch 1992:21).

Since Emancipation, Barbadians have lived up to their description as the "great emigrants of the Caribbean," in that their labor has found many outlets (Chandler 1946:124–130). Until the early 1920s, Barbadians supplied labor in Jamaica, Trinidad, Guyana, and Cuba. Tens of thousands went to Panama, Nicaragua, Honduras, Costa Rica, Venezuela, and the Bahamas. During the early 1940s, a plan called the Vieuxfort Scheme contemplated the resettlement of thousands of Barbadians in St. Lucia. The scheme intended to resettle the immigrants on an abandoned sugar estate at Vieuxfort acquired by the Barbadian government for that purpose. The plan was abandoned, however, because of the war and difficulties in the St. Lucian sugar industry. During World War II, Barbadian laborers moved to Trinidad, St. Lucia, Bermuda, Curaçao, and the United States. Beginning in 1944, the U.S. War Food Administration and War Manpower Commission recruited thousands of Barbadians for work in that country (Chandler 1946:124–130). After the war, thousands migrated to England and North America. Small numbers also migrated to the Bahamas.

The systematic migration from Barbados to the Bahamas began in 1892 when Barbadian men were recruited to augment the reorganized Royal Bahamas Police Force. Small groups of Barbadians continued to migrate first as policemen, and later as prison officers and skilled artisans, until 1968, when the newly elected, predominantly Afro-Bahamian government restricted the recruitment of foreigners to serve in the public service. Many recruits resigned after their contracts expired and pursued successful careers in other areas of the private and public sectors. Most who continued as police and prison officers rose through the ranks to assume very senior positions.

The Barbadians, initially welcomed upon arrival in New Providence, quickly became embroiled in conflict with the local police and the black majority. However, they generally retained favor with the local white oligarchy. In time, they used their advantages of superior education and a rigid work ethic to acquire social and economic status denied most black Bahamians. Successive generations of Barbadian immigrants gradually assimilated into Bahamian society and continued to emphasize the importance of education to their children. That emphasis became a key catalyst for educational reform in the Bahamas, especially from the 1920s through the 1960s. Consequently, by 1968 most Barbadian Bahamians had acquired a college education in the United Kingdom or North America, and returned to the Bahamas to hold important positions in the public and private sectors.

According to Frank (interviewed on August 15, 1997), then treasurer-secretary of the Barbadian Bahamian Association, most Barbadian Bahamians encourage their children to pursue professions such as law, medicine, business, and engineering. He estimated that 80 percent of the approximately eighty association members could boast that in each family most of their children were successful professionals, and at least one was a doctor, lawyer, or a certified accountant.

Recruitment of Barbadians as Police Constables, 1892–1908

The Police Act of 1891 required the establishment of a paramilitary police agency to assume the duties of the Second West India Regiment troops preparing to withdraw from the colony that year. In January 1892, inspector J. H. Learmouth returned to New Providence from Barbados with forty-two Barbadian recruits designated to form the nucleus of the constabulary force. The recruits were reportedly "young, intelligent, and of good character, presenting favourable material" [BR/COR, Royal Bahamas Police Force: Annual Report. 1890–1893 (Bahamas/PRO, 1971, p.4)]. They were described as "literate, as might be expected of the superior class from which they [were] drawn" "[BR/COR, Royal Bahamas Police Force: Annual Report. 1890–1893 (Bahamas/PRO, 1971, p.5)]. The emphasis on literacy was drawn as a comparison to the black Bahamian police of the late nineteenth century, who were generally semiliterate. All recruits were medically certified by the police medical officer and required to sign contracts. One account described the event as follows:

> For the first time in the history of this country, policemen were required to sign contracts. All persons below the rank of Inspector appointed under the Act had to undergo a probationary period of three months. During this period, all recruits were evaluated and those found to be unfit for service were immediately discharged. Those found to be fit were required to sign contracts for an additional six years until the individual attained 2l years of service, after which he received a pension or gratuity. (Pratt and Simmons 1990:30)

The constables, ranging in age from nineteen to twenty-two, were housed in the military barracks vacated by the Second West India Regiment troops, and provided with free meals and uniforms [Bahamas Police Force. *Annual Report, 1890–1893*, 7]. They were "not permitted to live outside of the Barracks and had to obtain permission to marry" (Pratt and Simmons 1990:30). They were regularly drilled in military tactics and allowed access to firearms and closely resembled the troops they replaced in many areas of operation. Conversely, the native police were not regularly drilled, had no formal training in the use of firearms, and were denied access to such instruments, even for use in the line of duty (Pratt and Simmons 1990:31).

The constables were responsible for firefighting and provided with horses to draw the fire engines. Previously, that responsibility rested with the volunteer fire brigade, which comprised mostly local police and volunteers from the community. One source noted: "At that time, the fire fighters had to draw the engines to the scenes of fires themselves. Under those conditions, when they arrived, they were too exhausted to effectively fight the fires (Pratt and Simmons 1990:31). Black Bahamian men reportedly resented the Barbadians because the latter were young, able-bodied men, well-fed, well-dressed and with plenty of money to spare. Therefore, they were likely to become "formidable rivals to the young men of the labouring class in the affections of the women" [BR/COR, Bahamas, CSOP. folio 23, (Enclosure no.2), Jackson to Ripon, July 1893, no. 94].

The recruitment of Barbadians for paramilitary service in the Bahamas concluded a series of discussions between colonial officials and the Bahamian white elite concerning the security of the colony following the imminent withdrawal of the Second West India Regiment. In 1888, Lord Knutsford, secretary of state for the colonies, suggested that the local police force be strengthened to fill the vacuum to be left by the troops [BR/COR, Bahamas. CSOP, Shea to Knutsford, November 12, 1888 folio 23. no. 230, [Confidential], (Bahamas/PRO. 1971)].

Sir Ambrose Shea, governor of the Bahamas, cautioned his superior that a strengthened police force of predominantly black Bahamians might encourage unity with the popular masses against white rule in the event of social unrest:

> In the proposal to increase the police organization as a substitute for the Military Force I feel there lies a danger that the public security would be weakened and not confirmed by such a measure. While I see no reason to complain of the general conduct of the black population, I am without much faith in the temper they would exhibit on any occasion in which their race prejudices were excited . . . I see peril in the increased efficiency their training would give them. [BR/COR, Bahamas. CSOP, Shea to Knutsford, November 12, 1888 folio 23. no. 230, [Confidential], (Bahamas/PRO. 1971)]

Sir Ambrose's comments reflected similar views the Bahamian elite expressed in an 1885 petition addressed in the House of Assembly to Governor Henry Blake: "Such a step [withdrawal of the troops] as this we cannot but regard as one that will be absolutely fatal to the future progress of the Colony: its good government will be placed in jeopardy, and insecurity to life and property will, under these circumstances universally prevail" [BR/COR, Bahamas, CSOP, Blake to Stanley, September 4, 1885. folio 23. no. 226. [Confidential]. (Bahamas/PRO. 1971)].

On August 8, 1885, Governor Blake reported these fears to his superiors: "While [I] cannot speak too highly of the general conduct of the population, the fact remains that there is strong feeling on the part of the black and coloured peoples against the white population of Nassau" [BR/COR, Bahamas, CSOP, Blake to Stanley, September 4, 1885. folio 23. no. 226. [Confidential]. (Bahamas/PRO. 1971)].

In 1886, racial tensions heightened when a white Bahamian named Sands who fatally shot a black policeman was subsequently released from custody on his plea of momentary insanity. L. D. Powells, a former circuit judge in the Bahamas—and himself a victim of white Bahamian social injustices—commented on the event: "A member of the New York Yacht

Club, who knows the Bahamas thoroughly once said to me, 'I was [t]here the day Sands was arrested and I never shall forget it as long as I live! No one who saw that crowd could doubt there was an undercurrent of race hatred with which the white Conchs [Bahamian whites] will have to reckon sooner or later" (Powells 1888:41).

Efforts to recruit policemen in other British West Indian colonies generally failed. The inspector general of constabulary in Jamaica remarked that "suitable recruits from that colony were unlikely to be attracted by the low salaries which were being offered by the Bahamas" (Johnson 1992:118). Eventually, the colonial authorities and Bahamian elite compromised to recruit Barbadians to form the core of the constabulary force. Bahamian whites and the colonial authorities agreed that men recruited outside the colony were less likely to become sympathetically involved with the local communities they policed. The Bahamian elite were convinced that foreign, black police could control the predominantly black Bahamian population just as the West India Regiment suppressed the 1865 Morant Bay (Jamaica) Rebellion. Furthermore, Barbadians were successfully recruited as police to replace the West India Regiment in British Honduras and Trinidad (Johnson 1973:19–20).

The recruits received a warm welcome from most residents upon arrival in New Providence [Bahamas Police Force. Annual Report, 1890–1893]. In 1893, a House of Assembly select committee confidently reported that the Barbadian recruits were an impressive paramilitary force, which offered a "guarantee both to the local public and to investors abroad, that their interests will be safeguarded by an efficient administration of the law" [BR/COR. Bahamas. House of Assembly Minutes: "Select Committee Report on the Progress of the Colony during the Past Five Years," folio 23. no. 236. (Enclosure no. 39), 15 April 1893 (Bahamas/PRO. 1971)].

The favorable report ignored the concerns of H. M. Jackson, colonial secretary of the Bahamas and architect of the reorganization of the Royal Bahamas Police Force. Jackson noted that the relations between the local black communities and the constables had become alarmingly strained and threatened to erupt into open hostility [BR/COR, Bahamas, CSOP, Jackson to Ripon. 8 September 1892 folio 23. no. 234 (Bahamas/PRO. 1970).129]. Jackson's fears became a reality in July 1893, when a confrontation between the constables and residents of the black community of Grants Town developed into three days of civil unrest. Mobs of black Bahamians armed mostly with wooden clubs and stones attacked the small police substation in Grants Town and constables on patrol in the community.

Investigation into the disturbance revealed that the constables often displayed excessively aggressive and abusive behavior toward Bahamian blacks. Deep resentment arose between the two groups which at times threatened to develop into open conflict. Jackson suggested that the local police resented the constables because: "They [local police] know that they are to be gradually replaced by the Constabulary and thus feel themselves looked on as an inferior Force. They regard the Constables as interlopers, who [are] taking the bread out of their mouths by depriving them and their friends of a convenient means of earning a livelihood" [BR/COR. Bahamas. CSOP, Jackson to Ripon, 8 July 1893. folio 23. no. 237. (Enclosure no. 2) (Bahamas/ PRO. 1971). 97].

Colonial officials, in an effort to control hostility between the two groups while still encouraging continued Barbadian migration, allowed the old police force to survive, but restricted its duties to policing the predominantly black communities. The primary responsibility of the Barbadians "remained the protection of the property interest of the white minority" (Johnson 1992:119). The division of responsibilities suggested the colonial authorities and white Bahamians had greater confidence in the Barbadians. When interviewed on May 18, 1997, Dale noted that many Barbadians married into affluent colored Bahamian families, where parcels of land were customarily distributed as dowries. Invariably, this situation allowed the Barbadian relatively easy access to land at a young age—an accomplishment that ordinarily would have been improbable to accomplish in Barbados. Moreover, the Barbadians became a buffer between the local whites and blacks and a diversion of black hostility from whites to the foreigners. The division remained in effect until 1909, when a new Police Act integrated the force and extended equal privileges to all servicemen. The small-scale migration of Barbadians to the Bahamas continued to consist of policemen until the 1920s, when favorable economic conditions in the colony attracted Barbadian skilled laborers in search of economic opportunities.

The Barbadian constables affected life in the Bahamas at the turn of the century both socially and economically. One immigrant, Charles Odle, married a Bahamian, fathered ten children, and settled just south of Mason's Addition. Odle became prominent in the community, and a street was named Odle Corner in his honor. Similarly, Gibbs Corner, located in the same area, honored another Barbadian immigrant. The recruits brought an unprecedented level of discipline and education to the police force which, in turn, established improved standards for future recruitment. The integration of the force in 1908 created an environment that allowed Bahamian recruits to benefit from the experiences and examples of their Barbadian counterparts. The exposure resulted in a more informed and educated police force, better equipped to execute its duties, and capable of mounting successful challenges to the social inequalities fostered by the ruling white minority (Pratt and Simmons 1990:45).

Barbadian constables, typically between eighteen and twenty-six years of age, migrated every three years in groups averaging twenty-five men. Many viewed the Bahamas as an underdeveloped, "back-water" colony, where "Yankee dollars" were readily available and entry into the United States was easy. Most considered the quality of society in the colony to be inferior to that of Barbados and the crime level intolerably high (Powells 1888:61–69). Kendrick noted in a May 23, 1997, interview that most Barbadian immigrants to the Bahamas were aware of the general geographical location of the colony, but were usually ignorant of the social and political norms of the islands. He noted that very few Barbadians expected to remain in the Bahamas beyond the terms of their contracts. Instead, many intended to follow the paths of economic opportunity to North America or Great Britain.

Some Barbadian recruits remained in the Bahamas after their contracts expired. Generally, they retired to the more affluent "colored" communities of Mason's Addition and Delancy Town located on the southern fringes of Nassau, just a short distance from where the more privileged white Bahamians resided, but north and socially separate from the black communities to the south. The Barbadians displayed a propensity for discipline and "things English" which was generally demonstrated in their well-kept residences. Their homes were usually brightly painted and often featured English-style gardens. Gmelch (1992:25–26) noted that the description of Barbados as "Little England" has "some legitimacy (based on) comparisons between the two landscapes, both green and rolling hills and everywhere showing the hands of humans. . . . Barbadians, more than any other Caribbean people, are similar to the English in their reserved civility, and in having an unshakable belief in their own superiority." John Wickham said Barbadians possess a "distinct penchant for priding themselves on their moral excellence" (1975:223–230). They demonstrated a strict regard for punctuality and lines of authority, according to an interview with Jason in 1997, unparalleled in a society where time and authority were lightly regarded.

The Migration of Barbadian Artisans, 1920s–1930s

Beginning in the 1920s and extending throughout the late 1930s, scores of Barbadians, together with other skilled artisans and general construction workers, migrated to the Bahamas in search of economic opportunity. The Volstead Act of 1922, which ushered in a decade of "Prohibition" in the United States, transformed the Bahamas into a significant entrepôt for smuggling illegal alcoholic beverages. Rum running produced a period of unprecedented prosperity in the colony (Tinker 1982:25–68). The new wealth encouraged substantial investments in construction projects, primarily in New Providence. Foreign laborers had to be recruited because the local labor market could not adequately accommodate the construction boom.

In 1922, small groups of Barbadian skilled artisans began to migrate to the Bahamas in response to the demand for skilled labor to rebuild the Colonial Hotel, which had been destroyed by fire in March of that year. Others came in successive years during the 1920s to work on the construction of the Fort Montagu Hotel, the development of exclusive communities for American winter residents, and other projects designed to accommodate the expanding tourist industry and pleasures of the Bahamian nouveau riche. Many Barbadian workers were recruited from Cuba, and had previous experience on the Panama Canal. The U.S.-based Purdy and Henderson Company, which was contracted to rebuild the Colonial Hotel, operated sub-offices in Canada and Cuba. It was from the latter office that most artisans (including British West Indians and Cubans) were recruited. Some Barbadian police who were skilled artisans resigned from the force after their contracts expired and secured employment in the more lucrative construction industry. Alfred King, a carpenter for over seventy years, reminisced in 1997 that many of the skilled carpenters and masons working in Nassau during the 1920s and 1930s were West Indians. He noted that several artisans like Messrs. Beckles, Carter, Wilshire, and Ellis were Barbadians originally recruited as policemen.

Despite the influx of Barbadians, Bahamian administrators continued to lament the chronic shortage of local skilled labor. In 1924, the editor of the *Nassau Tribune* noted that "today there are too few thoroughly competent native skilled mechanics and the number is decreasing." On April 8, 1926, the *Nassau Guardian* reiterated the prevailing concern for the inadequate supply of local skilled artisans: "No one who takes the trouble to inform himself of the actual trend of public interest can doubt that in the next few years will see a very great increase of winter residents in New Providence and many other Bahamian islands. Houses will be needed. Boats will be in demand. Craftsmen of all kinds will all be required to meet the need of enlarged population. Where will they be found?"

According to Howard Johnson, several factors contributed to the shortage of skilled labor in the Bahamas during the 1920s:

> First, there was competition for the available skilled labour from private individuals and from the colonial government which had undertaken an expansive programme of public works. Even more important in explaining the shortage was the fact that the colony's educational system made no provision for technical education. . . . Finally, the system of apprenticeship by which young men had earlier learned the trades after a period of attachment to a skilled artisan had broken down by this period (Johnson 1991:150; Powells 1888:52–53).

Johnson also notes that the white elite, through their control of politics in the colony, resisted the appropriation of funds for any program, including vocational education, which would allow the black majority a means of social and economic upward mobility and promote a challenge to their control (Johnson 1991:150; Powells 1888:52–53). The labor situation was further aggravated by the migration of many skilled Bahamians seeking work on the development of projects in other countries. As noted in chapter 2, beginning in the 1890s, some Bahamians sought employment in Central American and Caribbean countries, such as Panama, Cuba, and Curacao. The majority, however, migrated to south Florida, where salaries were comparatively higher than at home.

Like the police recruits earlier, the predominantly colored Barbadian artisans generally settled in the more affluent colored communities, such as Delaney Town and Mason's Addition. The local coloreds and black elite accepted them largely because their skills made them highly marketable and their skin color made them socially acceptable. The black Bahamian elite comprised mainly descendants of liberated Africans. The coloreds were mainly the descendants of Hispanic San Domingan and Cuban émigrés and the product of black-white miscegenation. Most, through success in business, had accumulated considerable property which, in turn, made them eligible to vote and provided them with a level of social and economic affluence second only to the white elite.

Additionally, the Barbadians were welcomed because their Yankee dollars—earned primarily in South and Central America and Cuba—coupled with their comparatively superior level of education, made them eligible for marriage to the young women of the communities.

Many West Indian builders and contractors who migrated to the Bahamas in the 1920s were formally trained and reported years of experience and expertise in modern techniques of construction. For instance, C.A. Prescod, a Barbadian, advertised "13 years Practical Experience in Cuba, Panama, Honduras (Spanish), and Mexico," according to a *Nassau Guardian* article on October 3, 1924. Clement T. Maynard advertised in the *Nassau Tribune* on April 7, 1925, that he had worked in France, Brazil, Panama, and Cuba before migrating to the Bahamas. Some Barbadian artisans married into the more prominent colored and black Bahamian families. Over the years these marriage alliances produced some of the more socially distinguished and financially successful families in the country, such as the Goodings, Marshalls, Maynards, Rokers, and Watsons, who have produced several prominent lawyers, businesspersons, medical and academic doctors, and politicians.

Perhaps the most enduring legacy of the Barbadian artisans of the 1920s and 1930s was their contribution to the reestablishment of the apprenticeship system, which helped to produce a new cadre of young, skilled Bahamian tradesmen. Many artisans (especially carpenters, stone masons, tailors, and dressmakers) operating from the 1940s to the 1960s could attribute their successes in part to being apprenticed to Barbadian artisans (*Nassau Guardian* October 3, 1924; *Nassau Tribune* April 7, 1925). Under the apprenticeship system, young men and women were attached to a skilled artisan for periods ranging from five to ten years. After the apprenticeship ended, the recruit was locally acknowledged and respected as a skilled artisan.

The apprenticeship system was not purely altruistic. According to an interview with Alfred in 1997, most recruits endured long hours of labor from exacting patrons for little or no salaries. Some unscrupulous artisans were accused of abusing apprentices as a source of cheap labor. Reportedly, many skilled artisans systematically and in a limited way exposed their apprentices to trade secrets to ensure that only a few would become accomplished masters of and competitors in the professions. According to George in 1997, there were reportedly several cases where apprentices were discharged by their masters (presumably without just cause), allegedly to limit competition within the profession, and to ensure the necessity to recruit foreign labor. The apprenticeship system successfully helped to replenish the local supply of skilled laborers and eventually diminish the need to recruit foreign labor. In 1935 a group of leading Bahamian carpenters petitioned the colonial authorities to restrict the further migration of foreign carpenters to the Bahamas [BR/COR, Bahamas. CSOP. Petition from Bahamian Carpenters Regarding Employment of Aliens. 1935. folio 8871. (Bahamas/PRP. 1970)]. As a result, few Barbadian skilled artisans were recruited for work in the Bahamas after the 1930s.

Barbadian shoemakers, tailors, and dressmakers were some of the more successful artisans in the colony. Most, according to Edna in 1997, operated businesses from selected side streets off Bay Street (the main business thoroughfare dominated by the white elite), and catered exclusively to colonial officials, affluent Bahamians, and winter residents. The opportunity to establish businesses near Bay Street (which almost certainly assured success) was a highly coveted privilege accorded only to selected artisans by a largely paternalistic white elite. The artisans continued the practice of apprenticeship and trained many young Bahamians in the respective trades. In a 1997 interview, Francina stated that by the late 1950s, some of the most prominent shoemakers and tailors in the Bahamas were former apprentices of Barbadians.

British residents especially patronized Barbadian tailors because of their familiarity with British cloths and fashions, and dedication to the trade. The tailor, like his construction counterpart, did not encourage his sons to apprentice with him. There is evidence to suggest that some tailors developed other economic interests and left the businesses for their apprentices to manage or acquire [BR/COR, Bahamas, Census of the Bahamas taken in the year 1953, 12 February 1956 (Bahamas/ PRO. 1971)]. A review of the 1953 census indicates that by that date many Barbadian artisans and civil servants who immigrated to the Bahamas during the 1920s had become small grocers and entrepreneurs in other small businesses. Few black Bahamian tailors operated businesses near Bay Street before 1950, or catered to an affluent clientele. Instead, most operated within the predominantly black communities where most of their patrons resided.

The Barbadian dressmakers—mostly the wives of skilled construction workers and policemen—catered almost exclusively to the Nassau elite and rich tourists. Most accepted colored Bahamian girls as apprentices, often a decision based on the girl's social status, skin color, and the relationship that existed between their families and that of the dressmaker. In some instances, the daughters and sisters of senior Bahamian policemen were apprenticed to the dressmaker wives of Barbadian policemen. According to one account, apprenticeship to Barbadian dressmakers, although a coveted privilege, usually involved long, exhausting hours for minimal wages. Most apprentices eventually established reputable businesses patronized by affluent clients. In an interview on July 18, 1997, Edna, a black Bahamian and the daughter of a police sergeant, recounted that it was rare for a black Bahamian girl to be selected for apprenticeship. She noted that she overheard other dressmakers question her apprenticeship. She remains convinced that her apprenticeship to the wife of a Barbadian policeman was largely the result of her father's rank and influence on the police force.

The apprenticeship system encouraged rigid economic class distinctions. For instance, most black Bahamians could not successfully compete with the foreigners and their apprentices for the upscale market. Invariably, said Edna, many local artisans established businesses in the black communities where they lived, and grudgingly accepted lifestyles considerably less attractive than those enjoyed by their more privileged counterparts. The black Bahamian dressmaker, for example, was generally poorer, less educated, and less privileged than her colored counterpart, and seldom married anyone of social or economic distinction. Instead, most remained on the economic margins of Bahamian society.

Interestingly, very few Barbadian artisans encouraged their children to follow them in trade. Instead, they encouraged them to pursue such traditionally white professions as medicine, law, and engineering. The experience of the electronics technician, Ralph Gooding and his wife, Eileen, is illustrative of this. The Gooding children include two medical doctors, a pharmacist, and an accountant. Mrs. Gooding, an educator, noted that most of the family resources were devoted to the education of their children. She resigned from a teaching position with a private school and devoted her full attention and care to the upbringing of the children. It was only after the last child had completed high school that Mrs. Gooding sought reemployment. She claims that her experience is typical of many Barbadians in the Bahamas. Within successive generations, the children of Barbadian immigrants became some of the more renowned professionals in the Bahamas.

Evidence suggests that some Barbadian immigrants were economically established in the Bahamas by the late 1920s (Bonacich 1973:585). Bonacich theorized that migrant professionals and artisans accumulate wealth, which they carry with them during the course of migration. A review of the Sun Life Assurance Company records revealed that some Barbadians, after a decade of residence in the Bahamas, paid as much as $77 per month to maintain policies worth as much as $5,000 [The Moseley-Cuevas Collection, Policy Register: Sun Life Assurance Company (Bahamas) Limited (Nassau: Department of Archives, 1984)]. Additionally, by the 1930s some Barbadian immigrants owned extensive parcels of land in New Providence [BR/COR. Bahamas. Register General Department: "Double General Index. 1927–1930." 24 March 1931. (Bahamas/PRO. 1971)]. The "Double General Index" contains miscellaneous legal documents, including land grants and purchases. Joseph Nathaniel Gill, for example, was a Barbadian carpenter who migrated to the Bahamas via Cuba in 1923. By 1930, he had purchased considerable property (twelve acres in one instance) in various sections of New Providence.

In an interview with my grandmother (1997), the foster daughter of Joseph Gill, she recalled that he was an economically secure man when he came to the Bahamas. She speculated that Gill probably accumulated monies working in Panama and Cuba, prior to immigrating to the Bahamas. Such economic indicators suggest that some Barbadian immigrants were able to accumulate significant funds in Panama and Cuba, which they invested in their adopted country. Otherwise, some immigrants presumably made significant economic sacrifices during a period when the average wage of a carpenter or a stonemason was less than fifty shillings per day [BR/COR. Bahamas Blue Book, 1927 (Bahamas/PRO. 1971). 213].

Barbadians in Politics and Medicine

Generally, Barbadian immigrants avoided active participation in local politics and the public debate of social issues. It appears from interviews with Barbadians who immigrated to the Bahamas before the 1940s that many Barbadians reportedly advocated social and political enfranchisement for Bahamian blacks. Most, however, avoided active public support for fear of reprisals from the white elite. Some of this sentiment persisted even to an August 1997 interview with a Barbadian who insisted on anonymity in order to protect their economic and social status.

There is evidence to suggest that Barbadian immigrants justifiably feared reprisal from the white elite. One exception was Ernest L. Bowen, a tailor and the son of Barbadian immigrants, who represented the southern district of New Providence in the House of Assembly from 1903 to 1925. Another exception was Robert M. Bailey, who was allegedly victimized for his political campaign against a white Bahamian candidate. Bailey, a tailor by profession, emigrated to the Bahamas in 1898. He was an active leader of the local chapter of Marcus Garvey's Universal Negro Improvement Association (Hill 1983:282). In 1924, he unsuccessfully contested a seat on the legislative council (Hill 1983:148). The whites, led by Bailey's political opponent in the election, reportedly decided to punish him for his political opposition to them: "After the election was over, the Bay Street Boys [white Bahamian oligarchy] put the fire on Robert M. Bailey. They took away the contract from him to make clothing for the Police Force. Ralph Collins, a rich white man, had Robert M. Bailey on a retainer to make between ten and twenty suits per year. After the election, he took away his contract and so Robert M. Bailey had to face near starvation." This was a clear case of victimization (Hill 1983:148).

In 1928, Bailey lobbied the colonial authorities to permit Garvey to address a rally in Nassau. The event was reportedly the largest mass gathering in Bahamian history (Martin 1983:179–181). Bailey actively participated in the movement to introduce the secret ballot box into Bahamian politics. The "Ballot Box Party," as the lobbyists for the introduction of the ballot box in the Bahamas called themselves, included several Haitian, Barbadian, and British Guianese proponents (Saunders 1991:147). According to Saunders, at the public clinics, when other doctors refused to go into poor neighborhoods, Dr. Worrel went (Saunders 1991:147). During the early decades of this century, Barbadians contributed to the advance of medical services in the Bahamas. G. S. Worrel, a graduate of Boston University, emigrated to the Bahamas in 1915. Subsequently, he served as a doctor for over four decades, often in the more rural islands. According to one account: "The Worrels served the Bahamian people for over forty years as a Doctor and Pharmacist and served freely as the prison physician and as Welfare officer" (Bethel 1997:40).

Barbadians and Secondary Education

Barbadians played a significant role in the establishment of secondary education in the Bahamas. Primary education, compulsory for children between the ages of six and fourteen since 1877, was provided free by the local board of education. Mary Moseley noted, however, that "secondary education [was] mainly in the hands of the various religious bodies" (Moseley 1926). In the 1920s, the three secondary schools in the Bahamas were all located in Nassau and included the Wesleyan Methodist-operated, co-ed Queen's College, and two schools run by the Church of England—St. Hilda's for girls and Boys Central. The schools catered exclusively to the white elite and did not encourage the enrollment of blacks (Saunders 1991:159–162). Barbadians such as R. M. Bailey, Clement T. Maynard, and E. L. Bowen agitated along with Bahamian coloreds and blacks for the establishment of a public high school in the colony (Saunders 1991: 159–162).

In 1924, the Government High School was established presumably to serve the educational needs of local coloreds and blacks, to provide non-white Bahamians with secondary education, and to train teachers for service in the public system. It was obvious from the beginning, however, that the institution was established to serve the black and colored elite and exclude the majority. It offered a limited number of seats (fifty in 1928 and fifty-one in 1932). The few scholarships offered were selectively determined by the social and economic status of students' parents within the community, and the patronage of politicians. Interestingly, the student population included the children of most Barbadian and other West Indian immigrants.

Between 1925 and 1950, approximately 30 percent of the students were children of Barbadian immigrants [Government High School Student Records. 1925–1950. microfilm edition (Bahamas/PRO, 1988)]. By the mid-

1930s, economic conditions worsened because of the Great Depression and the threat of global conflict, which influenced a slowdown in construction. The economic situation was exacerbated by the return of Bahamian artisans and laborers to the colony, and the migration of hundreds of people from the outer islands to Nassau. These combined factors forced colonial officials to restrict the migration of West Indians to the Bahamas. It was in the 1950s when the Bahamas entered another period of relative prosperity. But the final and largest wave of Barbadian immigrants soon arrived.

The Impact of Later Immigrants. 1952–1968

Significant Barbadian migration to the Bahamas resumed in the 1950s. Repeating the experience of the 1890s, most immigrants were recruited as police and prison officers. Some retired officers explained that the almost exclusive recruitment of Barbadians as police and prison officers was partially attributable to the efforts of B.J.H. Colchester-Wemyss, commandant of police in the Bahamas from 1955 to 1963. Colchester-Wemyss was an Englishman who had worked in Barbados before coming to the Bahamas. According to the informants, he married a Barbadian, admired the Barbadian work ethic and demonstrated an "appreciation for things English." Consequently, he reportedly convinced the colonial authorities to increase the recruitment of Barbadian police and prison officers from a three-year routine based on perceived labor requirements to an annual exercise. Furthermore, Colchester-Wemyss reportedly influenced the upward mobility of Barbadians within the service to the disadvantage of local officers.

Three interviewees requested anonymity during May 1997 in order to protect their social and economic positions. Their allegations, in the absence of documented proof, are difficult to substantiate. It is a fact, however, that most of the police and prison officers sent overseas for advanced training during the Colchester-Wemyss tenure were West Indian immigrants [BR/COR, Bahamas, CSOP. folio 9363. Colonial Police Service Courses of Training in the U.K. and Caribbean, 1950–1960 (Bahamas/PRO. 1971)]. A smaller number of Barbadians were recruited to work in the tourist industry as waiters, cooks, stewards, and maintenance engineers. Those who worked in the outer islands represented the second largest group of West Indians living in the rural Bahamas. Haitians have traditionally represented the largest ethnic group of foreign origin in the Bahamas, as will be examined in a later chapter. This last wave of immigrants made significant contributions to the development of the economy, government, and society in the Bahamas. Perhaps their most significant was to the development of education in the outer islands.

The postwar Barbadian immigrant to the Bahamas differed from earlier Barbadian immigrants in several significant areas. For instance, some brought their wives or soon after arrival "imported" wives from Barbados. Typically, the 1890s-1930s immigrants left wives in Barbados and produced second families in the Bahamas; many married (or lived in common-law relationships with) local women and eventually became assimilated into Bahamian society. Average postwar immigrants were older, and often had several years of work experience as low-level government officers, teachers, hotel-workers, and technicians. In comparison, the earlier immigrants—especially the police recruits—had the educational equivalent of high school degrees.

Artisans who arrived in the 1930s were the obvious exception to this rule, since most had had considerable work experience in countries such as Panama and Cuba. The later immigrants used the advantage of their previous work experience to move rapidly from the police and prison services into other sectors of government and private enterprise. Especially significant was the impact of those recruits who became teachers in the outer islands.

The term "outer islands" was introduced by British colonial officials to refer to all islands in the Bahamian archipelago other than New Providence. Literally, it meant islands lying off Nassau. Over the years, the term took on economic connotations to mean those islands where the American influence was relatively small and where social and economic development lagged (in some cases) considerably behind New Providence. In the period following Independence, former prime minister Pindling, in recognition of the negative connotation that the term had assumed and the social and economic disparity it had come to represent, officially reclassified all islands in the Bahamas as the "Family Islands."

Most Barbadian teachers in the outer islands were totally unprepared for life in those underdeveloped communities. Many expected to work in islands considerably larger than Barbados. Transportation between the islands, which was often sporadic and unpredictable, was by boat. On land, it was almost always over seemingly impassable roads. Hurricanes occasionally wreaked havoc and at times forced residents to abandon their homes and take shelter in more secure buildings such as schools and churches, and sometimes caves. Evans Cottman, an American doctor who practiced in some of the islands, noted that the prosperity affecting the Bahamas was generally confined to New Providence and some islands in the northern Bahamas.

Typically, the islands to the south (with the possible exception of Inagua) remained in a state of social and economic depression (Cottman 1979:68–122). Perhaps, none were prepared for the general isolation from civilization and friends that life on the outer islands created, and the fact that supplies depended entirely on the frequently unreliable scheduled visits of mail boats.

The Bahamian government offered incentives to attract teachers to outer islands, including free transportation of dependants and furniture, housing, and a "hardship allowance" that was designed to compensate for general discomfort. Some Barbadian police and prison officers requested redeployment as teachers in the outer islands because of the advantages offered. The anonymous interviewees in May 1997 suggested that most postwar Barbadian police and prison officers came to the Bahamas expecting to be transferred to other sections of the public service. According to the source, the anticipation was based on information that a shortage of trained teachers and technicians existed in the colony. Such requests were frequently accommodated because many trained Bahamian teachers rejected work in the outer islands because of the gross underdevelopment that existed in many. The story was told of one Bahamian teacher who was "banished" to an outer island in 1961 on charges of insubordination. On the island, he complained about his appointed residence, where "chickens and goats and everything [slept] in the bloody place" (Ferguson 1974:32). The teacher reportedly refused to remain on the island, and as a result was suspended without pay for three months. Most Bahamian teachers chose, instead, to work in the metropolitan areas of Grand Bahama and New Providence.

Many of the trained teachers in the outer islands during the 1950s and early 1960s were Barbadians. The Civil Service List for the 1950s reveals that a minimum of seven of the twenty-three trained teachers stationed in the outer islands were Barbadians [BR/COR, Bahamas, CSOP, folio 13289. no. I-IX. Bahamas Civil Service List. 1947–59, (Bahamas/PRO, 1971)]. The Civil Service List for the 1950s reveals that while seven of the twenty-three trained teachers (+33 percent) stationed in the outer islands were Barbadians, five of the remaining teachers were recruits from other West Indian islands. Many were deployed to schools staffed almost entirely by untrained Bahamian teachers called "monitors." Frank, a Barbadian initially recruited as a police officer in 1955, taught for many years in the public school system in the Bahamas. Frank claimed in a 1997 interview that during his tenure in Cat Island from 1962 to 1968, Barbadians were the only trained teachers on that island.

Most Barbadian teachers struggled to cope at schools which were grossly understaffed, had insufficient resources available, and little opportunity for receiving substantial support from the central educational agency in Nassau. Teachers like Kendrick, Albert Bullen, Leon Price, Lawrence Gibson, and Ivan Holder designed curriculums and gradually improvised more efficient systems of education in the outer islands, according to an interview with Kendrick in 1997. Some Barbadian teachers spearheaded community efforts to upgrade the physical conditions of their schools and others established evening classes for promising students. Many outer island students were admitted to the prestigious Government High School in Nassau during the 1960s as a result of the discipline and high academic principles taught by Barbadian teachers. This argument is supported by the fact that many Bahamian social, economic, and religious leaders of the 1970s and 1980s were students of Barbadian teachers.

Barbadian police and prison officers made significant contributions to other areas of the public service. Neil, interviewed in 1997, was recruited as a prison officer in 1956, and worked as a finance officer in Barbados before coming to the Bahamas. He was transferred to the Bahamas public treasury after working as an officer for nine months in the prison system. Neil eventually worked for over twenty-four years in the treasury and was largely responsible for upgrading the systems of accounting and recruitment at that agency. Among other things, Neil introduced a system for grading accountants which remains in effect. Additionally, he trained a cadre of young accountants that included the future administrative heads of the public treasury and department of audit, several bank managers, and private accountants.

Some Barbadians took advantage of the opportunities for advanced training available locally to upgrade their skills or acquire new ones. Advanced training strategically positioned them for upward mobility within the government service and employment in the private sector. Dolton Chandler, for example, recruited in 1952 as a police officer, was granted scholarships to study automobile mechanics at the Nassau Technical College and at the Metropolitan Police Driving School in England in 1959. Dolton admitted in his interview in May 1997 that he had limited skills as an auto mechanic prior to his immigration to the Bahamas and that he borrowed automobile manuals and taught himself the basics of auto repair. In 1968 Dolton became the supervisor of the auto mechanics section of the Bahamas Industrial Training Center. Some of the leading auto mechanics in the post-Independence Bahamas emerged under his tutelage.

Small numbers of white Barbadians migrated to the Bahamas during the 1950s and 1960s. Their skin color and professional skills allowed them to easily assimilate into upper-class Bahamian society. They resided in the most affluent areas of New Providence, attended the Anglican Cathedral, and were members of elite organizations. Some, like the civil engineer Edward Boyce, were recruited for the government service. Private firms recruited others, such as Oswald Bancroft and James Ince, as accountants and administrators. In most cases, white Barbadians remained in the colony and established businesses or became partners in existing firms [BR/COR. Bahamas. Report on the Census of the Bahama Islands Taken on the 12th April 1953 (Bahama/PRO. 1953)]. The 1953 census report provides significant information on the country of origin of the respondent, professional background, social and civic affiliation, and domestic (family and household) statistics. Based on available information, the white Barbadians were socially and politically conservative, and their presence in the Bahamas was relatively insignificant. In the 1950s and 1960s, Barbadian immigrants helped shape the demographic composition of several communities in New Providence, including the expansion of the Chippingham and Palmdale districts, the Palmetto Village, and the Danottage Estates. Streets in these communities, such as Davis Street in Chippingham, Arundel Street in Palmdale, Watson Way in Palmetto Village, and Conliff Court in Danottage Estates still bear the names of some of these early pioneers. According to one informant, Ellen, interviewed by the author on May 28, 1997, Barbadian immigrants typically purchased property in areas adjacent to each other, developed community watch groups to guard their properties, and offered assistance to each other's families.

Summary

Unquestionably, Barbadians contributed significantly to the development of society, politics, and economics in the Bahamas. Beginning in the 1890s, three small waves of Barbadian migration to the Bahamas occurred. In 1892, systematic migration began when forty-two Barbadians were recruited as constables to replace the West India Regiment troops stationed in the colony. The constables, generally encouraged by the Bahamian white minority, quickly demonstrated prejudices toward the less-educated local police and black Bahamian majority. Consequently, the Barbadians became the objects of distrust and occasional aggression by the Bahamian majority. The simmering animosity began to fade after the police and constabulary forces were equitably amalgamated by the Police Act of 1908. The recruitment of Barbadian men, mostly as police and later as prison officers, continued until the 1930s, when systematic migration was interrupted by the events of World War II.

During the 1920s, groups of Barbadian skilled artisans responded to job opportunities created by the development of public and private projects in New Providence. The artisans, mostly carpenters and masons, worked on the construction of new hotels, public projects, and private homes throughout the island. The Barbadians contributed substantially to the revival of the apprenticeship system, under which many young Bahamian artisans were trained. Many apprentices eventually became the leading artisans in the country from the 1940s into the 1960s. Some Barbadian artisans migrated to North America and England after the construction boom ended in the early 1930s. Those who remained became absorbed into Bahamian society.

The third group of Barbadians, mainly recruits for the police and prison services, immigrated to the Bahamas during the 1950s and 1960s. They differed from former groups in several areas. First, they were older than the earlier groups with an average age of twenty-four. Second, most were previously employed in Barbados as low to mid-level professionals: some used employment in the Bahamas as a stepping-stone to North America and England. Third, the majority of the later immigrants remained in the Bahamas, some married local women or imported wives from Barbados, and either transferred to other sectors of the public service or resigned to work in the private sector. Generally, the Barbadian experience in the Bahamas exemplified an unassuming modesty in the face of obviously significant contributions to the social, economic, and political development of their country of adoption. The next chapter will trace the history of Jamaican migration to the Bahamas from the 1920s to Bahamian Independence in 1973. It will demonstrate how illegal Jamaican migration into the colony created serious labor imbalances, motivated public resentment against Jamaicans, and forced colonial officials to implement restrictive immigration laws.

4

Jamaican Migration to the Bahamas

General Overview

Jamaican migration to the Bahamas became significant during the 1920s, when Jamaicans and other skilled workers sought employment in the construction of tourist and public works projects in the colony. At that time, most Jamaican immigrants may have come via Cuba. In an August 1997 interview, Pearl, the widow of Daniel, a Jamaican carpenter who migrated to the Bahamas during the 1920s, said that most Jamaican immigrants to the Bahamas during the period came from Cuba to escape the economic depression that followed the fall of sugar prices in that country. Others may have come from the Canal Zone or directly from Jamaica. Jamaicans worked as butlers and maids to the winter residents, skilled artisans in the construction industry, and as tailors and dressmakers. Others were recruited as police and prison officers. A limited number of Jamaican professionals were employed in the private and public sectors.

Groups of unskilled Jamaicans also entered the Bahamas illegally during the 1920s, and seriously challenged the potential of the local labor market to absorb the significant increase in unskilled labor. Subsequently, native laborers, including migrants from the outer islands, returnees from agricultural and construction work in Florida, and, ironically, earlier West Indian immigrants publicly protested the presence of the undocumented Jamaicans in the Bahamas. Consequently, by the 1930s, documented Jamaican migration into the Bahamas was reduced to a small number of professionals.

During the 1930s, Jamaicans who entered the colony illegally were routinely deported. Restrictions on West Indian migration in general—and Jamaicans in particular—remained in effect until the late 1960s when the Pindling administration initiated a program to recruit teachers, mostly Jamaicans, for employment in the civil service. Jamaican immigrants contributed to the political and social advancement of black Bahamians and the ultimate reshaping of politics and society in the Bahamas. Jamaican-Bahamians produced some of the most prominent political leaders in the Bahamas during the 1960s and 1970s. In 1973, the son of a Jamaican immigrant and a Bahamian woman became the first prime minister of the independent Bahamas. Additionally, some members of his cabinet trace their heritage to early Jamaican migration to the Bahamas.

Country Profile

When first discovered by Columbus on May 3, 1494, Jamaica was populated by its original Indian inhabitants. The island was initially called St. Jago, after the patron saint of Spain. The name was eventually replaced with the indigenous Xamayca (well-watered), which was later anglicized as Jamaica. The Spaniards established the first European settlement in 1509. From 1509 until 1655, when it was captured by the British, Jamaica was a Spanish colony. Under British administration, it became known for the wealth of its sugar plantations, which lasted throughout the eighteenth century until the emancipation of slaves in 1838. In the subsequent years, setbacks to the sugar industry brought the island economic hardship from which it has never fully recovered.

After a long period of direct British colonial rule, Jamaica began to gradually achieve local political control in the late 1930s. That was a time of social unrest marked by violence. During that time the foundations for Jamaica's leading political parties were formed by Alexander Bustamante (Jamaica Labor Party—JLP) and Norman Manley (People's National Party—PNP). In 1958, Jamaica joined the West Indian Federation, but withdrew in 1961 following a referendum. Complete independence from the United Kingdom was attained in August 1962. In the 1970s, Jamaica, under the socialist administration of Michael Manley, was economically and politically ostracized by the United States, with the effects of exacerbating political and economic turmoil in that country. As a result, many wealthy Jamaicans migrated with their capital, thus effecting a severe economic drain on the financial resources of the island nation. The migration of the wealthy was subsequently imitated by thousands of intellectuals and laborers who migrated mostly to North America and other destinations that included the Bahamas (Stephens and Stephens 1986:57–73).

Migration in the 1920s

Prior to the 1920s, few Jamaicans were attracted to employment opportunity in the Bahamas. In the 1890s, for example, efforts to recruit policemen from Jamaica were unsuccessful because "suitable recruits from that colony were unlikely to be attracted by the low salaries which were being offered by [The] Bahamas" (Johnson 1992:118). In 1907, in one notable exception, the Sisal Fiber Company recruited fifty Jamaican men to work on a sisal plantation on Little Abaco Island. The Jamaicans were housed in barracks and paid daily wages of two shillings and six pence [GB/COR, Bahamas. Governor's Dispatches. no.39. "Emigration. Migration. Repatriation and Labour. 1803–1921." 1907 (Bahamas/PRO, 1971)].

The company was unable to recruit locally, because many Bahamians were already employed in south Florida or successfully cultivating acres of sisal on family property and engaged in sponge fishing. By the 1920s, however, job opportunities in Panama and Cuba had become scarce, and some Jamaican laborers looked to the Bahamas for employment. Jamaican skilled artisans migrated to the Bahamas in small, yet significant numbers in response to the demand for skilled labor (Hall et al. 1971:10). The migration movement of the 1920s reversed that of the 1830s when, in the aftermath of Emancipation, small groups of black Bahamians were recruited to Jamaica under contract (Hall et al. 1971:10). The development of tourist and public works projects in New Providence created employment opportunity for thousands. Approximately 1,800 persons were employed in the course of the Colonial Hotel reconstruction (*The Tribune Handbook* 1924:173–177). Additional thousands were employed in other areas.

Included among the Jamaican immigrants were artisans recruited by the Purdy and Henderson Company to work on the reconstruction of the Colonial Hotel. The artisans were generally highly skilled and experienced in modern techniques of concrete and steel construction (Johnson 1992:150–152). Most had accumulated monies from work in areas of Latin America and the Caribbean where Yankee dollars were heavily invested.

The Jamaicans, like other British West Indians, received lower wages than their North American and Cuban counterparts. According to a contemporary employee, the West Indians in general, and Jamaicans in particular, became angry that the Cubans received higher wages for performing similar tasks. Subsequently, according to an interview with Alfred in September 1997, Jamaicans reportedly organized strikes in demand for equal pay. Alfred was employed on the reconstruction of the Colonial Hotel as an apprentice to his foster father, a Barbadian carpenter who was previously employed in Cuba. Alfred noted that most of the West Indians employed on the project were Jamaicans. The few Barbadian and Trinidadian artisans employed in the reconstruction did not actively support the strikes, perhaps to protect their jobs.

Jamaican artisans, according to Alfred's contemporary, Joseph, interviewed on November 2, 1996, introduced Bahamians to the potential of collective bargaining and unionized efforts. Joseph, a retired Jamaican carpenter who was employed on the hotel reconstruction project during the 1920s, argued that the success of the Jamaican-led agitation for equal pay demonstrated to black Bahamians that they could use organized industrial action to combat the economic inequalities perpetrated against them by the ruling white elite. This suggestion is debatable because many Bahamians, who had been employed in New York and Florida, were active in the development and administration of unions.

There is evidence to support the argument that Jamaicans contributed to the development of trade unionism in the Bahamas. The Working Man's Union, the first labor union established in the Bahamas, was organized during the 1920s to "classify labour according to trades and skills" (Saunders 1991:162). Interestingly, subsequent labor movements were organized during the 1930s to protest foreign competition. The principal organizers of the union included two Jamaicans. The union was not successful, primarily due to the covert opposition of the white elite. According to one report (Saunders 1991: 162), union members contended with threats that bank loans would be denied them, and that they might be fired, and possibly evicted from rented homes. The same source noted that the general objective of the elite was to prevent the American investors from paying black Bahamians relatively high salaries which could not (or more probably would not) be continued by local employers when the projects were completed. According to a September 30, 1996, interview with William, a white Bahamian and son of a merchant who became successful during the 1920s, the elite routinely cautioned potential investors of the delicate socioeconomic balance that existed in the Bahamas at the time.

During the 1920s, many wealthy Americans established winter homes in New Providence and recruited the services of experienced Jamaican butlers, maids, gardeners, and chauffeurs. It was expected that these domestics would be suitably equipped with references from previous employers, be willing to live on the premises, and possibly travel with the employer to a summer residence (often for several months) in the United States. Most Bahamians were inexperienced and thus ineligible to work as maids and butlers to the Americans. Furthermore, many were reluctant to leave their families and properties for employment overseas. Sandra, the daughter of Jamaican immigrants to the United States, said during an interview on April 22, 1995, that during the 1920s and 1930s there were "hushed" conversations between her parents and family friends about Jamaican acquaintances and family members who were recruited for domestic service in the Bahamas. She said they sometimes discussed how the domestic employees, once their American employers returned to the United States, absconded and assumed illegal residence in that country. Sandra claims that in 1926 her father worked in the Bahamas as a truck driver for a local business. She stated that her mother worked as a maid for a Jamaican cousin (who had reportedly "done [financially] well in Panama") and his family, before securing employment in Nassau as a construction foreman. Sandra said the cousin and his family eventually migrated from the Bahamas to New York.

Generally, skilled Jamaican artisans recruited other Jamaicans (usually family members and friends) to work as apprentices, nannies, and maids. The decision to recruit fellow Jamaicans was reportedly motivated more by economic considerations than social bias. Archer alleged in an interview with the author on September 17, 1996, that Jamaican employers recruited domestic employees from among friends and family members because they provided a source of cheap, dependable labor. The domestic employees were reportedly eager to accept the jobs, because employment in the Bahamas provided an opportunity to eventually obtain jobs with persons other than their original employers, and possibly migrate to the United States. Archer's father worked as a stonemason in Nassau from the 1920s until the 1950s. He claims that his father sometimes complained about the influx of skilled and presumably illegal West Indian immigrants to the colony "taking away Bahamian jobs." Some Jamaican domestic servants were reportedly family members and acquaintances of the employers. Archer said colonial officials often "turned a blind eye" to the fact that many of the domestics remained in the colony after their original employers had left, and secured employment with other West Indians, winter residents, Bahamian elite, and other skilled artisans. Some domestics, reportedly, accumulated sufficient funds to finance their eventual migration to the United States.

In the late 1920s the colonial government in Jamaica expressed alarm over the migration of professionals to the Bahamas and elsewhere, such as in 1927, when the Bahamian government attempted to recruit a small number of Jamaican agriculture teachers. The colonial secretary of Jamaica expressed concern that the Bahamian advertisement for teachers would attract some of the best Jamaican professionals. He opined that "the minimum salary offered by [the Bahamian government] is the maximum to which the most qualified teachers in Jamaica can attain and . . . therefore the terms offered will probably attract the best men here and create discontent among the rest [GB/COR, Bahamas, CSOP, folio 4712. no. 6, 25 November 1927, (Bahamas/PRO. 1971)]. The Bahamian government attempted to assure the Jamaican authorities that there was no need for concern: "It should be impressed upon all candidates that the life on an Out Island is in most cases a somewhat lonely and difficult one, the people being as a rule, uneducated, and scarcely suitable as companions for the school teachers. For this reason it would be advisable that a married man should be accompanied by his wife, and if she happens to be a qualified teacher, the government would be prepared to pay her a small salary as an assistant teacher" [GB/COR, Bahamas, CSOP, folio 4712. no. 4, "School Teachers from Jamaica," October 19, 1929 (Bahamas/PRO, 1971)]. The teachers were expected to be men no older than forty, with "two or three years teaching experience . . . capable of teaching agricultural science using 10–15 acre farms" [GB/COR, Bahamas, CSOP, folio 4712. no. 8, "School Teachers From Jamaica. 1927–1929." 16 May 1929 (Bahamas/PRO, 1971)]. The chairmen of the boards of agriculture and education convinced the governor-in-council that the introduction of agricultural education would motivate out islanders to remain at home and engage in agricultural enterprises. The colonial secretary was directed to secure assistance from his Jamaican counterpart to recruit the services of five teachers. They received annual salaries of approximately £250-£300 and prepaid passages for themselves and their dependents.

More than thirty Jamaicans applied for the five teaching positions. Most applications were rejected because the applicants were too old, unqualified, or attempting to renege on their contracts with the Jamaican government. One applicant, the father of five children, claimed to have served fourteen years as the principal of a grade school. Another applicant admitted that although his age was forty-two, he was suitably qualified for the position. He reported that he was a graduate of Mico College (a prestigious teacher training school in Jamaica), the recipient of honors in government examinations, and a twenty-year veteran educator [GB/COR, Bahamas. CSOP, folio 4712. "School Teachers from Jamaica, 1927–1929," May 27, 1929. (Bahamas/PRO. 1971)]. One successful applicant, in anticipation of hardships in the outer islands, brought furniture, including a bed and piano, to the Bahamas.

In the 1920s, the board of agriculture, wishing to develop a botanical garden and plant nursery, recruited Jamaican horticulturist Leonard Jervis. Jervis traveled extensively throughout the islands collecting species of plants and advising the colonial administration on the condition of agriculture in the colony. According to John, in an interview with the author on September 18, 1997, Jervis introduced into the colony new ornamental plants and crops from Jamaica, and implemented a structured policy on the organization of local agriculture. John, a leading Bahamian horticulturist, said that in the 1970s, when he worked for the Department of Agriculture, he heard about the innovations in horticulture Jervis introduced. In the early 1990s, John headed the botanical gardens in Nassau. Jervis married a local woman, raised a family, and retired in the Bahamas. His descendants include his grandson, a prominent Bahamian historic preservation architect.

Beginning in the early 1920s, scores of illegal West Indians (especially Jamaicans) entered the colony, including a high number of women. Most found refuge from the authorities in the homes of other Jamaicans, or as concubines and wives to Bahamian men. Some reportedly deliberately produced children with Bahamian men to ensure against deportation. According to Eliza, age eighty-eight at the time of the interview on September 18, 1996, most foreign women were aware that the Bahamian authorities were reluctant to deport any alien women who could prove that their children were born in the colony and fathered by Bahamians. In some cases, the women allegedly paid as much as £50 to be smuggled into the colony, usually via Inagua and the Ragged Islands. Eliza claimed that in 1928 she, along with two other Jamaican women, paid a Ragged Island ship captain to smuggle them from Cuba to Inagua in the southern Bahamas. From Inagua, they reportedly worked their way north to Nassau "where the real money was." Eliza declined to elaborate on the type of work she and her companions engaged in.

Some employed interesting methods to remain in the Bahamas. Miriam, ninety-two at the time of the interview, told the author on September 18, 1996, for example, that she was recruited in 1922 as nanny to the three daughters of her father's carpenter friend. She stated that other young Jamaican women employed in the Bahamas during the 1920s deliberately married Bahamians to ensure that they could remain in the colony. However, after her employer migrated to the United States, she rented lodging from another Jamaican family and worked illegally as a dressmaker for almost ten years before her marriage to Bahamian Howard Fernander.

In another case, Samuel, a Jamaican butler, worked for a winter resident family, but subsequently terminated his employment after only three months. The immigrant, denied further employment in Nassau, migrated to an outer island, where he changed his name and engaged in farming. He eventually married a local woman, acquired land, and thus legitimized his position in the community, according to an interview with the author on September 17, 1997. Samuel is the son of a Jamaican recruited in 1923 as a butler. He stated that his father migrated from New Providence to an outer island (the name of the island is kept anonymous to protect the identity of the family), where he married "Samuel's" mother five months after arrival in New Providence.

Some Jamaican women allegedly joined with Bahamian women to establish prostitution rings that catered almost exclusively to the artisans and laborers from the construction sites. Joan remembered, in an interview with the author on September 17, 1996, that there was a house near Hay Street (a predominantly black community in Nassau) which was occupied by three Jamaican women. The women reportedly worked as dressmakers, but their mostly male "clients" allegedly appeared after dark and left during the early morning hours. Davis, a retired Jamaican stonemason who came to the Bahamas in 1925, similarly recalled in a September 20, 1996, interview, that Jamaican and Bahamian prostitutes "set up shop" to meet the sexual demands of the construction workers. He claimed that

Jamaican women operated separately from Bahamian counterparts in small groups from rooms rented in such predominantly black neighborhoods as Bain and Grants Towns.

Davis, eighty-seven at the time of interview, alleged that many of the Jamaican prostitutes followed the immigration circuit of West Indian laborers to countries where employment opportunities existed. Davis referred me to two of his contemporaries and former laborers for interviews. Both, with the promise of anonymity, corroborated Davis' allegations. The editor of a local daily, in an apparent reference to illicit activities perpetrated by foreigners, complained: "There are at present in Nassau, quite a number of undesirables, who roam the city and suburbs at nights and make things very unpleasant for the women folk especially. There are also, we regret to say, some of our own ladies of the species, who were objectionable enough; but since there have been so many foreigners of the lower type continually coming and going, it has become positively unbearable" (*Nassau Daily Tribune*, November 4, 1923).

The illegal migration of West Indians into the Bahamas provoked public protest, mostly by black Bahamians, that specifically targeted Jamaicans. Hundreds of predominantly black Bahamians, who had been seasonal laborers on farms in Florida, returned home. They were prevented from returning to the United States by legislation that required passing a literacy test as a standard for entry. Generally unemployed, this group protested the West Indian presence in the colony. In 1926, three successive hurricanes crippled the once lucrative sponging and agricultural industries in which many outer islanders were engaged. The demise of these industries and the inaccessibility of the Florida job market motivated many Bahamians to flock to Nassau in search of employment, which had become hard to find by the late 1920s (Albuquerque and McElroy 1986:172).

On December 4, 1926, Mary Moseley, editor of the *Nassau Guardian* and a prominent white Bahamian, expressed concern that West Indian laborers deprived native Bahamians of employment opportunities. She said "the point which occurs to the Bahamian is that the resources of this Colony are not unlimited; and our duty being to our own people first, it follows that every alien drawing a wage from a Nassau industry is restraining a Bahamian from the opportunity of filling that position." The editor warned that the entry of "the more or less unskilled labourers who wanders to Nassau from one of the other West Indian islands because he has heard that Nassau is a sort of Tom Fiddler's ground should be rigorously discouraged." "Tom Fiddler's ground" is an obscure English expression that denotes a place where law and authority are lightly regarded, and "Tom Fiddler" was one of the main characters in an English story that featured such a fictitious place.

R. J. Bowe, a colored businessman and member of the House of Assembly, demanded the enforcement of restrictions on West Indian migration. In a letter printed December 8, 1926, to the editor of the *Nassau Guardian,* Bowe reminded the government that it was its responsibility to provide employment for Bahamians rather than for foreigners and aliens. Howard Johnson (1992:154) confirmed that the fear of some Bahamians that foreigners were being employed at the expense of local laborers was justified. He noted that in 1926 only thirty-nine of the 277 Colonial Hotel employees were Bahamians.

In January 1927 the executive council issued legislation which specifically prohibited the entry of immigrants traveling from Bermuda, Cuba, Jamaica, and British Honduras for a period of one year, without prior permission from the Bahamian colonial government. The executive council, comprising the governor, colonial secretary, receiver general/treasurer, and leading white Bahamians, dictated the direction of politics, society, and economics in the colony. Only passengers traveling first class were exempt from the restriction. The *Nassau Daily Tribune* editor commented on January 19, 1927, that no more than "a dozen British Hondurans, Bermudans, and Cubans" were in the colony at that time. Jamaicans were the obvious targets of the immigration restriction, since immigrants from other countries and colonies composed a small percentage of the immigration population in the colony.

The *Nassau Daily Tribune,* February 26, 1927, carried the story of Fred B. Spence, a Jamaican and former resident of Nassau, who expressed amazement that the Bahamian government enacted restrictive immigration legislation "directed at us Jamaicans." Immigration historian Howard Johnson (1992:115) commented on the immigration restriction: "The reference to immigrants traveling from Cuba was possibly intended to block the entry of Jamaican immigrants who were leaving Cuba in the aftermath of the depression in the sugar industry. The need for these regulations must have seemed urgent to the colonial authorities for Jamaica was also directly connected with [the] Bahamas by two ships . . . which plied between the two colonies fortnightly."

The *Nassau Daily Tribune,* which published a weekly column featuring news from the courts that provided encapsulated reviews of the cases, reported that in 1927 a number of Jamaicans were arrested, imprisoned, and (in some cases) deported for mostly minor crimes and infractions. For example, it reported that Jamaican Sinclair Seely (an unskilled laborer) was arrested for stealing groceries (30 April); Bahamian Joshua Anderson and Jamaican Ralph Fabre were charged with unlawful possession of stolen goods (4 May); and Kenneth Craydock (unskilled laborer) was "sentenced to five strokes of the birch for being found on the grounds of the Fort Montagu Hotel and unable to explain his presence there" (3 August).

Anonymous writers and the Jamaican press questioned the restrictions on immigration into the colony that seemed to target Jamaicans. One letter to the editor in the January 26, 1927, *Nassau Daily Tribune*, signed "Ashamed to be a Bahamian," outlined Jamaican contributions to the Bahamas and lamented the restrictive immigration laws:

> I say at the outset they are not undesirable. They are not monopolizing the courts, the jails, the hospital, the asylum nor the ranks of the beggars. They do not swell the ranks of the illiterate, they are intelligent and well-schooled. Most of them have a trade and some of them have qualifications that are scarce here. We have them in industry, and we have them on our police force with creditable records. In the erection of the Hotels New Colonial and Montagu we could not supply labour familiar with steel construction, the Jamaicans supplied it.

The writer, in obvious favor of lifting the immigration restrictions, continued: "And it is noteworthy that since their ingress into this Colony many of them have acquired property, and have not become paupers, some have married and in all the social activities of the people they are prominent." The Jamaican press castigated Bahamians for their apparent victimization of Jamaicans. The *Nassau Daily Tribune* published on February 4, 1927, the following excerpt from the Jamaican *Daily Gleaner*: "The population of [The] Bahamas numbers about forty thousand: those make their living by catering to tourists, by rum-running—a decayed industry in these days, we are afraid—and by curing sponges. A few Jamaicans have periodically emigrated there, but almost invariably they had obtained employment before leaving Jamaica. For instance, people from [The] Bahamas would engage Jamaica[n] cooks, butlers and housemaids and pay their passage over." In a later edition, February 12, 1927, the *Nassau Daily Tribune* printed another excerpt from the *Daily Gleaner,* which noted that the Jamaican legislative council passed a resolution protesting against "recent Legislation of the Panama Government excluding Jamaicans and other West Indian Negroes from Panama."

Jamaicans, despite the restrictions on immigration, continued to seek (and in some instances gain) employment in the Bahamas. In one advertisement on February 13, 1927, in the *Nassau Daily Tribune,* a Jamaican "colored couple" requested positions with a "good" family. The wife offered services as a "Lady's maid, nurse, or first class cook;" the husband claimed to be an "experienced valet, chauffeur, butler, or all round man." The couple expressed a willingness to travel. In another advertisement on April 6, 1927, the applicant offered himself as a "very good, all rounded, and reliable man (from Kingston, Jamaica). [seeking employment] as a clerk or manager of any merchant or liquor Department, also office, etc., and a good road foreman, not afraid of hard work." Another Jamaican applied for a position as a chauffeur on August 22, 1927, stating ten years' experience and the ability to supply references upon request. Most applications for entry, however, were rejected.

Bahamian officials, alarmed at the migration of Jamaicans and other West Indians to the Bahamas, passed the Immigration Act of 1928 [GB/COR, Bahamas. Executive Council Minutes. 1927–1931 (Bahamas/PRO. 1971)]. According to these minutes, almost 60 percent of all applications for entry into the Bahamas during the period came from Jamaicans. The act required all immigrants traveling second class to produce landing and health certificates and to pay a significant head tax prior to entry [GB/COR, Bahamas. CSOP. folio 6005. no. 29. "Immigration Act, 1928," 1930. (Bahamas/PRO. 1971)]. In 1929, the colonial secretary notified the managers of the major hotels that every person recruited to work in the hotels during the 1929–1930 season was required to be "furnished with a letter or identification card to be handed to the Immigration Officer upon arrival in Nassau, in order that he may be satisfied that the passenger is a bona fide employee of your Company" [GB/COR, Bahamas. CSOP. folio 72. "Charles Dundas. Colonial Secretary to H. E. Aspinall. Manager in Nassau. Munson Steamship Line." November 10, 1929. (Bahamas/PRO, 1971)]. Thus, by the end of the 1920s, considerable official and unofficial apprehension with respect to Jamaican migrants existed in the Bahamas.

Migration in the 1930s and 1940s

During the 1930s and 1940s, the migration of Jamaicans to the Bahamas was seldom officially documented. One reason for this scarcity of information is the fact that few Jamaicans were interested in migration to the colony. In 1930, few employment opportunities existed in the construction industry and even fewer in the hotel industry. Subsequently, many Bahamians and most West Indian immigrants were left unemployed. Most Jamaican artisans sought employment in other countries. Some, mostly unskilled (and generally illegal) Jamaicans, however, employed a variety of methods to remain in the colony. They were joined by other illegal aliens, predominantly Cubans, Haitians, and Turks and Caicos Islanders. In 1931, circuit magistrate E.H.M. McKinney noted concern for the proliferation of illegal immigration into the Bahamas. He reported that "Inagua and Ragged Island, Grand Bahama, and Bimini are open doors by which aliens of all types easily find their way to Nassau. . . . To illustrate, Inagua is the door by which persons from Haiti, San Domingo, Turks Island, Jamaica, and Cuba enter" [GB/COR. Bahamas. CSOP. Folio 6005. no.137. E.H.M. McKinney, Acting Stipendiary and Circuit Magistrate to Colonial Secretary, September. 1931 (Bahamas/PRO. 1971)].

Generally, the Bahamian colonial government ignored local and international criticism and continued to control West Indian migration. The Immigration Act of 1930 recommended that plumbers and painters be prohibited from entry into the colony without special permission [GB/COR, Bahamas. Executive Council Minutes, Folio 7147. no.24. 7 November 1930 (Bahamas/PRO. 1971)]. Restrictions were extended to the first class West Indian passenger, who was "if required, [expected to provide] an assurance in writing that he will not stay longer than four months in the Colony" without special permission from the governor-in-council [GB/COL Bahamas. CSOP. folio 78b. "Immigration Act 1930" (Bahamas/PRO. 1971)]. The following year, restrictions covered "Builders, Contractors, Electricians and Tailors" [GB/COR. Bahamas, Executive Council Minutes. folio 7157. no. 11. 18 May 1931 (Bahamas/PRO. 1971)].

Jamaicans continued to apply for employment in the Bahamas until the outbreak of World War II. Applications for employment, made through the office of the Jamaican colonial secretary, included those from scores of government employees. One such employee was Louis A. McKenzie, who submitted the following application: "having read in today's issue of the *Daily Gleaner* the big expansion programme in telephone facilities by the Bahamas Government, I hereby beg to apply for a position in the Telephone Department. I have great experience in telephone Operations. At present I am employed by the Jamaican Government in the Colonial Secretariat" [GB/COR, Bahamas. CSOP. folio 10136. "Application for Employment. Louis A. McKenzie." October 3, 1937 (Bahamas/PRO, 1971)]. During the war years, West Indian migration to the Bahamas temporarily ceased. Significant migration did not resume until the 1950s.

Postwar Migration to Independence, 1945 to 1973

Jamaican migration to the Bahamas resumed in the 1950s, when a small number of immigrants were recruited for employment in the public and private sectors. In 1949 the Bahamian colonial government embarked on an ambitious program to promote the islands as a major tourist and financial center. The action that followed produced employment opportunity in many sectors that, as in the 1920s, the small local labor market could not adequately fill (Albuquerque and McElroy 1986:187–191). Beginning in 1943, thousands of Bahamians were employed in the United States as farm laborers. Scores of "undocumented others" were living in the "Overtown" section of Miami. Invariably, West Indians, including Jamaicans, were recruited to partially fill the void. Most were recruited into the government service as police and prison officers.

The inspector of prisons, in his *Annual Report* for 1951, reflected the crisis that then existed in the local labor market: "The same difficulty in securing satisfactory recruits exists in the Prison as in the other Departments of the Government, and it is largely due to the fact that eligible persons can do better in Civil (private) life" [GB/COR. Bahamas. House of Assembly Minutes. folio 19. "Annual Report on Nassau Prison." April 1951. (Bahamas/PRO, 1971)]. The decision was made to recruit officers from throughout the British West Indies. Interestingly, Jamaicans were not highly regarded as suitable recruits. In a September 20, 1997 interview with three anonymous retired Trinidadian prison officers who were recruited in the 1950s, it was suggested that the government perceived Jamaicans as a troublesome, potentially disruptive people, who might incite other officers to agitate for better working conditions and wages. The men requested anonymity because, as one explained, "we don't want any trouble with our friends because of what we say."

Beginning in the postwar years, and continuing into the 1950s, the white-controlled Bahamian government faced serious challenges to its control of politics and society from an increasingly militant black majority. Understandably, it would have demonstrated a reluctance to recruit Jamaicans, who were widely perceived by many to be the most militant of all West Indians. In October 1997, the author met a Grenadian visitor to the Pompey Museum of Slavery in Nassau. During the course of conversation, the visitor, a history professor, noted that most English-speaking West Indians detest—and in many cases, fear—Jamaicans because of their "over-aggressive and individualistic nature." The visitor, in his late sixties, reportedly lived in England for thirteen years before moving to Canada. He noted that the friction between Jamaicans and other West Indians was most evident in England when he lived there. Consequently, the decision was made to obtain "recruits from Trinidad, [where it was] understood that there [was] a surplus of suitable material" [Annual Report on Nassau Prisons, April 1951. 3].

In succeeding years, recruitment prioritized Trinidadians, Barbadians, and Grenadians over Jamaicans. Between 1950 and 1973 Jamaicans represented less than 7 percent of all West Indians recruited into the public services [GB/COR, Bahamas, CSOP. "Colonial Service General Employment Status List. 1950–1968." folio 10999. (Bahamas/PRO, 1971)]. During the 1950s, Barbadians and Trinidadians were heavily recruited for the prison and police forces. In the 1960s, Grenadians became the more widely recruited. It should be noted, however, that annual recruitment was low, averaging approximately twenty officers. The few exceptions were specialized teachers, such as R. A. Shirley and G. B. Grant, who conducted courses in visual aids at the Board of Education summer school for teachers according to a notice in the August 5, 1961 *Nassau Guardian*.

Jamaican women competed with Bahamians for jobs in the hotels and restaurant industry. Scores of undocumented Jamaican women were also reportedly employed in private residences as domestic workers. The Browns (white Canadians) were recruited in 1953 as caretaker/managers of a condominium situated in the exclusive Cable Beach section of New Providence, according to an interview with the author on September 13, 1996. The Browns alleged that many winter residents and elite Bahamians exploited the women through long hours of work for low wages. They noted that approximately 50 percent of the domestic staff complement of cooks and maids in the industry were illegal Jamaican women. The couple alleged that the women were required to sometimes work eighteen-hour days to prepare for, serve at, and clean up after the frequent dinner parties the residents held. Some Jamaican domestic workers reportedly became permanent staff who traveled with their employers. They amusingly remarked that some domestic workers "vanished" shortly after arrival in the United States.

Bahamian domestic workers reportedly resented the competition from the Jamaicans. According to Alma in a September 1997 interview, some Bahamian women were denied employment in some residences because the Jamaicans were willing to work longer hours for less money than the average Bahamian would accept. At the age of eighty-seven at the time of interview, Alma still demonstrated contempt for some Jamaicans she knew more than forty years ago, and she said that the presence of the Jamaican women "caused plenty [Bahamian] women not to find jobs."

In 1966, the Bahamian authorities initiated a systematic program to detain and deport illegal Jamaicans and Haitians. Jamaicans, unlike the Haitian illegal aliens, entered the colony on visitor visas and deliberately overstayed their officially allotted time. The authorities reacted to constant complaints from the public of competition in the employment market from illegal Jamaican immigrants. One Jamaican's complaint to the editor of the *Nassau Guardian* on July 25, 1966, offers invaluable insight into the dilemma of the Jamaican "visitor" to the Bahamas in the late 1960s:

Sir, I am a scared Jamaican, who is afraid to reveal his name or whereabouts for fear of being hunted down like a dangerous wild animal and thrown into Fox Hill Prison. Yet I would like to know why at this very moment there are some of my countrymen and women in Fox Hill Prison, locked up like common criminals. They have committed an offence, yes. They came into this country as tourist. They overstayed the allotted time. They worked honestly, though illegally, filling jobs that Bahamians did not want, or did not have the skills to fill. As a result, people from my country that is a part of the British Commonwealth of Nations, with passports, are hunted down like dogs and are made into jailbirds. Every Jamaican who worked on the dredging project has been ordered home. Why is it that Jamaicans employed by the Bay Street Boys have not been ordered out of the country?

The "dredging project" mentioned by the correspondent referred to the expansion of the main docks in Nassau, which included dredging of the harbor. As mentioned earlier, the "Bay Street Boys" were the Nassau-based, white Bahamian elite who operated their economic interests mostly from Bay Street, which is the main street and business district in the Bahamas.

The annual reports from the prisons for the years 1967 and 1968 reflect the concern officials had about illegal Jamaican migration and the subsequent overcrowding of the prisons their arrest and incarceration created. For example, the report for 1967 noted that "there was an influx into the [Nassau] Prison of Jamaican nationals who were found in . . . contravention of the Immigration Act. . . . This led to overcrowding" [Annual Report on Nassau Prison, January 1968]. The report for 1968 stated: "we also have to accommodate female Jamaican nationals who overstay their time. The Haitian and Jamaican nationals seem to keep coming and this is leading to great overcrowding in the female Prison" [Annual Report on Nassau Prison, January 1969].

The prison reports reveal some of the "delay tactics" illegal Jamaican immigrants (notably women) used to frustrate efforts to deport them from the Bahamas. The 1968 report, for example, went on to note that "the Jamaican nationals have started a new thing in that they are either destroying or purposely losing their passports. This is causing great delay in having them processed for return to Jamaica." It was alleged during an interview with Perry on October 6, 1996, that some Jamaican female visitors deliberately became pregnant in the Bahamas. Perry, an immigration officer at the time of interview, stated that it was common for Jamaican women to visit the Bahamas, become pregnant, and (if marriage was not offered) request asylum based on the "presumed Bahamian nationality" of the child. The Jamaican women apparently hoped that either the Bahamian father would marry them, or that their Bahamas-born child would make them eligible for special immigration consideration. The report [Annual Report on Nassau Prison, January 1969] noted that "the ones [Jamaicans] who have delivered babies while in the Bahamas have not registered their births thus causing delay in obtaining traveling documents for these children and subsequently contributing to our problem of overcrowding."

Illegal Jamaican migration to the Bahamas created mixed reaction among Bahamians. Most whites did not come in direct social or economic contact with Jamaican immigrants, and so were generally indifferent to their presence in the colony. Both Jamaicans and Haitians, however, competed with blacks for employment opportunities, and in some instances, low-cost housing and the affections of eligible mates. Understandably, blacks issued the most vociferous protests against the migration to the Bahamas of any West Indians. One black, in a June 20, 1967, letter to the *Nassau Daily Tribune,* demanded that the government deport all (legal and illegal) West Indians from the Bahamas.

Some West Indian immigrants were concerned that the government might tolerate reprisals against them. One West Indian, in a letter to the *Nassau Daily Tribune,* reminded Bahamians on July 16, 1967, that the "Beloved Premier [Pindling] promised a square deal for all Belongers." "Belongers" were non-Bahamians who were given official resident status. Interestingly, the term "Expatriate" was used to describe whites, such as Europeans and North Americans, with similar immigration status. The writer noted that "it is not only Bahamians [needed to efficiently] run the country" and reminded Bahamians that "many Belongers voted for the Progressive Liberal Party in the last election and, therefore, had a right to live in the Bahamas." After Independence in 1973, the Bahamian government recruited hundreds of Jamaican teachers to fill vacancies existing in the science and technical fields. The recruitment of Jamaican teachers declined in the 1980s, when teachers from Guyana became the most frequent recruits.

Summary

Small numbers of undocumented Jamaicans migrated to the Bahamas during the 1920s and 1930s. Many engaged in a variety of mostly criminal misdemeanors. Some paid relatively large sums of money to be smuggled into the colony, while others, recruited for employment in one specific area, absconded to more lucrative jobs. Some undocumented Jamaican women engaged in prostitution, and others became the concubines and wives of Bahamian men and skilled artisans. Some Jamaicans relocated to the outer islands, where they assumed new identities.

In the late 1920s and early 1930s, a small number of Jamaicans were recruited to develop a new approach to agriculture in the Bahamas. The horticulture and agriculture teachers introduced a variety of new plants to the colony. The agriculture teachers, in particular, encouraged out-islander youth to remain in the rural islands and become self-employed in agricultural production. Agriculture education had the long-term effect of encouraging entrepreneurial initiative and curbing mass migration from the outer islands to New Providence.

In the late 1920s, Bahamian colonial officials introduced immigration restrictions that appeared to especially target Jamaicans. The new immigration laws responded to growing public protest over competition from West Indians for limited jobs. Despite protest from the Jamaican press and unidentified Bahamians, the restrictions eventually prohibited the entry of most skilled artisans into the colony. Thereafter, Jamaican migration was reduced to a small number of professionals recruited primarily for the government service. Many others, however, came as visitors, gained illegal employment, and overstayed the time allotted for their visits.

Despite their small numbers, Jamaicans significantly affected economics, society, and politics in the colony. During the 1920s, immigrant skilled artisans introduced black Bahamians to innovations in modern construction. The artisans provided a supply of skilled labor that satisfied an existing labor shortage necessary to facilitate economic development in New Providence. More importantly, their presence in Nassau demonstrated levels of professionalism to which black Bahamians could realistically aspire. Most Jamaican artisans remained in the colony for an average of five years, and then departed to other countries in search of employment opportunity.

Perhaps the most significant Jamaican contribution was made to the development of politics and society. Evidence suggests that the early artisans, primarily through the establishment of trade unions, encouraged black Bahamians to resist white political and social domination (Saunders 1991:78–85). In the 1920s, Jamaican artisans collaborated with black Bahamians to facilitate Marcus Garvey's appearance at a predominantly black political rally. Furthermore, according to Saunders, Garvey addressed what was reported to have been the largest crowd ever assembled for any event in Bahamian history; he inspired the masses to address the social, economic, and political barriers that separated them from the white elite.

The nearly xenophobic Bahamian reaction to the Jamaican-led, West Indian migration of the early decades of this century demonstrated a carefully considered Bahamian immigration policy of "open doors" when convenient and "closed doors" when a threat to employment and the social status quo was perceived. The next chapter will examine Bahamian reaction to Haitian migration. It will demonstrate how language, as well as ethnic and socioeconomic differences, served to relegate an entire minority group to the subservient role of social inferiors.

5

Haitian Migration to the Bahamas, 1793–1956

Migration from St. Domingue

Until the 1950s, migration between Haiti (Figure 5.1) and the Bahamas represented a reciprocal and constant flow of human traffic. The human linkage between the two countries began in the pre-Columbian era, when groups of aborigines migrated north from Española and established Lukku-cari (also known as Lucayan) subcultures in the islands that now make up the Bahamas. The Tainos, as the Lucayan migrants were also called, continued to war and trade with their cousins in the western part of Española now called Haiti (Craton and Saunders 1992:3–18). These authors claim that the two subgroups traded extensively in salt, dried shellfish, and possibly sea-island cotton, in exchange for hard stones, pottery, and an alloy of gold and copper called *guanin*. In the sixteenth and seventeenth centuries, after Europeans populated the islands, the human linkage expanded to include the interisland migration of buccaneers, pirates, privateers, and traders.

In the eighteenth century, the French (to whom Spain ceded the western section of the island in 1697) established a naval curtain to protect their economic interests in St. Domingue. Consequently, this curtain effectively interrupted the interisland linkage. Significant numbers of African slaves were forcibly migrated to work sugarcane and coffee plantations. The slave population, mostly led by Toussaint L'Ouverture, Jean-Jacques Dessalines, and Henri Christophe, revolted against the French in 1791, and in 1804 independence was established. The island, renamed Haiti, became the first black republic and the second republic in the New World.

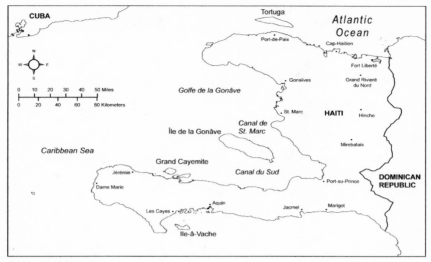

Figure 5.1. Haiti.

Following independence, two separate regimes (North and South) existed until Haiti was unified in 1820. From 1822 to 1844, Haiti and the eastern part of the island were temporarily reunited. In 1844, the Dominican Republic and Haiti became separate countries. Haiti entered a period of chaotic political and economic turmoil that was accentuated in 1915 by U.S. military intervention and occupation. The occupation ended in 1934 (Geggus 1982).

Haitian-Bahamian Relations and the Haitian Revolution

Ironically, the revolutions of the late eighteenth century reestablished the Haitian-Bahamian human linkage. One consequence of the Haitian Revolution was an exodus of white planters with their slaves and groups of free people of color (Geggus 1982:40). Further, according to Geggus, slave owners brought their slaves out of St. Domingo because slaves were chattel property. The immigrant slaves accompanied their masters for a variety of reasons, but many slaves did not willingly leave St. Domingo. Perhaps there was sufficient semblance of authority (or coercion) remaining on the plantations or in Cap Français to enable masters to leave with their slaves.

Some historians, however, suggest that loyalty may have motivated some slaves to voluntarily accompany their masters. A French fleet, anchored off Cap Français in anticipation of possible British and Spanish invasions, rescued thousands of terrified St. Domingans from the revolutionary carnage. The refugees escaped in over 200 French naval and private ships (Nash 1988:141). Most refugees fled to Cuba and the United States (Hunt 1988:24–30). Almost 4,000 whites and 2,000 blacks and *gens de coleur* sailed with the French fleet to Charleston, Baltimore, Philadelphia, New York, and Boston. A small number of St. Domingans emigrated to Jamaica. According to an article in the *Royal Gazette* (July 9, 1799) a smaller number migrated to the Bahamas; some because they were unable to finance relocation to their first choice of refuge. Most, however, were captured and landed in the colony as prizes of privateering (McWeeny 1994:2). Some refugees were white French colonists accompanied by their African slaves. Others were royalist coloreds fleeing probable reprisal by militant slaves [GB/COR. Bahamas. Debates in the Courts of Vice-Admiralty. 1798–1805 (Bahamas/PRO. 1971)]. Many St. Domingan refugees escaped St. Domingo aboard American ships chartered for that purpose.

The indiscriminate and predatory nature of Bahamian privateering—particularly targeting French shipping from St. Domingo—exposed the colony to the threat of military retaliation by offended states. In 1779, for example, it was discovered in letters confiscated from French prisoners that as many as six contingents of mostly free blacks and mulattos planned to escape from St. Domingo. According to the report, the plans called for an attack on Nassau to free as many slaves as possible, acquire loot, and subsequently attempt to establish a free black settlement in west Florida [GB/COR. Bahamas. Debates in the Courts of Vice-Admiralty. 1798–1805 (Bahamas/PRO. 1971). June 24, 1779. folio 23. no. 191]. The governor's report on the incident demonstrated, among other things, that local fortifications and the militia had fallen into a state of gross disrepair. In September 1793, the colony was in a state of military alert. Residents were alarmed by news of an armed attack from "a considerable [French] force [assembled] at New York for the purpose of invading this Island [New Providence] and avenging the depredations which [Bahamian] privateers had committed against the trade of Saint Domingue" (*Bahama Gazette*, January 19, 1794). Interestingly, The Earl of Dunmore, governor of the Bahamas, enlisted the aid of privateers operating within the Bahamas, and stationed privateer ships in strategic locations throughout the archipelago [GB/COR. Bahamas, CSOP. folio 23. no. 32. Dunmore to Dundas [Confidential]. September 1793. (Bahamas/PRO, 1971), 153.]. The governor requested additional assistance from Jamaica and the Spanish government at Havana. The privateers provided some 1,200 men to augment the poorly organized local militia, which was estimated at only 230 men.

Generally, Haitians were held imprisoned aboard the ships until the colonial authorities decided their fate. Most prisoners, however, did not wish to remain in the Bahamas. The more affluent prisoners made financial arrangements with the authorities to have their slaves and some personal possessions released. Repatriation negotiations were executed primarily through the office for prisoners of war located in Nassau. In 1805, R. Lord, an "agent for Prisoners of War for the Bahama Islands," issued the following notice, which provides insight into the process to which prisoners were subjected: "Notice is hereby given to all Commanders and Agents of privateers who shall neglect to report at this Office, immediately on the arrival of any Prize or Privateer the number of Prisoners that may have on board the prison ship, or who shall permit all prisoners to land, that their bonds may be put in suit" (*Royal Gazette*, July 6, 1805).

The repatriation process was reportedly a protracted exercise that could last several months. According to McWeeny (1994:3), there would have been delays in deportation arrangements, and in the interval, opportunities and incentives would have been presented for residents looking for cheap labor. Some officials, probably "impatient with the hassles of deportation arrangements and the expense to the public purse of maintaining large numbers of refugees," made concerted efforts to accelerate the deportation process (McWeeny 1994:3). Some unscrupulous officials, however, probably solicited bribes from the émigrés to hasten the process. Others, probably motivated by surreptitious incentives from residents who wished to delay deportation in hopes of acquiring confiscated Haitian slaves inexpensively, prolonged the process. Most of the less affluent Haitians, unable (or unwilling) to pay for their release, made numerous attempts to escape captivity.

Initially, Bahamian authorities appeared to be sympathetic to the plight of the white Haitian émigrés. It should be noted, however, that the sympathy exhibited was influenced by a perception that the Haitian whites were generally successful planters and businessmen who could contribute to the development of the colony. In 1797, Governor Dunmore, in recognition of this potential contribution, proposed a plan to attract Haitians to the Bahamas. He informed the council that: "It has occurred to me that it might be desirable for Administration, in the event of the cession of

St. Domingo, or any other of the French islands on the conclusion of the Treaty of Paris, to establish in some of the Bahamas for such of the French as many have attached themselves in most of [the] . . . Islands to the English Governor, as well as for certain meritorious French immigrants [BR/COR, Bahamas, CSOP, folio 23. no. 35. Outline of a Plan for the Settlement of the Bahamas by means of French Immigrants and Reduced Officers of Army and Navy. July 1797. [microfilm edition]. (Bahamas/PRO. 1971), 97.].

As reported in this same document, the governor proposed the establishment of a French settlement at Inagua, which he claimed was "well suited for a French settlement, particularly from St. Domingo, [as it] contains many thousands of acres well adapted to the culture of cotton." He noted that Inagua was "supposed not to be unhealthy, as none of the causes unfavourable to the constitution of Europeans appear to exist there" and he proposed to give the Haitians generous land grants and authorization to relocate with their personal property, including slaves and houses. The plan proposed the settlement of fifty French families on Inagua; forty on Acklins "on which there are only four settlers;" and fifty on Andros "where the number of settlers are also inconsiderable." He went on to include military officers, who were to be enticed by land grants "in a manner similar to that adopted in the Grant made by this Colony to the American Loyalist."

The continuous and overwhelming influx of Haitian refugees, however, caused colonial officials to reconsider plans to establish Haitian settlements in the Bahamas. According to McWeeny (1994:3), "the privateers had proven themselves too industrious; there were now too many [Haitian] immigrants to attend to and economic distortions resulting from the privateering boom, not the least of which was runaway inflation, had become alarmingly evident" in Nassau. Colonial officials decided that deportation was the most feasible method of controlling Haitian migration to the Bahamas.

The Bahamian attitude concerning the influx of Haitian immigrants is reflected in one of the governor's reports to the colonial secretary: "The incredible number of French prisoners and passengers we have had here has raised the price of every kind of provisions enormously and I am using every means in my power to get [them] sent to America, the original place of their destination" [GB/COR. Bahamas. CSOP. folio 23. no.32. Dunmore to Dundas. July 1793. (Bahamas/PRO. 1971), 124]. McWeeny noted that, although the "white émigrés from Saint Domingue [Haitians] doubtless stood an infinitely better chance of settling in the Bahamas if they were so inclined," public anxiety over the large number of refugees created a "clamor for more effective exclusionary action" (1994:3).

Nassauvians, fearing attacks by the French from within and without the colony, protested the presence of the Haitians. They complained that "the dangerous consequences that results from so many French prisoners being confined on board prison ships in [Nassau] harbour, and the state of alarm in which the inhabitants of this Town are kept arising from the dread of prisoners who are rendered in great degree desperate" [GB/COR. Bahamas. CSOP, folio 23. no. 64. February 10, 1796 (Bahamas/PRO. 1971), 260]. The protesters recounted cases in which groups of Haitian prisoners escaped in locally owned ships stolen from the Nassau harbors, such as the theft of a ship belonging to prominent residents William and James Moss "laden with cargo and anchored in fortified Fort Montaigue" [GB/COR. Bahamas. CSOP, folio 23. no. 64. February 10, 1796 (Bahamas/PRO. 1971), 260]. The residents reminded the [governor-in-] council that Haitian prisoners had occasionally set their prison ships ablaze in desperate attempts to escape [GB/COR. Bahamas. CSOP, folio 23. no. 64. February 10, 1796 (Bahamas/PRO. 1971), 260].

Local slaves were discouraged from association with the Haitian slaves and *affranchis* (non-white, free Haitians) as a means of limiting the opportunity for black rebellion. Conversely, they were encouraged to report the "suspicious movements" of French prisoners. In one recorded case, a group of local slaves was publicly applauded for its recapture of a group of Haitian escapees. The *Bahama Gazette* reported the event as follows:

On Sunday night . . . we were informed that nine French prisoners of war, effected their escape from on board the prison vessel situated in the harbour, and evaded every attempt made by the keepers of the ship to regain possession of them. We are . . . happy to inform our readers that three of the said prisoners were apprehended in a boat they had stolen from Mr. Fernander . . . by the bravery, good conduct and judgment of three slaves belonging to Robert Rumer, Esq., one belonging to Mr. Samuel Moxey and one belonging to Mr. Taylor, who observed a suspicious boat approaching them . . . repaired to Mr. Rumer's house, . . . got arms, pursued in a boat belonging to their master, the suspicious boat, with which they came up, and after firing three rounds with balls cartridges, the Frenchmen surrendered, and were conducted back to their abode on board the prison ship by the faithful negroes, where they obtained a receipt for the delivery of them (July 5, 1804).

The editor noted that he "took pleasure in relating the conduct of the above slaves, in hopes that they were or will be rewarded equal to their deserts."

Just a year later, the *Bahama Gazette* (July 7, 1805) reported that Bahamian authorities, in an obvious effort to quiet public alarm at the influx of mostly colored and black Haitians, levied taxes of £30 upon each slave, and £100 on each *affranchis*. Slaves for whom taxes were not paid were arrested, confiscated as state property, and sold at public auctions to the highest bidder. Defaulting *affranchis* were also arrested. Unlike slaves, however, these free people could not be sold as chattel property. Instead, they were deported to neutral ports such as those in the United States. Those prisoners unable to pay the deportation cost were "apprenticed" to local residents until they had accumulated sufficient funds to pay the cost of transportation from the colony. In 1796, for example, the *Bahama Gazette* advertised the "apprenticeship" of an *affranchi* (named Joe), who was sentenced to deportation from the colony. The advertisement stipulated that the "Negro man [was] sentenced to be transported out of the Bahama Islands, [but] must not be sent to any of the French or Spanish Islands" (*Bahama Gazette*, November 23, 1796). The decision to prohibit the deportation of Joe to "any of the French or Spanish Islands" is unclear. Perhaps it was made on the assumption that the deployment of blacks to territories controlled by economic rivals would strengthen the economic base of that colonial power.

In 1793, colonial authorities amended the Immigration Act as a measure "essential to the security and peace of these Islands" [GB/COR. Bahamas, Minutes of the House of Assembly "An Act For Laying Certain Duties And Impositions On All French Negroes, And Other French Persons Of Colour Now Within These Islands Or May Hereafter Be Brought Within The Same" September 1793. (Bahamas/PRO, 1971)]. The *Bahama Gazette* reported on September 18, 1793, that under the amended act, the taxes levied on the immigrants generated substantial revenue. They reported that in 1793, for example, taxes and duties on "French Negroes" amounted to £1,156,195. The receiver general, in his dual capacity as treasurer (and in probable recognition of this source of potential revenue) cautioned Bahamian purchasers of St. Domingan slaves to pay outstanding taxes in order to "prevent further trouble." The act further required ship captains bearing French slaves to "provide a detailed report on the slaves within twelve hours of arrival in port." The Immigration Act of 1793 became, as one author described it, a "discriminatory, anti-Haitian immigration policy . . . armed with the bludgeon of draconian taxation, presumably on the theory that few would be able to withstand the financial blows inflicted and thus be beaten back into the sea from whence they came" (McWeeny 1994:4).

In 1795, reports McWeeny, the Immigration Act was revised to empower all British subjects to "arrest on sight any Haitian slave found at large and promptly commit him to the common jail to await deportation at his own expense" (1994:4). The legislation declared it illegal to purchase, hire, or employ any St. Domingan slave who entered the colony after February 1793. Interestingly, the act exempted St. Domingan slaves living in New Providence, Harbour Island, Eleuthera, and Watlings Island, where a number of planters had protested the prospect of losing their investments in St. Domingan slaves already employed in the mentioned islands. The majority of the Bahamian population lived in these islands. Many employed confiscated St. Domingans as a source of cheap labor. McWeeny suggests that the public outcry influenced the broad concession granted.

The revised immigration policy was especially restrictive against the *affranchis*. Those entering the Bahamas after 1795 were granted an amnesty of two months to leave the colony, after which they were subject to arrest and deportation. The colonial authorities may have exerted exclusionary pressure against the free, colored St. Domingans as one means of establishing social control. McWeeny argues that "free negroes were not under the proprietary superintendence of a master and were therefore, if not theoretically, in a better position [than St. Domingan slaves] to resort to subversive activity undetected" (1994:5). He opined that "the Haitian mulatto . . . actually started all the trouble in Saint Domingue when they [took] up arms against the French colonist well before the slaves."

In 1797, Bahamian colonial authorities discovered a plot by St. Domingans to lead an insurrection against white authority. An intelligence report claimed that: "French negroes (most of whom were captured by privateers of this port [Nassau] and brought to this Island in the commencement of the War) had entered into a conspiracy, immediately to seize the ordnance stores, to put the sentries to death, and after providing themselves with a sufficient quantity of arms and ammunition to attack Fort Charlotte and set fire to the east end of town in order to divert the attention of the inhabitants" (*Bahama Gazette*, August 3, 1797).

Evidence given at the inquiry that followed, and reported on September 14, 1797, in the *Bahama Gazette*, identified and convicted five St. Domingans of plotting to organize "the Destruction of His Majesty's subjects, the white inhabitants of these Islands." Evidence came primarily from Bahamian slaves, some of whom testified that they had attempted to discourage the treasonous act. The defendants, Baptiste Perpall, Baptiste Tucker, Police Edgcombe, Tom Bethune, and Tom Lockhart allegedly "resolved to 'fight and take the country from the white people' and thereby put themselves in the same situation as the black people were in the Cape [Français]" (McWeeny 1994:6). Three of the defendants were found guilty of treason and executed by hanging. The corpses of Perpall and Tucker (the acclaimed leaders) were prominently displayed in chains at a place called Hog Island Point as a warning to others of the price of treason. Two suspected co-conspirators were saved from execution, but summarily deported from the colony. Although the records do not specify, the deportees were probably *affranchis*, because slaves in the Bahamas (as in most other slaveholding areas) were traditionally condemned to death for treason.

Typically, in that period of apprehension of a revolt, free blacks would probably not be reprieved. However, if reprieved, the persons would probably not have been allowed to remain in New Providence or any of the more populated islands where they could become a symbol of rebellion and resistance to white rule.

Bahamian whites, alarmed by the prospect that the St. Domingans might collaborate with slaves in New Providence in a bloody rebellion against them, relocated the remaining refugees to sparsely inhabited islands in the southern Bahamas, distant from New Providence. The incident temporarily cemented official resolve to stringently enforce restrictions against St. Domingan migration into the colony. McWeeny noted that the resolve to restrict Haitian migration to the Bahamas was short-lived because "political resolve in the Bahamas [was] seldom sustained for long stretches. Tending instead to ebb into the customary pattern of slack indifference . . . once a given crisis and the public hysteria associated with it had passed" (1994:7). The many islands of the Bahamas and their location along the major shipping lanes connecting the Americas, how-ever, combined with the economic prosperity that privateering generated in the islands, militated against a successful immigration policy.

In 1801, Bahamian whites were shocked by the announcement that the predominantly white 47th Regiment would be removed from the Baha-mas, and subsequently replaced by a contingent of black troops. They feared that the local blacks, St. Domingans, and the black troops would conspire against them. Most Bahamian whites ignored the fact that the British intended to replace the contingents of white troops stationed throughout the West Indies with troops from various West India Regi-ments. The replacement of white troops with black troops recruited from the West Indies and Africa was designed to reduce the high mortality from tropical diseases which occurred among white troops [GB/COR. Bahamas. CSOP, folio 133. no. 47. April 11, 1801 (Bahamas/PRO, 1971)]. The British decided that soldiers of the 5th and 6th West India Regiment stationed at the Bay of Honduras should replace the troops stationed in the Bahamas.

Nevertheless, white Bahamians petitioned the governor to retain the white troops for protection against a possible invasion of the Bahamas by rebel forces from St. Domingue. The petitioners complained that "it is not easy to conceive a more general panic, than the appearance of these [black] detachments excite the agitation of the public mind could not have been greater had Touissaint [*sic*] himself have come with all his force" [GB/PRO, Bahamas, CSOP, folio 23. no. 39. "Petition Against the Removal of the 47th Regiment." May 12, 1801. (Bahamas/PRO, 1971), 132–33]. Whites were especially fearful that the St. Domingans' domicile in the Bahamas would incite the black troops to destabilize white oligar-chic control over the colony. They protested that: "the great numbers of French negroes . . . who have within these few years found means to in-troduce themselves to this Colony, afford sufficient grounds for apprehen-sion, and if they should by any artful practices, and they are not deficient in cunning, ingratiate themselves with the black Troops, the situation of these islands would be truly alarming [GB/PRO, Bahamas, CSOP, folio 23. no. 39. "Petition Against the Removal of the 47th Regiment." May 12, 1801, (Bahamas/PRO, 1971), 132–33]. Some petitioners threatened to aban-don the colony with their property should the "black Troops of the West India Regiment be allowed to be stationed in Nassau" [GB/PRO, Baha-mas, CSOP, folio 23. no. 39. "Petition Against the Removal of the 47th

Regiment." May 12, 1801. (Bahamas/PRO, 1971), 132–33]. In 1801, despite the protests, the West Indian troops replaced their European counterparts without incident.

Throughout the early decades of the 1800s, some white Bahamians continued to express paranoia over the prospect that Haitian immigrants could instigate insurrections against them. One of the numerous petitions to the governor on the subject noted that "merchants and traders live in apprehension of having their stores and property destroyed by fire. The planters fear a spirit of licentiousness will be disseminated amongst their slaves" [GB/COR, Bahamas/ CSOP. folio 23. no. 40 (Bahamas/PRO. 1971), 116]. One petitioner went on to claim that families were greatly "disturbed at the idea of a Revolt similar to what happened in St. Domingo [happening in the Bahamas]" Some expressed concern with what they perceived to be growing *affranchis* influence on the colored middle class and threats to white monopoly on trade and politics (Craton and Saunders 1992:204–210).

Privateers continued to bring St. Domingan émigrés to the Bahamas even in the years following the establishment of the Republic of Haiti. After 1805, Bahamian privateers increasingly preyed on Spanish shipping. By 1804, however, Haitian migration to the Bahamas had slowed significantly. Most of the earlier immigrants were settled in Inagua and the Turks and Caicos Islands. Some Haitian whites and *affranchis*, however—largely because of their light skin color and highly demanded trade skills (tailors, jewelers, shoemakers)—remained in Nassau and became assimilated into the Bahamian middle class. In January 1799, one immigrant, Monsieur Le Bastier, was reported in the *Bahama Gazette* to be sufficiently established as a businessman to announce that he made "Elastic Truffles upon an Improved Plan, which were found at St. Domingo to be superior to any ever used." Another immigrant reported in that same newspaper on January 18, 1799, that Monsieur Peries, reputedly the former receiver general of St. Domingue, became established within the Long Island plantocracy as a "French Gentleman . . . with the most engaging manners, and an appearance uncommonly respectable, possessed of a liberal and cultivated mind."

Most Haitian immigrants, despite the anxiety expressed by some white Bahamians, peacefully assimilated into Bahamian society. A minority, however, became involved in anti-white activities. One such case was that of Joseph Duty, an *affranchi* who arrived in the Bahamas in 1807 but resided intermittently in Cuba [GB/PRO. Bahamas, CSOP, folio 23. no.118. Matthews to Lord Stanley. September 13, 1844. (Bahamas/PRO,1971), 94–100]. In 1844, Duty was court-martialed in Cuba in absentia and subsequently banished from Spanish West Indian territories for ten years on charges of conspiracy to incite armed rebellion against the whites in Cuba. Duty unsuccessfully appealed to the Bahamian authorities to intervene on his behalf. Subsequently, Duty became a permanent resident of the Bahamas in 1836 and a naturalized Bahamian in 1844.

After 1834 in the British Empire, the gradual and limited freedom of mobility, speech, and social and political opportunity that Emancipation accorded people of color, allowed some Haitian immigrants to succeed in economics and politics. Among the most successful of the Bahamian *affranchis* in the Bahamas were half-brothers Edward Laroda, John Goodman, and Stephen Dillet. Laroda became one of the first colored members of the House of Assembly. Goodman was a successful merchant who owned large acreage of land. In Nassau, a popular public seaside picnic area (Goodman's Bay) is named in honor of Goodman. Arguably, Dillet and his sons were the most notable of the early Haitian immigrants to the Bahamas. The son of French army officer Etienne Dillet, Stephen was born in St. Domingue in 1797. He and his mother, Mary Catherine Argo, while sailing to Cuba, were captured and brought to New Providence in 1802 aboard a privateer. During the 1820s and 1830s, Dillet distinguished himself as a successful businessman, politician, and civil rights activist. He is credited as the first colored Bahamian elected to the House of Assembly.

In 1833, Bahamian whites, indignant that Dillet defeated a white opponent and won a place in the House of Assembly, refused to allow him to take his seat. A special election was called in which the white elite threw their entire support behind the white contestant. Dillet, however, won the second election by a clear mandate and was only then allowed to assume his place as a member of the House of Assembly. He represented one of the city districts of Nassau for twenty-five consecutive years. Dillet, who also served as the first black Bahamian postmaster, died in 1889. His early political accomplishments were monumental for a period in Bahamian history when slavery had only recently been abolished, and the minimum eligibility to vote was ownership of real property valued at £200. In the years immediately following Emancipation, only a small number of black Bahamians possessed property valued at £200. Dillet's sons, Thomas William Henry and Stephen Albert, became distinguished in a number of professions. James Johnson (Johnson 1933:3–5), an African American of Bahamian extraction, married Stephen Albert's sister. The couple later relocated to Jacksonville, Florida, where their son James Weldon Johnson was born.

Thomas William Henry distinguished himself as a House of Assembly representative, first for the western district of Nassau and later for a district on the island of Abaco. In 1864, he was elected chairman of the Board of Health and an acting assistant judge. In 1865, he became the first Bahamian of color promoted to the Legislative Council (Saunders 1991:71). At age twenty-three, Stephen Albert was appointed acting deputy inspector of lighthouses. He became an accomplished navigator, and mastered several lighthouse tender ships in the Bahamas, England, and the West Indies. He was a prolific writer who distinguished himself as a correspondent to and periodic editor of six local newspapers. Known to many as "Captain Dillet, Admiral and Our Grand Old Man," Stephen Albert died in 1930 at the age of eighty-five. The *Tribune* (November 2, 1930) honored him as "a writer who wielded a trenchant pen, an orator and a politician . . . a temperance reformer and a musician."

Haitian Migration: 1838 to 1922

The Haitian-Bahamian human linkage continued throughout the 1800s through continuous trade between the two countries. Seamen from the southern Bahamian islands traded salt, fish, and British and American manufactured goods for fruits, vegetables, rum, and livestock with Haitian merchants in the northern port towns of Haiti [GB/COL Bahamas, CSOP, folio 277. no. 90 Governor's Annual Report for 1898, June 18, 1899. (Bahamas/PRO, 1971)].

The geographic proximity of Inagua and Long Cay in the southern Bahamas and Ile de la Tortue (Tortuga) less than sixty miles off northwest Haiti played a special role in fostering constant interisland migration between Haiti and the Bahamas. In the late 1800s and early 1900s, Tortuga was one of the most important centers for the production of breadbasket foods, for shipbuilding, and for maritime commerce in Haiti. Tortuga and port towns in northern Haiti supplied the southern Bahamas with food, boats, and handicraft. Port de Paix and Cap-Haïtien, in particular, were then more accessible to residents of the southern Bahamas than Nassau.

In 1898, acting governor Churchill reported that "so many steamers from New York en route to the Gulf Ports now call at Inagua for labourers that the inhabitants of that place can import their goods direct from New York and also make a profitable trade by exporting American goods to Hayti" [GB/COL Bahamas, CSOP, folio 277. no.90. Governor's Annual Report for 1898. June 18, 1899. (Bahamas/PRO, 1071)]. Inagua served as an important entrepôt from which deck hands could be recruited for ships sailing to South and Central America, and agricultural laborers for plantations in those countries. It also offered facilities for the exchange of foreign currencies (Albury 1976:36–65).

Beginning in the late 1800s, Haitians began a small, yet constant migration to the southern Bahamas in search of economic opportunity. In 1901, the enumerator of census for the District of Inagua and Long Cay reported the presence of approximately 300 West Indian immigrants, which included an undetermined number of Haitians: "There were absent from the island at the time the census was taken about 1,000 men, employed in Mexico, Central America, and on steamers; of this number at least 300 were residents of this Island (and will be back in a few months), about 400 are from other islands of the Bahamas, and the remainder were from Haiti and other West Indian Islands" [GB/COR. Bahamas. CSOP, Report on the Census of the Bahama Islands taken in 1901. (Nassau: *Nassau Guardian* 1901)].

Despite apparent language differences, there is evidence to suggest that the Haitian presence in the southern Bahamas was as significantly high throughout the late nineteenth and early twentieth centuries as was the Bahamian presence in northern Haitian ports during the same period [GB/COR. Bahamas. CSOP, Report on the Census of the Bahama Islands taken in 1901. (Nassau: *Nassau Guardian* 1901)]. Haitian-Bahamians and older Bahamians who were interviewed reported cases in which Bahamians from the southern Bahamas fathered (and later abandoned) children in Haiti while working as stevedores in Haitian ports, or during regular trading excursions to that country. Evidence of this reciprocal migration is revealed in a series of taped interviews with Bahamian-Haitians conducted and sponsored in the Bahamas by the Department of Archives. In one case, an interviewee claimed that in 1915 his Bahamian father migrated from Inagua Island to Haiti where he established a pharmacy with goods imported from the Bahamas. The Bahamian, being an English speaker, reestablished himself as a tailor with a contract to produce uniforms for American soldiers stationed there (Sherene Thompson, interview with the proprietor of Jasmine Florist, Nassau, the Bahamas, December 11, 1995, copied transcript in Bahamas/PRO, 1997). Another interviewee, Jacques Cadet, remembered a business establishment in Haiti called the "All Day, All Night" that was reportedly owned and operated by a Bahamian called Marcey Myer. Cadet reported that as a child in Haiti, he remembered Bahamians living in Haiti and those trading there or employed as stevedores and deck hands on visiting ships congregating at this store to share news about the Bahamas. He mentioned an "old [Bahamian] lady name Mary, a dressmaker, who used to tell us stories about Cat Island, the island in the Bahamas where she was born." He claimed it was in that environment that he learned to speak English (Thompson interview with Jacques Cadet, Haitian-born, Bahamian entrepreneur, Nassau, the Bahamas, December 12, 1995, copied transcript in Bahamas/PRO, 1997).

Some Haitians in Inagua married Bahamians and produced families. Others established relationships with local mistresses. It should be noted that few Haitian immigrants intended to remain in the Bahamas after current job opportunities ceased to exist. The Haitian-Bahamian linkage resulted in the proliferation of children sired by Bahamians and Haitians [Thompson, Taped interview with Captain Victor Lockhart, January 15, 1966, copied transcript (Bahamas/PRO, 1997), 3]. Many Bahamian traders and crews of trading ships reportedly frequented Haitian brothels or maintained Haitian mistresses during excursions to that country. The high level of human interaction between Haitians and Bahamians would have provided numerous opportunities for social contact at all levels and would have facilitated subsequent migration. The large number of Bahamians with Anglo-French names, such as Bode (now anglicized as Bodie), Deleveaux, Dillett, Dupuch, Duvalier, Godet, Laroda, Moree, Marche, and Poitier strongly supports the argument for a large Haitian influence in the Bahamas. Despite strong evidence to the contrary, some Haitians in the Bahamas insist that former Haitian dictator François "Papa Doc" Duvalier was born in the southern Bahamas. Yvon Cherenfant states that the name "Duvalier," which is common in the Bahamas, is uncommon in Haiti. Haitian-Bahamian businessman Jacques Cadet insists that Duvalier was born in Inagua: "We [Haiti] don't have no Duvalier but you come to [the] Bahamas all you have is Duvalier[s]. Only Duvalier we had was him [the former Haitian president] and when he left that's it, nobody else. All the Duvaliers are here in Nassau."

By the turn of the twentieth century, Haitian (together with other West Indian) migrants began to fill the labor vacuum existing in Nassau that was created by the exodus of Bahamians in search of employment opportunities in south Florida. Albury noted (1976:169) that "records are scant but perhaps ten to twelve thousand Bahamians emigrated during the first two decades of this century." Bahamas governor W. Grey-Wilson, in 1908 and 1911 reports, noted that the migration destination of Bahamians from the southern islands had shifted from Central and South America to the United States. He noted that an economic downturn in the United States had "paralyzed" the Central American logging industry, while fruit steamships which had previously recruited Bahamian stevedores had ceased to call at Bahamian ports [GB/COR, Bahamas. Governor's Despatches, 1904–1912: Grey-Wilson to Lewis Harcourt, June 1911 (Bahamas/PRO, 1971)]. Haitians followed the northbound labor migration trail and secured employment in the northern Bahamas mostly in the agricultural sector, clearing farm acreage for large American-owned industries.

Haitian Migration: 1922–1956

Before the 1950s, few Haitian migrants demonstrated a desire to remain in the Bahamas. In fact, the comparatively insignificant disparity of wealth and development could possibly have made Haiti more attractive to Bahamians [Interview with Captain Victor Lockhart, 5]. In 1931, the Bahamas' colonial government compiled an immigration list which supports this argument. The list (complete with names, addresses, nationalities, and dates of arrival) included approximately 2,000 West Indian immigrants in the colony, of which fewer than ten were Haitians [GB/COR, Bahamas, CSOP, folio 23. no. 57. List of Unregistered Aliens in the Bahama Islands, 1931 (Bahamas/PRO, 1971)]. In each case, the Haitian was registered with an anglicized (as opposed to francophone) name, such as Samson Brown, Samuel Davis, Edgar Henderson, Emerald Johnson, and Fritz Sears, suggesting that some of the Haitians may have descended from British West Indian immigrants to Haiti (Fraser 1988:79–94). Haitian immigrants, in the absence of laws restricting their migration to the Bahamas before the turn of the century, had little need to anglicize their names (as is a common practice today).

As previously discussed, beginning in the 1920s, with expansion in the construction of public and private projects, the migration of Haitians to the Bahamas concerned colonial officials. This was not a novel phenomenon. Colonial officials had expressed concern over the migration of Haitian laborers to Inagua and Long Cay before the turn of the century. Acting Governor Churchill, in his *Annual Report* of 1898, alluded to the "introduction of criminal classes from Haiti who have to be kept in prison at Nassau. . . ." (Fraser 1988:79–94). Authorities, however, were particularly concerned with the migration of increasing numbers of undocumented Haitian laborers. After 1920, Haitians registered with the immigration authority gave predominantly francophone names, such as Sairville, Leradeau, and Thervial. It could be inferred that the migration of Haitians of non-Bahamian ancestry to the Bahamas might have begun in the 1920s.

In 1929, the Bahamas' colonial secretary directed the commissioner at Inagua to report on the migration of illegal Haitians through that island [GB/COR, Bahamas. CSOP, folio 8810. no. 60. "Commissioner at Inagua: Report to the Colonial Secretary." June 1929. (Bahamas/PRO. 1971)]. Commissioners are the chief government representatives on the outer islands. No directives were issued, however, to vigorously arrest and deport the illegal Haitians identified [GB/COR, Bahamas. CSOP, folio 8810. no. 59. Report of the Immigration Officer for the Year 1929. January 1930. (Bahamas/PRO. 1971)]. In 1929, the twenty-three illegal aliens deported from the Bahamas included twelve Jamaicans, seven Cubans, and one Haitian (the latter was imprisoned on charges of petty larceny and deported after his one year of imprisonment ended). One possible reason for the apparent official duplicity may be the fact that Bahamian-Haitian mutual interisland migration was still in effect in the late 1920s. This argument is supported by a story that appeared in the *Nassau Daily Tribune,* which told of a boy injured at Mayaguana, situated in the southern Bahamas, whose parents found it more convenient to take the child to Haiti for medical help rather than to Nassau. The story, reported in a matter-of-fact tone in the *Nassau Daily Tribune,* July 23, 1929, suggests that in the 1920s, Bahamians continued to visit Haiti routinely for a variety of services. It should be noted that this event occurred during the U.S. occupation of Haiti, when the Americans established better medical facilities—at least temporarily.

Bahamian migration to Haiti subsided during the war years (1939–1945) and practically ceased by the end of the conflict. In addition to military conscription, a major exodus of Bahamians occurred with the 1943 introduction of the U.S. Farm Labor Program, which between 1943 and 1953 recruited more than 5,000 Bahamians seasonally. The migratory flow became predominantly one of Haitians entering the Bahamas in varying numbers. Haitian sloops continued to ply between northern Haitian ports and the Bahamas. The direction of the traditional trade routes, however, shifted increasingly from the southern Bahamian islands to Nassau and destinations in the northern Bahamas. Simultaneous with the shift of Haitian trade from the southern Bahamas to Nassau, was the gradual shift of Bahamian trade from Haiti to Cuba (it should be noted that Bahamians had trade ties with Cuba that predated the era of piracy). Invariably, Haitian migrants flocked to the Bahamas to seek employment in jobs left vacant by Bahamian migrants to the United States.

During the 1940s, Haitian migration to the Bahamas had become significant. In 1948, Maxwell J. Thompson was made honorary vice consul to Haiti, with responsibility for the administration of affairs concerning the growing number of Haitians migrating to the Bahamas. Later that year, the Haitian government reciprocated with the establishment of a Haitian consul in the colony.

In 1953, there were perhaps fewer than 500 Haitians (documented and illegal) living and working in the Bahamas [BR/COR, Bahamas Immigration Department. Annual Report, 1953 (Bahamas/PRO, 1971)]. Haitian-Bahamian relations continued to be cordial, and as late as 1955 Haitian immigrants were marginally tolerated in the Bahamas. The level of cordiality which existed between Bahamians and Haitians was demonstrated, according to a news story in January 21, 1955, when the editor of the *Nassau Daily Tribune* made an unsuccessful attempt to influence the Haitian and Bahamian authorities to include the Bahamas in Haitian president Paul Magloire's international tour.

Beginning in 1956, Bahamian attitudes toward Haitians became increasingly intolerant. In the 1950s, hundreds of Bahamians migrated from the outer islands to Nassau in search of employment. Hundreds of others returned from seasonal labor in the United States, unemployed and angry that Haitians and other West Indians were securing employment in cases where they were unable to do so (Johnson 1972:28–36). In December of that year, more than 100 undocumented Haitian immigrants were arrested and deported. The *Nassau Daily Tribune* reported on May 18, 1957, that Bahamian immigration officials "rounded-up" approximately 140 undocumented Haitians for subsequent deportation. By 1957, with the onset of the lengthy dictatorship of François Duvalier (1957–1971) and his son Jean-Claude Duvalier (1971–1986), Bahamian immigration officials complained of having to contend with "floods" of Haitian immigrants who continued to invade the colony. The *Nassau Daily Tribune* (May 24, 1957) attributed the "unprecedented influx of illegal Haitian immigrants. . . . to the turbulent political and economic conditions then existing in Haiti." The late 1950s in Haiti, preceding the election of Duvalier as president, was a period of social, economic, and political disorder. At the end of 1957, immigration officials estimated the total number of illegal Haitians in the Bahamas at 1,000. The annual report demonstrates the shift in Bahamian attitudes toward Haitians in 1953, when a small number of Haitians were reportedly living in the Bahamas, and the obvious alarm that the immigration of several hundred in 1957 created [BR/COP, Bahamas Immigration Department: Annual Report, 1957. (Bahamas/PRO, 1971)]. A steady increase in illegal Haitian emigration to the Bahamas had begun and was to continue in varying numbers to the present.

Summary

Historically, since the first group of aborigines migrated northward from northwestern Española, the Bahamas and Haiti have been linked by centuries of mutual trade and migration. The Bahamian-Haitian linkage was strengthened during the Haitian Revolution, when hundreds of St. Domingans were forcibly exiled to the Bahamas by the Revolution. The émigrés significantly influenced politics and economics in the colony. Many became refugees of the state. Others, in rebellion against imprisonment aboard prison ships and forced exile in the Bahamas, staged many attempts to escape. Invariably, the escape attempts, together with the presence of a large number of non-white foreigners in the colony, created discontent and fear among the white residents.

During the post-Emancipation period and later in the nineteenth century, Haitian sloops frequently visited southern Bahamian ports laden with agricultural produce and rum, which were traded for a variety of European and U.S. manufactured goods. Most Haitian traders made no attempt to settle in the Bahamas. Beginning in the late 1950s, however, the mutuality of the linkage began to shift, as the Bahamas became economically prosperous, while Haitian economic depression intensified under the Duvalier dictatorships. The concentration of Haitian trade with the Bahamas shifted to the northern islands of New Providence, Grand

Bahama, and Abaco. The influx of Haitian migrants caused Bahamian officials to initiate restrictive policies against Haitians. The following chapter discusses efforts by Bahamian officials to control immigration during the 1950s and early 1970s.

6

Haitian Migration to the Bahamas, 1957–1973

Haitian Migration, 1957–1967

From the late 1950s to the 1970s, Haitian migration to the Bahamas affected society and economics in the colony, with repercussions that resound to the present. Beginning in the 1950s, the Bahamas enjoyed a period of economic growth that involved significant expansions in the financial and tourism sectors. Islands in the north of the archipelago profited especially from the investment of predominantly North American and British capital. Consequently, the colony experienced significant demographic shifts as residents from the southern islands flocked to the north in search of employment and improved living conditions [BR/COR. Bahamas Census Reports for the years 1940 and 1953 (Bahamas/PRO, 1971)]. Substantial investments produced significant disparities in wealth and development between the northern and southern Bahamian islands in general, and the Bahamas and Haiti in particular. Haitians, who traditionally traded with the islands, increasingly migrated in large numbers to New Providence, Abaco, and Grand Bahama islands, the areas of greatest investment. Consequently, thousands of Haitians migrated to the Bahamas to escape the abject poverty and political chaos which enveloped Haiti immediately before and during the repression of the Duvalier regime.

Beginning in the 1950s, a significant increase in Haitian migration to the Bahamas began with the ascendancy to power in Haiti of François Duvalier. Born in 1907, Duvalier graduated from the University of Haiti School of Medicine in 1934, where he served as a hospital staff doctor until 1943. A contributor to the Haitian daily *Action Nationale* (1934), he was influenced by the scholar Lorimer Denis and became a member of Le Groupe des Griots, an organization of writers who embraced Black Nationalism and voodoo as the foundations of Haitian culture. A supporter of President Dumarsais Estimé, Duvalier was appointed director general of the national public health service in 1946, under minister of labor in 1948, and minister of labor in 1949, a post he retained until 1950, when President Estimé was overthrown by a military junta under Paul Magloire.

In 1945, Duvalier, who had become the central opposition figure, went underground. After the military forced the resignation of Magloire in December 1956, however, he reemerged as a prominent political leader. His followers participated in most of the six governments that were formed in 1956. In September 1957, running on a program of popular reform and Black Nationalism, Duvalier was elected president of Haiti. In an effort to consolidate his power, he reduced the size of the army and, with the assistance of his chief aide, Clement Barbot, organized the Tontons Macoutes ("Bogeymen"), a private paramilitary force responsible for terrorizing and assassinating most opposition to Duvalier. In 1964, Duvalier declared himself president for life.

Duvalier's manipulation of legislative elections in 1961 to have his term of office extended to 1967, as well as other corrupt and despotic acts, resulted in a temporary termination of U.S. aid to Haiti. In 1963, he promoted a cult of his person as the semidivine embodiment of the Haitian nation. The Vatican excommunicated him in 1964 for repression against Roman Catholics in Haiti, but Duvalier persuaded the Vatican to lift the sanction in 1966. The Duvalier regime, although threatened by conspiracies and terror, lasted longer than any of its predecessors. His rule of terror, while eliminating most political dissent, provided Haiti with an unprecedented period of political stability. As of his death in 1971, power was transferred to his son, Jean-Claude.

In February 1986, after nearly thirty years of dictatorship by the Duvaliers, a mixed military-civilian National Council of Government was established. In 1988, a problematic general election brought Leslie Manigat to power. Manigat was removed by a military coup four months later. In September 1988, the government of Manigat's predecessor, led by Lieutenant-General Henri Namphy, was similarly deposed and replaced by Lieutenant-General Prosper Avril. Avril resigned in 1990. In March 1990, the judge Ertha Pascal-Trouillot was named president of a temporary government consisting of a nineteen-member Council of State. Following general elections in December 1990, Roman Catholic priest and popular leader Jean-Bertrand Aristide was inaugurated as president of Haiti (Nicholls 1996, 56; Trouillot 1990: 38).

According to Dawn Marshall, 90 percent of the immigrants to the Bahamas came from northern Haiti, with 77 percent of that total coming from areas such as Môle Saint-Nicolas, Cap-Haïtien, and Tortuga. She argues that, contrary to popular belief in the Bahamas, few immigrants came from south of Gonaïves and Port-au-Prince. Haitians from the southern region, she contends, were more likely to migrate to the Dominican Republic, Cuba, and the rest of the world (Marshall 1979:21–60). Marshall goes on to argue that, until 1968, most Haitian migrants to the Bahamas were economic and not political refugees. She says the northwest, the home of most Haitian emigrants during the period, was isolated from the rest of the country by poor roads and mountainous terrain, and that deforestation, overtaxed soil, droughts, official neglect, and seasonal hurricanes have rendered the areas very poor, even by Haitian standards. She notes that the predominantly subsistence peasants of the region, isolated from Port-au-Prince, naturally regarded the Bahamas as a land of opportunity.

Most migrants were attracted by information via the Haitian *telediol* (word of mouth), a verbal communication system that disseminated news from one person to the next. Word spread of job opportunities in forestry, sugar cultivation, provision farming, gardening, and general labor in the northern Bahamas. The jobs reportedly paid at least twice the amount Haitians expected to earn in Haiti. In the author's interview with John in September 1997, age seventy-two at the time of the interview, he said he migrated to the Bahamas in 1959 in search of employment opportunity. He claims his intention was to make sufficient money to establish a family, a home, and eventually a business in Haiti. Thousands of Haitians were employed as *sales* (common laborers) in labor camps in Abaco, Grand Bahama, Andros, and Eleuthera. Recruits were temporarily housed with Turks and Caicos Islanders and Bahamian laborers, although the Bahamians and Turks and Caicos Islanders protested Haitians being housed in the same quarters. The Haitians were unceremoniously relocated to overcrowded, unhygienic camps (such as that at Campbell Town, Abaco), in virtual isolation from the neighboring communities and camps.

Beginning in 1957, Bahamian officials began to demonstrate concern over the estimated 1,000 Haitians reportedly living in the Bahamas. The colonial authorities were particularly concerned that the existing immigration laws inadequately addressed the Haitian problem. At that time, Bahamian immigration policies were dictated by the Immigration Act of 1928 and the Immigration Rules of 1938. The laws required a ship captain to present a correct and detailed list of passengers, together with a duty of £1 for each passenger seeking employment in the colony. Passengers were required to present valid health certificates and character references, a landing permit, and pay a £20 surety deposit. Violators of the act and rules forfeited their deposits and risked fines of £25, a possible jail sentence, and subsequent deportation [BR/COR. Bahamas. CSOP, Immigration Act. 1928 and Immigration Rules. 1938 (Bahamas PRO. 1971)]. One official, Magistrate Mr. St. George, suggested in an article in the *Nassau Daily Tribune* on June 14, 1957, that "the only solution to the problem of the illegal entries from Haiti was to keep increasing the prison term."

The situation, widely referred to as the "Haitian Problem," became particularly acute in 1958, when the Bahamas suffered a period of economic recession after crop failures in the United States resulted in the repatriation of hundreds of Bahamian farm laborers from the United States simultaneously with a sharp decline in the Bahamian tourism industry. The House of Assembly amended the immigration laws "to deal effectively with the large numbers of Haitians who have entered the Colony illegally" [GB/COR, Bahamas Executive Council Minutes: Votes of the House of Assembly. May 1958 (Bahamas/PRO, 1971)]. One newspaper concurred with public opinion that by accepting lower wages and at times offering bribes to foremen to remain employed, the Haitians undermined the ability of Bahamians to become employed. It was noted, however, that the immigrants accepted the very menial tasks most Bahamians generally refused. In the *Nassau Daily Tribune,* May 30, 1958, the editor argued that Haitians worked in logging and salt industries because Bahamians generally discounted such tasks as "slave labor" for low wages.

In 1959, officials, influenced by growing public protest over the Haitian influx, strengthened the immigration requirements for entry into the colony (Diederich and Burt 1970:137–138). According to these authors, in 1959, Haitian migration increased substantially as thousands of economic refugees escaped probable starvation caused by a severe drought that ravaged the northwestern Haitian communities near Jean Rabel. American-based charitable organizations reportedly fed some 75,000 in the affected area. Illegal immigrants now faced fines of £50–100 and six to twelve-month imprisonment. According to the *Nassau Daily Tribune*, on January 26, 1959, one magistrate, apparently disgusted by repeat offences, imposed the maximum penalty on two Haitians. The magistrate, in passing judgment, reportedly commented: "It seems to me that by now it should be well known throughout Haiti that entry permits are in [the] Bahamas. Yet only last week 87 passengers came in on a single day without permits." For the first time in Bahamian history, immigration efforts were coordinated through the police, immigration, and customs departments. A boat, chartered and manned by immigration officers, was assigned to patrol Nassau harbor in search of Haitian sloops and illegal aliens. The *Nassau Daily Tribune* article went on to state that early in the operation, the patrol vessel intercepted a Haitian sloop with ninety-five illegal aliens, including two infants. The immigrants reportedly carried small packages of food, makeshift knapsacks made of cloth, and very little money. The prisons became overcrowded with illegal immigrants, and the cost of deportation created an unexpected economic strain on Bahamian government resources. In a May 18, 1960, letter to the *Nassau Daily Tribune* editor, an observer complained that in 1959, the £6,400 spent on deportation could have been used as partial payment on an official patrol boat. Magistrate Maxwell Thompson allegedly complained in the June 13, 1960, *Nassau Daily Tribune*, that "every month large numbers are coming in and all that happens is that they get free passage back to Haiti."

In 1960, Haitian migration to the Bahamas threatened to reach catastrophic proportions. That year, the May 18th *Nassau Daily Tribune* alluded to the raising of the curtain on the second act of the "Haitian Invasion." On June 10, according to the paper, a group of sixty illegal Haitians were arrested as they emerged from a congested public landing site. The Haitians, upon interrogation, reported that they had escaped from the poverty-stricken northwest of Haiti, where the only real income was a maximum of $10 earned when an occasional Dutch or French ship visited the area. On July 11, the paper carried the sarcastic headline "More Haitian Tourists In," and reported the capture of another fifty-one illegal immigrants. The journalist, who reported that the illegal aliens appeared before the court, reckoned that "Haitians are, of necessity and by training, a fatalistic, patient people who take life as they meet it." By 1961, immigration officials were confronted with the problem of inadequate jails in which to house illegal aliens awaiting deportation. The problem became obviously acute when fifty-four illegal Haitian immigrants held at the central police station had to "sit in the corridor of the cell block" (Marshall 1979:101).

Annual Haitian migration increased from an estimated 1,000 Haitians living in the Bahamas in 1957 to over 10,000 in 1962, and accounted for almost 15 percent of the total population of the Bahamas [BR/COR. Bahamas Immigration Department: Annual Report. 1962 (Bahamas/PRO, 1971)]. The estimated increase of 9,000 Haitian immigrants within the short span of six years—while appearing small in comparison to the numbers migrating to the Dominican Republic and the United States—was considered overwhelming in the Bahamas. Bahamian colonial officials resolved to address what was increasingly perceived by many Bahamians to be an ineffective Haitian immigration policy. Interestingly, in the early 1960s, Haitian-Bahamian relations were still cordial, despite increasingly questionable Bahamian efforts to control illegal Haitian migration and existing tension between the Haitian government and the United States. The level of cordiality is demonstrated in an advertisement in the *Nassau Herald* on July 16, 1961, which offered "10-day vacation cruises to Haiti aboard the *MV Lady Baillou*—only £10 round trip." In 1962, the Bahamian government appointed a special task force to "inquire into the entry of Haitians into [the] Bahamas and their effect on local employment [BR/COR, Bahamas, CSOP, folio 8828. no. 22. Minutes of The Executive Council. June 1962 (Bahamas/PRO, 1971)]. Additionally, this same council reported a vote to appoint a committee consisting of the commissioner of police, the chief immigration officer, and the superintendent of prisons to "prepare comprehensive recommendations for action to enable that a drive against illegal Haitians be initiated." One recommendation of the task force was the mass deportation of offenders.

In 1963, the immigration department initiated its "Operation Clean Up," which was designed to repatriate the estimated 10,000 illegal Haitians living and working in the Bahamas. Security forces collaborated with judicial agencies to deport hundreds of Haitians. One skeptic noted in the *Nassau Guardian* on January 4, 1963, that several of the deportees were repeat offenders who had been deported to Haiti at least twice and that the deportations merely allowed the Haitians a free vacation south for the winter. "Operation Clean Up" was aborted after less than a year because the threat of conflict between Haiti and the Dominican Republic preoccupied Haitian officials and apparently prevented them from effective cooperation in the deportation process. The *Nassau Guardian* reported on May 8, 1962, that Bahamian magistrate Mr. J. Bailey refused to allow further deportations while the possibility of conflict between Haiti and the Dominican Republic persisted. It noted further on May 14, 1963, that, because of overcrowding in the prisons, convicted offenders were detained under house arrest aboard Haitian sloops anchored in Nassau harbor to await deportation. Although never specifically mentioning "Operation Clean Up," the paper continued to issue occasional reports on illegal entries and deportations. The Bahamian government, unable to effectively continue its policy of systematic mass deportation, crammed offenders in already overcrowded prisons.

In 1963, a new Immigration Act was introduced under a revised constitution to specifically target Haitian immigration. The Immigration Act of 1928 had defined a Bahamian as a native of the colony who was a British subject. The new act, however, redefined the conditions under which a person could claim Bahamian citizenship, or "belonger" status. The authority of the immigration officer was increased to allow for search without a warrant. Additionally, the immigration officials were authorized to interrogate prospective immigrants, request medical certification, and arrest persons in cases of reasonable suspicion. Also, immigration officials were empowered to demand letters of intent from non-Bahamians whenever the occasion arose [BR/COR, CSOP, folio 345. no. 56. Bahamas Immigration Act. 1963 (Bahamas/PRO. 1971)]. The Vessels Restrictions Regulations that accompanied the new act (1963) required all vessels of less than 100 tons entering the Bahamas from Haiti to clear customs and immigration at Matthew Town, Inagua. There, the captains were required to present a manifest signed by the Haitian authorities that described the cargo, crew, and passengers. The crews (not to exceed nine members) were required to present appropriate documentation certified by the British consul in Haiti. The *Nassau Guardian* reported on September 8, 1964, of the apprehension of a Haitian sloop that carried a crew of twenty-six, including thirteen women. It could be inferred that a seaman's passport was fairly easy to obtain in Haiti, and that obtaining such documents was one method Haitians used to obtain entry into the Bahamas. Contravention of the new laws resulted in fines of £1,000. In effect, the new regulations were specifically designed to discourage most Haitians from entering the Bahamas. The new immigration legislation, however, was unsuccessful in deterring illegal Haitian migration to the Bahamas. A variety of clandestine methods were used to circumvent the immigration laws.

The daily newspapers consistently reported such cases, which included Haitian refugees coming ashore on deserted islands or at remote areas of New Providence and entering Nassau Harbour on Haitian sloops in secret compartments.

The Progressive Liberal Party and Haitian Migration, 1967–1973

In 1967 and 1968, Haitian migration to the Bahamas was directly affected by the emergence of the Progressive Liberal Party (PLP) as the ruling party of the Bahamas. In January 1967, the predominantly black PLP replaced the predominantly white United Bahamian Party (UBP) as the government of the Bahamas. Haitians were encouraged to migrate by rumors of numerous jobs made available by a sympathetic black government. In an interview with Robert on October 24, 1996, he noted that the adverse economic condition of Haiti and the rumor of well-paying jobs in the Bahamas motivated many Haitians to migrate. Robert, who migrated in 1964, confirmed that it was rumored in Haiti that a bridge linking New Providence and Grand Bahama was proposed and promised to employ thousands of laborers. The rumor, which was incorrect, may have been based on misinformation concerning the construction of a bridge linking Nassau with the outlying Paradise Island, less than one mile away. The new government, despite public recognition of the social and economic problems created by Haitian migration, appeared eager to demonstrate sympathy for the economic plight of other black West Indians. In an early statement, Senator, the Honorable Dr. Doris Johnson, leader for the government in the Senate, declared that Bahamians had to decide either to accept or expel the Haitian immigrants. She claimed that expulsion was not an option her government wished to seriously consider because "many Haitians here are raising families." The senator concluded that: "There must be some way to legalize their staying in this country." The senator added, according to the *Nassau Daily Tribune* coverage of April 29, 1967, that a committee was formed to consider the presentation of Haitian literature and art to the Bahamian public.

Some PLP parliamentarians attempted to embarrass the former government by accusing some of its members of profiting from the Haitian problem. In July 1967, for example, Cecil Wallace-Whitefield, the minister of works in the new government, accused former premier Sir Roland Symmonette of the unethical abuse of his office while functioning as minister of immigration in 1965. According to Wallace-Whitefield, "the Government had a tender, which could be used for [repatriation], but instead of using the tender and saving Government money, Sir Roland used his own vessel." The *Nassau Herald*, on July 13, 1967, seemed to confirm this when it reported that in 1965, former premier Sir Roland Symonette, while he had direct responsibility for immigration matters, reportedly leased his tender vessel *M.V. J-de-V* to the government to transport repatriated Haitians. In other cases of alleged abuse of office, opposition members allegedly recruited Haitian tailors and barbers in direct competition with black Bahamian artisans. On July 16, 1967, Bahamian tailor William O. Newton, in a letter to the editor of the *Nassau Herald*, appealed to the government to remove unfair competition from Haitian tailors and barbers he alleged were introduced by the former government. In the 1960s, it was widely known that white businessmen recruited and employed Haitian tailors and barbers to produce and repair shoes, and to service the needs of their tourist and winter resident clientele.

The PLP government initially demonstrated an apparent commitment to Haitian integration into Bahamian society by employing a few Haitians in the civil service. Most Haitians were employed in the Public Works Department as "weekly" laborers. Civil servants classified as "weekly" are temporary workers with limited benefits. Conversely, the "monthly" worker is a permanent employee, eligible for full benefits such as pensions, etcetera. In early 1967, it was common to see Haitians sweeping the streets of Nassau, working on waste disposal vehicles, digging ditches, and cleaning public properties. Haitian artisans, including wood carvers and straw vendors, were allowed to sell their work in public markets. Anton, a Haitian woodcarver, said in a September 13, 1997, interview with the author, that during the 1960s he and other Haitians were allowed to trade their wood and straw products from sloops anchored in Nassau harbor. Haitian produce vendors without permits were allowed to sell fruits and vegetables from sloops anchored at the Nassau wharves and at dilapidated stalls erected along some of the minor throughways.

The government sponsored a committee to foster closer Haitian-Bahamian cultural ties. The committee secretary was Haitian Roman Catholic priest Father Guy Sansaricq, who ministered to a predominantly Haitian congregation in New Providence. Father Guy, as the secretary was affectionately known among his parishioners, demonstrated a determination to effect total Haitian integration into Bahamian society. He insisted that

Bahamians become more humane to Haitian immigrants. He called for the government to institute adult education programs to familiarize Haitians with the culture of their new home and Bahamians with Haitian culture. He repeatedly urged the new administration to grant Haitian immigrants already in the Bahamas "alien resident status" and to provide legal permission for the absorption of additional Haitian immigrants. Father Guy argued in the *Nassau Guardian* on May 6, 1967, that: "A Haitian with an alien resident status would become immediately and genuinely interested in the lasting progress of the country." He promoted Haitian labor in the development of industries in the outer islands and the value of the Haitian immigrant as a consumer.

Most Bahamians opposed attempts to foster such relations. To some, Father Guy's position represented that of his committee and invariably the government. A steady stream of letters to the *Nassau Daily Tribune* expressed near-xenophobic reactions to Haitian immigrants. One writer suggested on May 24, 1967, that the Bahamas would become a "Bahati" if Haitians were given alien resident status. The editor replied on June 2, 1967, concluding that "the reaction among our people shows that there is a good deal of feeling in the Colony . . . against any effort that may extend a helping hand to these people." Public outcry reached a new crescendo when a "sudden increase in the number of illegal Haitian entrants" was reported on June 5, 1967, just ten days after the government announced the formation of the Haitian-Bahamian committee.

Some white Bahamians accused the PLP government of encouraging Haitian migration as a means of creating a voting population politically obligated to them. Chester, a retired white Bahamian merchant, reported in an interview with the author in September 1997, that many whites, especially those from the Abacos, believed the PLP deliberately promoted Haitian migration in early 1967 to establish sympathetic voting blocs in predominantly white communities in the outer islands. The *Nassau Guardian,* traditionally representing the views of the white elite, accused the government of not having a clearly defined immigration policy. In 1958, a consortium of white elite businessmen bought the *Nassau Guardian,* intending to transform the newspaper into their political voice in counteraction to the already established pro-black, pro-PLP *Bahamian Times.* Traditionally, the media in most societies influences politics in the respective country. Carl Stone and Aggrey Brown (1981:301–389) demonstrate the role that the *Gleaner* played in influencing politics in Jamaica during the 1970s. Some editorials suggested that the apparent lack of a definitive immigration policy was politically motivated and created uncertainty and supposition in the minds of Bahamians and Haitians. One reminded the public of "the record of present government's often vociferous standards, as an opposition, against bringing in persons from abroad to work in the Colony." In the February 27, 1967, issue of the *Nassau Guardian,* a story referred to a 1958 communiqué by the opposition PLP reported in the *Bahamian Times* of January 23, 1958, in which it advised the formation of a committee to investigate what it claimed was an unfair UBP government immigration policy. The article noted that "some of the more imaginative of them [PLP politicians] even thought they saw a diabolical UBP plan to match the fast-growing [black] Bahamian population with imported white and colored staff."

Interestingly, most black Bahamians directed their accusations away from the government in general to Senator Dr. Johnson and Haitian migrants in particular. Understandably, in 1967 the black masses were still euphoric over the political victory of the black government, and unwilling to blame their heroes collectively for the Haitian problem. Displeasure was especially directed against the controversial senator, whom one critic sarcastically dubbed "The Honorable Important Doctor," in the May 27, 1967, *Nassau Daily Tribune.* Gradually, government officials and party colleagues, sensing public displeasure over the Haitian influx, began to disassociate themselves from Senator Johnson's controversial solution to the Haitian problem. In the author's September 14, 1997, interview with a former senior official in the PLP during the 1960s and early 1970s, the anonymous ex-officer claimed that many in the PLP disliked Dr. Johnson, not because the senator was an articulate, educated woman, but because she spoke candidly on all issues and often offended many people. He claimed that many of her colleagues wanted to see her political demise, and he alleged that certain government members conspired to deliberately "set-up" the senator as a pawn in a secretly devised game designed to test public reaction to the controversial immigration policy. Since this interview, other former and current officials have corroborated this conspiracy theory. One of the more critical opponents of the senator's proposed Haitian policy was PLP politician and party spokesman Arthur Foulkes. Foulkes, in an obvious rejection of Dr. Johnson's proposed Haitian policy, attacked plans announced by the Haitian consul to the Bahamas for the establishment of a "cultural exchange programme" between Haiti and the Bahamas. He sarcastically stated that "we [Bahamians] trust that [the Haitian consul] knows the difference between cultural exchange and public relations for the Duvalier dictatorship." Foulkes concluded that "there [was] nothing wrong with culture . . . but [Bahamians did not] care to exchange it for boatloads of Haitians" as reported in the *Bahamian Times* on August 8, 1967. Foulkes was the editor of the pro-PLP *Bahamian Times* newspaper and chairman of several government boards and agencies. Interestingly, he conveniently (and, perhaps, deliberately) blurred the distinction between the Duvalier dictatorship and the Haitian people.

Haitian immigrants came under increased verbal (and sometimes physical) abuse by intolerant Bahamians. Most were denied access to adequate housing or relegated to dilapidated housing. In one documented incident, covered successively in the February 12, 26, and 27, 1967, issues of the *Nassau Guardian*, a prominent Haitian athlete and his family of four were unceremoniously evicted from a house they rented from a senior police officer. According to one report, the owner "ordered two men to remove the doors and windows from the house." Instances of the forcible eviction of Haitians from rented premises were common during the late 1960s and early 1970s. In some cases, furniture was destroyed, clothing tossed outside, and doors and windows sealed to deny entrance. It should be noted, however, that the methods of eviction mentioned were not exclusive to Haitians and foreigners, as Bahamians frequently suffered similar fates. One Bahamian politician publicly noted concern at the numerous acts of brutality and blatant discrimination perpetrated against Haitian immigrants. He urged police and immigration officials to demonstrate greater humanitarianism in their interaction with Haitian immigrants. The politician noted in the November 4, 1967, issue, that, while the letter of the law called for specific action against offenders, it was the moral duty of the respective officials to demonstrate compassion in the execution of their duties.

In June 1967, the minister of internal affairs, speaking in the House of Assembly, announced a new immigration policy. Among other things, the new policy called for more consistent "round up," the need for stiffer penalties against smugglers of human cargoes, and public cooperation. The *Nassau Daily Tribune*, on June 17, 1967, reported that it was widely rumored (but officially denied) that the immigration department offered a bounty of $2 per (illegal Haitian) head to members of the public. The minister of agriculture complained that the captains of "Haitian vessels lying in port, in some cases for weeks, in order to sell their produce and other goods over the side" violated trade laws. He asserted that the vessels were targeted for immediate removal and their owners and captains for possible punishment [BR/COR, Bahamas. Votes of the House of Assembly, 8 June 1967. (Bahamas/PRO, 1971)]. The article went on to say that the minister of internal affairs, concurring, informed Parliament that his ministry was prepared to take action against the Haitian sloops, which created "congestion in Nassau ports [and attracted] illegal immigrants believed to be sheltering there."

Some Haitians, rather than face continued verbal and physical abuse, volunteered for repatriation. In the July 16, 1967, newspaper, immigration officials reported that illegal Haitian migration to the Bahamas was being contained: "304 Haitians were deported via the *M. V. New Providence,* while 41 left voluntarily on a Haitian sloop." Illegal Haitian immigrants were only allowed to voluntarily repatriate on Haitian sloops on the assurance of the Haitian consul that the passengers would be deposited at a Haitian port. One senior immigration officer alleged in the August 23rd edition that he "has had instances in the past where illegal Haitians were turning themselves in at police stations across the island." He claimed that on several raids, police and immigration officials "found illegal Haitians with suitcases and parcels packed, waiting to be taken away."

Notwithstanding the developments of July 1967, in 1968, the PLP, having won a landslide victory in the general elections of that year, increased efforts to control the influx of Haitian migration into the Bahamas. Combined forces of immigration and police officers conducted systematic raids on unsuspecting Haitian communities, usually during the early hours of the morning. Periodic roadblocks were established at major roadways to intercept public transportation and arrest undocumented aliens. Regular marine patrols were maintained to intercept Haitian sloops smuggling illegal passengers into the colony. Reports of hostile public reaction toward Haitians decreased, and confidence in the government's commitment to the control of illegal Haitian immigration appeared to grow as evidenced by fewer complaints against Haitian migration to the Bahamas appearing in the local newspapers. Illegal Haitian migration into the Bahamas, however, continued almost unabated.

According to two anonymous informants, known to the author for almost twenty-five years and interviewed officially on September 18, 1996, beginning in the late 1960s, illegal Haitians employed more subtle and clandestine methods to enter the Bahamas. Instead of the traditional direct entry into Nassau harbor aboard provision sloops, aliens were generally landed in remote areas off the southern coast of New Providence during the early hours of the morning. The newly arrived were usually met by a Haitian contact and conducted to small Haitian shantytowns. Some captains left their passengers on remote cays, cleared customs and immigration at Matthew Town, Inagua, whereupon they retrieved their illegal human cargo for the furtive voyage to Nassau. According to informants, residents in the Haitian communities (through continuous contact with Haiti) expected the sloops to bring relatives and friends and made provisions for housing and identified possible employment opportunities. These two informants are undocumented Haitian laborers who were smuggled into the Bahamas in 1966 and 1968 respectively, and they granted interviews on the condition that anonymity be maintained.

The processing of undocumented Haitians demanded substantial increases in the Bahamas' public resources. On June 28, 1968, for example, the *Nassau Guardian* reported that more than 300 Haitian detainees had to be accommodated in a makeshift detention camp because the local prison was overcrowded by hundreds of other illegal Haitian aliens, leading Bahamian premier Lynden Pindling reportedly to allude to the influx of illegal Haitians as "The beginning of a new silent invasion."

An additional 100 Haitians had to be accommodated in a temporary camp at an abandoned air base. The editor of the *Nassau Daily Tribune* complained in the July 13, 1968, issue that the Bahamas wasted thousands of dollars daily to incarcerate illegal Haitians. According to the editor, "the cost of feeding the Haitians in custody is costing the Bahamas government between two dollars and three dollars per head per day. This means that the government at present is paying out a thousand dollars a day in food costs alone." The estimates were based on every 500 illegal aliens jailed.

In 1968, Haitian migration to the colony was influenced by a series of anti-Duvalier incidents originating in the Bahamas. Beginning in March, local residents accidentally discovered and subsequently informed immigration authorities that small groups of anti-Duvalier activists had established military training bases in the northern Bahamas from which they allegedly intended to launch revolutionary attacks against the Haitian dictatorship. Bahamian officials arrested a total of seventy-seven self-proclaimed "freedom fighters," and sentenced each to one year in prison to be followed by deportation. The freedom fighters encouraged other Haitian prisoners to stage a hunger strike and demand freedom and asylum in "any country that would have them," according to a story that ran in the March 27, 1968, *Nassau Daily Tribune*. The protesters allegedly smuggled a letter from prison which was subsequently published in the local press. Among other things, it explained the objectives of the hunger strike and requested authorization to request political asylum through the International Commission of Human Rights. The letter included in the February 20, 1969, *Nassau Guardian* concluded: "By going back to Haiti, fighting Duvalier, a lot of us could die. We are not afraid by the idea of death. The watchword is 'Freedom or Death.' Since we can't have this freedom, we have decided to go to the death by this hunger strike . . . enough is enough. Freedom or death."

The United States consul in the Bahamas volunteered to repatriate the Haitians to the United States as political refugees. The *Nassau Daily Tribune* announced on February 23, 1969, that the prisoners "were to be processed through the [U.S.] Consulate in accordance with the ordinary immigration laws and controls." The repatriation process, however, was reportedly complicated by the influence of special interest groups in the United States opposed to the immigration of Haitians to that country. The process eventually took more than seven months. In 1963, Dr. Clement Benoit (the Haitian consul to the Bahamas) and twenty-five Haitian supporters were deported from the Bahamas on charges of "fomenting trouble among the Haitians." The group requested, but was denied political asylum in the United States. According to the *Nassau Daily Tribune* on September 3, 1963, two U.S. senators argued that the Haitians were prohibited entry to that country because their presence would "set off apprehension . . . that several thousand more refugees may be headed for south Florida." The U.S. position on Haitian immigration, which appears to have remained effectively the same throughout the 1960s, contributed to the delayed repatriation process. A more detailed perspective on U.S. immigration policies regarding Haitian migration can be found in Felix Masud-Piloto (1996). The minister of home affairs assured the public in an article in the *Nassau Guardian* on February 20, 1969, that "the Bahamas government has been pursuing intensive talks with other governments and the United Nations in an effort to alleviate the Haitian Problem here." Two weeks later, the minister announced the arrival of a United Nations representative to assist with the problem of repatriation. As late as December 11 that year, the *Nassau Daily Tribune* reported that thirty-three of the original ninety-three protesters still remained imprisoned in Nassau awaiting repatriation to the United States and Canada.

In May 1968, reported the *Nassau Daily Tribune* on the 20th, a group of insurgents arrested by the Haitian authorities for an unsuccessful bomb attack against the presidential palace in Port-au-Prince, were linked to the sinking of the yacht *Yorel II* in the northern Bahamas. The yacht reportedly landed two mysterious passengers on a deserted area in Grand Bahama before it sank at the entrance of the Lucaya marina. Haitian officials claimed that the two passengers were pilots involved in revolutionary action against the Duvalier government and operating from a secret base within the Bahamas. Bahamian officials denied knowledge of an abandoned airstrip and camp discovered in north Abaco.

By June 15, President Duvalier was quoted in the *Nassau Daily Tribune* as he accused the British government of allowing anti-Duvalier sympathizers to launch attacks against him and his government from bases within the Bahamas. In an apparent show of power, according to this same report, Haitian officials imprisoned David Knox, the director of information for the Bahamas, who was on an official visit to Port-au-Prince. Knox was accused of complicity in the bombing attack and subjected to a trial apparently choreographed for the international press. By September 6, 1968, President Duvalier, in a demonstration of uncharacteristic humanitarianism, publicly announced in the *Nassau Daily Tribune* his intention to pardon Knox.

In July 1968, the newly appointed Haitian consul for Abaco, Joseph Antoine Dorce, was murdered in Freeport. Dorce was on a familiarization tour with the Haitian consul general and the vice-consuls for Inagua and Grand Bahama when the attack occurred, according to the *Nassau Guardian* article on July 8, 1968. In 1968, both the Bahamas and Haiti operated small diplomatic missions in the respective countries. The missions were headed by a chief consul and support staff. Five Haitians were charged with the offense, and four were found guilty. A subsequent appeal, however, resulted in a repeal of that sentence. Some Haitian immigrants in the Bahamas were secretly delighted by the attack against the much-feared Duvalier regime.

Rose insisted that most Haitian officials stationed in the Bahamas during the 1960s and 1970s were members of the dreaded pro-Duvalierist, Tonton Macoute secret police. She stated in a November 4, 1996, interview with the author, that many Haitian immigrants were also members of this feared organization planted in the Bahamas to spy on other Haitian immigrants for the Duvalier regime. Rose's allegations were corroborated by most of the other Haitian-Bahamians interviewed for this research. She confided that Haitians in her neighborhood secretly celebrated the murder, because most "Haitians know that Dorce was a Tonton Macoute [sent to] spy on us [Haitians in the Bahamas]."

The Haitian government accused Bahamians of complicity in plots to destabilize the Duvalier regime, and suspended negotiations on Haitian deportation. A July 22, 1968, report in the *Nassau Daily Tribune* headlined, "Return to Haiti Talks Between Governments Hit Snag." The accompanying article quoted an official immigration statement that negotiations "were still underway, but officials still do not know when they [illegal Haitians] are likely to be deported." The nature of the snag was not revealed. Officials, however, discreetly hinted that the Haitian government demonstrated a reluctance to receive deported Haitian nationals. Two days later, the paper reported that forty captured aliens "were added to the numbers in Oakes Field [detention camp] bringing their total to 187 with approximately 130 waiting in Fox Hill [prison] for deportation." On August 15, the newspaper also noted that approximately 210 Haitians were deported. No mention, however, was made about the Haitian-Bahamian deportation negotiations.

Generally, the international press and community failed to condemn Bahamian officials for what in some cases was excessively harsh treatment of impoverished and politically repressed Haitian immigrants. According to Marshall (1979:61–94) informants revealed that voyages lasted as long as one month and sloops authorized to carry a crew of eight to ten were known to transport as many as eighty passengers. In some cases, food supplies ran short and some passengers starved to death. The dead were reportedly unceremoniously cast overboard. In one case, a crying infant was gagged with an oil-soaked rag to prevent detection by harbor patrols. An obvious lack of concern in international forums for the plight of Haitian immigrants was demonstrated, according to the June 29, 1968, *Nassau Guardian*, in the visit to the Bahamas of Dr. Francisco Urrutia of the United Nations Commission for Refugees. Urrutia arrived in Nassau on the morning of June 28, discussed the Haitian situation with government officials, lunched, and returned to New York at 5:30 P.M. the same day, "satisfied that the problems were those of migrants, not refugees."

The *Nassau Daily Tribune* reported on August 15, 1968, that the British government was compelled to focus attention—albeit briefly—on the Haitian problem in the Bahamas. The incident involved a rebellion by members of a group of 210 Haitian deportees, who, while being repatriated aboard the tender *Eastdore*, "rushed the bridge in an attempt to overthrow the crew and subdue the police guard." Bahamian police guards opened fire, killing one deportee and injuring eleven others. According to the August 19, 1968, *London Times*, the British Parliament demanded an investigation into the matter, which some of its members regarded as "an ugly business." The newspaper castigated the Bahamas for inhumane treatment of Haitian refugees. Among other things, the *London Times* article stated that:

> The deportation of illegal immigrants by the Bahamian Government back to Haiti has been revealed as an ugly business by the mutiny on one of the ships. the Bahamas government would argue that their case is not comparable with the political sympathy extended in the West to refugees from a Communist regime. The numbers are much greater than [the] Bahamas could absorb even if they wanted to. Those who run away from Haiti may not do so from quite the clear motives of those who cross Communist frontiers, but their readiness to resist forcible repatriation strongly suggests that they deserve more consideration than they have been getting from the Bahamas Government.

The Haitian government demonstrated a reluctance to resume negotiations on the matter of deportation with Bahamian officials, or to receive deported nationals. As early as June 7, 1967, a *Nassau Daily Tribune* editorial opined that "while the Government of President Duvalier has expressed interest in the idea of cooperative deportation, there has been no active response to this country's [the Bahamas'] call for official discussions either here or in Haiti." Arguably, this reluctance was influenced by economic considerations. Dawn Marshall (1979:117–121) argued that "Haiti [has traditionally] gained more by allowing the illegal migration to continue than by preventing it." Marshall, basing her argument partially on data collected from the Bahamas Public Works Department, noted that Haitian migrants officially remitted approximately US$1.7 million in 1968. She reported, however, that the official figures were probably underestimated, because trusted relatives or friends generally conveyed most remittances. Marshall recounted an incident in which a priest traveling to Haiti reportedly conveyed some US$5,000 for families in Port-de-Paix. Beside remittances, Haitian immigrants in the Bahamas sent articles of furniture, utensils, groceries, and appliances (for example, stoves and refrigerators) to Haiti for domestic usage as well as for resale. She concluded (1979:117) that "the migrants are on their own and become the concern of the Haitian Government only when they become involved in matters of interest to the Government."

Dawn Marshall also suggested that the apparent Haitian government "reluctance to receive its nationals" amounted to the "political blackmail" of receiving countries (1979:115) and argued that Haiti gains significant economic benefits from the substantial remittances sent there by immigrants employed in other countries. She noted (1979:116) that in the case of the Bahamas, "the emigration of 40,000 Haitians over a period of 15 to 20 years [did] little to relieve the population of Haiti." Marshall concluded that, because of the high level of poverty in Haiti, "the financial benefits of these immigrants could be significant to a country especially when concentrated in one region like the North-West." For 1969, Marshall estimated that Haitian immigrants in the Bahamas may have remitted as much as $1.2 million to Haiti—a decrease of about a half-million—again basing her estimations on data collected from the Public Works Department.

Marshall (1979:117) contended that the Duvalier government deliberately provided minimum resources to prevent illegal migration to the Bahamas. She presented a possible additional motive for Haitian reluctance to control illegal migration from that country: "In Port-de-Paix that money [Haitians refer to as *Yo di*] paid by captains to protect their boats from official seizure and to obtain clearance from ports find its way, via local officials, into the pockets of even the highest officials in Port-au-Prince. This is so said as to be accepted locally as truth. It should not be surprising then that the Haitian Government seemed to take no effective action toward preventing the migration." Marshall's assertion that her "interpretation of the attitude of the Haitian government rests on an amalgam of information, mainly Bahamian, but including some Haitian sources that cannot be revealed" is fully appreciated by this researcher, who is similarly bound to keep some information shared in interviews strictly confidential. Marshall concluded that the Haitian authorities would take definitive action to prevent out-migration only when it became politically and economically convenient.

In July 1973, the month of Bahamian Independence, the Bahamas government revised the constitution, and in the process, restricted the eligibility of many children born of Haitian [and other foreign] parents in the Bahamas to claim Bahamian citizenship. The revision stipulated that persons born in the Bahamas after Independence were eligible to become Bahamians, if at the time of birth at least one parent was a Bahamian citizen. Some Haitians, who had lived in the Bahamas for many years, complained that the Bahamian government was unfair in its immigration restrictions. This was particularly true of young Haitian-Bahamians. Many became traumatized by their preclusion from participation in local social, economic, and political activities.

During the 1970s, few Haitian-Bahamian youth participated in national sporting events, or were members of civic and political youth groups. Some (mostly young men) did not complete their formal education (and in some cases, could not for a variety of reasons). Many of the latter became despondent and rebellious. An anonymous police official, interviewed by the author April 13, 1997, confided that officials have accused (in some cases justifiably) members of this latter group as collaborators in and perpetrators of many of the crimes committed during the late 1970s and 1980s. The informant stated that many Haitian-Bahamian youth join gangs and commit crimes to "fit in with the young guys." He suggested that some steal from the more affluent homes in protest against the people they perceive to be the main perpetrators of discrimination against them and largely responsible for their marginalization and exclusion from society. Most Haitians, however, seemed unperturbed by the intended ramifications of the Independence Order, primarily because they still cherished the hope that some day they would be able to return to the land of their birth. According to an anonymous social worker, interviewed on April 14, 1997, many Haitian-Bahamian youth wage a campaign of rebellion and crime against Haitians and Bahamians because they were not fully accepted and trusted in the Haitian communities as true Haitians and were largely ignored by Bahamians and considered to be half-breed.

Haitian immigrants, at the time of Independence, represented the lowest echelon of Bahamian society. The vast majority worked as common laborers. One laborer, widely known in his community as Maxie, illegally migrated to the Bahamas in the late 1950s and has been known by this author since the 1970s. When interviewed in December 1997, Maxie was employed as a gardener, but was allowed to seek employment elsewhere within the immediate community during the days he was not obliged to work for his host family. He continued to operate in that role for successive family members and other families within the wider community. Maxie was allowed to live in a shanty on the extensive property his patron family owned. The family sponsored Maxie on an annually renewed work contract. He was expected to repay this "privilege" by performing the duties of a handyman for the patron family at minimal wages. Failure to reciprocate would be perceived as ingratitude and could probably lead the family to reject him. At the time of interview, Maxie was seventy-five years old, in poor health, with a poor command of the English language. He had no real hope of becoming a Bahamian citizen, without which he remained ineligible for pension and other social benefits the state offers. His was a very uncertain future, as he grew older and as his initial family patrons died and left him to the care and protection of younger, less paternalistic (and sympathetic) relatives.

Maxie's predicament is common among Haitians who arrived in the Bahamas during the 1950s and 1960s. Rejection is usually because of the withdrawal of the "paternalistic" support that patron families provide through employment and liaison with immigration officials. Rejection resulted in economic suffering for some pre-Independence West Indian immigrants to the Bahamas. It was particularly severe for the Haitian immigrant from the economically depressed areas of northern Haiti who had little prospect of achieving even a moderately comfortable standard of living in his native community. Most Haitian immigrants were confined to the positions of day laborers and forced to accept substandard wages without complaint and with little hope of redress by government officials, church, and civic organizations. Low wages, in turn, forced most to live in substandard housing without an adequate supply of water and electricity, and to subsist on meager diets supplemented by produce imported aboard Haitian sloops. Most often, immigrant families were forced to live in single-room accommodations within a larger house shared by other immigrant families. Single, male immigrants traditionally shared a rented room with one or more immigrants. Cooking was done on single and/or double-burner kerosene stoves and on open wood fires.

Some pre-Independence Haitian immigrants congregated in shanty villages located in remote areas of New Providence. Dawn Marshall, in her research of one such community in the Carmichael Road area, noted that the Haitian community there was relatively large, consisting of over 1,300 residents. She described the community as follows: "From the Carmichael Road, along which Bahamians whiz in their cars, there is little evidence of this Haitian community, other than a few occasional pedestrians. The Haitians live away from the main road . . . in buildings whose locations have to be known if they are to be found. Often there is no necessity for Haitians to use the main road because the area is covered by a network of foot-paths which provide the essential communications network in much the same way as do the *gran chemins* of Haiti. Here, too, the efficiency of the *telediol*, the Haitian grapevine, should not be underestimated" (Marshall 1979:143).

Marshall (1979:129) confirmed that the great majority of Haitian immigrants, regardless of their levels of education, were forced to work as unskilled laborers because of the limited employment opportunity available to them. She noted a number of factors that limited their upward mobility within Bahamian society: the Haitian immigrant had to battle competition for limited jobs from Bahamians and other immigrants, because their experience was generally limited to peasant farming and petty commerce, and by poor schooling, limited English, and the fact that they settled in the Bahamas illegally. The Carmichael district, located in western New Providence, is the site of several cow, pig, and chicken farms. Traditionally, these farms employed Haitians as a cheap source of labor.

Many pre-Independence Haitian immigrants, however, recognized the value of education and made determined efforts to ensure that their children were enrolled in public schools. Most were eager for their children to learn English and become better equipped to cope with life in an English-speaking society. It was a common practice, therefore, for Haitian parents (mostly mothers) to escort their children to and from the local public schools.

At the time of Independence, Bahamian economic capacity for welcoming Haitian immigrants had reached the saturation point. Most Bahamians accused Haitians of dominating public services such as free medical care and education, but not contributing toward the financing of the services. The most vociferous arguments against the Haitians came from the low-income Bahamians, who could not afford to send their children to private schools or medical facilities. In 1973, it was common to hear some Bahamian women from this income bracket accuse Haitian women of "breeding like flies, and then using up all the beds in the hospital." Others complained that the Haitians were "taking over" the public schools.

Most teachers at public primary schools complained about overcrowded conditions created by the influx of Haitian students. According to a December 11, 1997, interview with Karen, there were periods when Haitian students accounted for as much as 75–80 percent of total enrollment at the Fox Hill Primary school where she taught. Few, however, victimized the Haitian students.

Summary

Beginning in the late 1950s and continuing after Bahamian Independence in 1973, thousands of Haitians migrated to the Bahamas. Official reports revealed that the Haitian population in the colony increased from an estimated 1,000 in 1957 to over 40,000 by 1973. Successive Bahamian governments attempted to curb illegal migration through the use of systematic raids, arrests, and mass deportations. The Haitian government, however, demonstrated an apparent reluctance to cooperate in deportation negotiations with Bahamian officials or to receive its deported nationals. As a result, attempts by Bahamian officials to negotiate deportation arrangements with Haitian counterparts were constantly frustrated.

In the Bahamas, illegal Haitian migration is now a perennial problem that defies simple remedial action. A major, often ignored, factor in the immigration equation is Bahamian ambivalence and complicity. Steve Dodge (1983:883) aptly characterized the history of the "illegal, officially unwanted, but apparently necessary" Haitian laborer in the Bahamas. Dodge noted that "the Haitians perform useful work disdained by most Bahamians. They provide low-cost agricultural labour, collect garbage, scrape boat bottoms, and do other heavy and menial chores." Many Bahamians demand increased Haitian repatriation exercises, yet continue to hire the illegal aliens to perform menial tasks at low wages. It appears that as long as the Bahamas remains politically and economically stable, and Haiti continues to experience economic and political maladies, the "Haitian Problem" will persist. The next chapter will discuss the migration of Turks and Caicos Islanders to the Bahamas and how they successfully assimilated into a Bahamian society that is traditionally hostile to other West Indian immigrants.

7

Turks and Caicos Islands Migration

Historical Overview

Historically, Turks and Caicos Islanders represent the second largest group of West Indian immigrants to the Bahamas, after the Haitians. Significantly, they have experienced the smoothest assimilation into Bahamian society, traditionally intolerant of most West Indian immigrants. This immigration enigma is partially explained by the fact that the two countries are united by geographical and historical circumstances. The Turks and Caicos Islands (Figure 7.1), situated at longitude 71.4° W and latitude 21.26°N, are recognized geographically as the southern extension of the Bahamian archipelago. From the 1670s to separation in 1848, and from 1962 until Bahamian Independence in 1973, the Bahamas politically administrated the islands. Since 1973, the islands have been governed as a British colony.

The first section of this chapter will discuss the ten islands and cays that make up the Turks and Caicos, as politically and socially a part of the Bahamas, and will review early attempts at colonization, emphasizing Bermudan migration to those islands. The section will include aspects of social history, trade conditions, and the political relations between Nassau and its farthest outpost until political separation in 1848. The second section will focus on subsequent migration after political separation until Bahamian Independence in 1973. It will examine the social, political, and economic conditions that influenced the different periods of migration and the migratory route of the immigrants. The section will provide a comparative analysis of the economic conditions prevailing in the sending and receiving countries during the period under review.

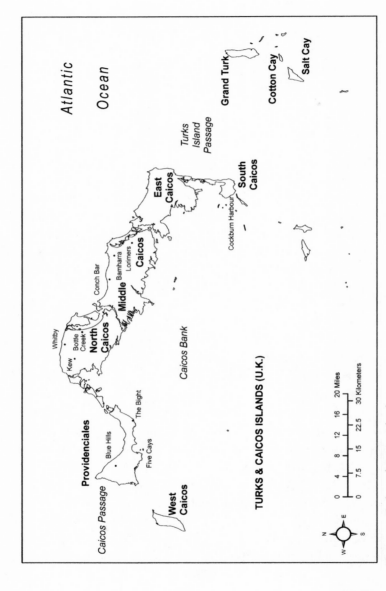

Figure 7.1. Turks and Caicos Islands.

Early Colonization

The Turks Islands are said to derive their name from a species of cactus *(Echinocactus myriostigma)* whose flower resembles a Turkish fez. The origin of the name "Caicos" is uncertain, but may be derived from the Spanish name *Cayos* for cays. Lucayans migrating northward from Española in A.D. 600 first settled the group of islands situated in the southernmost tip of the Bahamian archipelago (Aarons 1991:24). Juan Ponce de León visited the islands in 1512 while on a voyage from Puerto Rico. The first recorded English contact was reportedly made in 1585 by Sir Richard Grenville, "while enroute for Sir Walter Raleigh's Roanoke Island colony"[GB/COR, Annual Report for the Turks & Caicos Islands, 1966 (Bahamas/PRO. 1987), 39]; and two years later, other Roanoke-bound ships reportedly "searched for salt at the Islands Caycos" [GB/COR, Annual Report for the Turks & Caicos Islands, 1966 (Bahamas/PRO. 1987), 173].

Bermudans are traditionally credited with attempting the first permanent European settlement of the islands in 1678. The Bermudan "sojourners" were initially seasonal immigrants who visited the Turks Islands from March to November to rake salt at the numerous island ponds. They eventually developed a thriving salt industry that targeted lucrative markets primarily in the North American colonies. The success of the industry encouraged a continuous migration of Bermudans with their slaves. They were joined by a small number of immigrants from the Bahamas, Cuba, and Española. The continued success, however, caused other nations to view the prospects of colonization on the islands more favorably. Consequently, during the mid-seventeenth to early eighteenth centuries several European nations vied for political (and ultimately economic) control of the islands.

In 1710, the Spanish, who claimed sovereignty over the group, temporarily expelled the early Bermudan settlers from the islands. Attacks by Spanish forces continued during the succeeding decades. In 1764, a French expeditionary force led by the Comte d'Estaing invaded and claimed the islands as French territory. The Saint Domingue-based French established a settlement on Grand Turk called Fleur-de-Lis. The Comte d'Estaing was subsequently forced to vacate the island following vehement protest by the British to the French government that the settlement was established in violation of the terms of the Treaty of Paris [GB/COR. Bahamas. Votes of the House of Assembly 1848–1850 Appendix 1848 (Bahamas/PRO, 1971),

1–2], and the French government directed d'Estaing to retract any claim to the islands and to make reparations to the Turks Islanders who suffered damages as a result of the invasion.

In 1766, the British board of trade, in an attempt to establish a British territorial claim, initiated measures to annex the islands economically to the Bahamas. Andrew Symmer was appointed "to reside there, and by his presence on the spot, to ensure the right of the islands to His Majesty" and to oversee British economic interests [GB/COR, Annual Report for the Turks & Caicos Islands, 1966. (Bahamas/PRO. 1987), 173]. In 1781, by order-in-council, regulations were approved for the management of the salinas (salt ponds) and for the preservation of order. A plan was prepared by the imperial authorities to further colonize the island with loyal British subjects. In 1790, a group of Loyalists, primarily from the American colony of Georgia, obtained grants in the Caicos Islands, where many established plantations. A contingent of troops stationed in Jamaica was committed to the protection of the colonists. The British authorities, however, were primarily concerned that the troops be available to ensure the enforcement of taxes levied on the lucrative salt trade, which by the 1780s exceeded 500,000 bushels each year. During the early years of British administration little was done to improve social and economic life in the islands. According to Craton (1992:209), "the rule of Nassau in the Turks had never been either popular or efficient."

Beginning in the late 1700s, immigrants—mostly Bermudans—protested the excessive taxes levied on salt production. Some refused to pay salt taxes; others refused to export their salt. Most, however, defied British regulations and exported their salt on ships bound for the markets of France and Spain, countries then hostile to the British crown [GB/COR. Bahamas, CSOP. folio 23. no. 42. Halkett to Hobart. September 9, 1902. (Bahamas/PRO. 1971)]. In the late 1700s, the British were preoccupied with political dissent in their North American colonies, participation in European wars, and economic interest in the West Indies. Less valuable colonies like Bermuda, the Bahamas, and the Turks and Caicos Islands were often given only casual attention. Bermuda, allowed internal self-government, attempted to annex the Turks and Caicos Islands. The local British representative, motivated by political and economic self-interest, supported the Bermudan cause and instead of enforcing British control, established himself as the chief administrator of the islands, independent of British authority. The Bermudan immigrants continually displayed open disregard and contempt for British authority. They declared political allegiance to the government in Bermuda and expressed a desire to be administrated by the political authority in that island. The immigrants claimed to be "alarmed to the greatest degree" that they must be subject to the legislative authority of New Providence, in which case "they were unanimously determined to leave the islands" [GB/COR, Annual Report for the Turks & Caicos Islands, 1966. (Bahamas/PRO. 1987). folio 23. no. 42. Chalmers to Hobart, June 13, 1802 (Bahamas/PRO. 1971), 186–87].

The Bermudan government, encouraged by the protests of Bermudan immigrants in the Turks and Caicos Islands and the possibility of acquiring new revenue from taxes levied on the salt industry, made repeated claims to the crown for control of the islands. The Bahamian government counterprotested Bermudan interference in the political affairs of the islands. In 1790, the Earl of Dunmore, governor of the Bahamas, complained to the colonial secretary that he was "not a little astonished at [the] interference of Bermuda nor could [he] conceive what claim [Bermudan immigrants could] possibly have to any exemption from the payment of the same duties and taxes which other persons within the government are liable to" [GB/COR, Annual Report for the Turks & Caicos Islands, 1966. (Bahamas/PRO. 1987), folio 23. No. 30. Dunmore to Grenville, September 1, 1790. (Bahamas/PRO, 1971), 232]. Governor Hamilton of Bermuda insisted that "the Bermudas have for a number of years enjoyed the possession of these [Turks and Caicos] islands undisturbed" [GB/COR, Annual Report for the Turks & Caicos Islands, 1966. (Bahamas/PRO. 1987), folio 23. no. 42. Chalmers to Hobart, June 13, 1802 (Bahamas/PRO, 1971), 186].

In the early 1790s, the Turks and Caicos Islands were temporarily placed under the administration of the Bahamas government. The Bermudans especially "resented Bahamian control because it meant that they would be subject to Bahamian laws and taxation and not the laws of Bermuda, their former homeland" (Craton 1992:137). The protesters reiterated their claims that since Bermudans settled the group of islands, they were, therefore, entitled to sovereignty over them [GB/COR, Bahamas. CSOP, folio 23. no. 40. Memorial from certain Inhabitants of Bermuda to Lorimer, H. M. Agent and Commander for the Turks & Caicos Islands, 1801 (Bahamas/PRO, 1987), 236]. The petition claimed that nineteen out of every twenty-nine persons living in the Turks Islands at the time were Bermudans. Some non-Bermudan Turks and Caicos Islanders sympathized with the Bermudan immigrants, primarily because most were workers or investors in the Bermudan-dominated salt industry. Some were accomplices in the prosperous trade of contraband to communities in North America and the Caribbean. According to Craton (1992:137), Bahamians collaborated with the Turks and Caicos Islanders in both salt raking and the sale of contraband salt. He noted that in the 1790s, there was a demand for salt in the eastern Canadian territories and United States for use in the fishing industry. Ships from these areas visited the Turks and Caicos Islands to trade contraband salt for manufactured goods. Others recognized the high level of interest that the Bermudans exhibited toward the development of the islands in comparison with the general disinterest manifested by the Bahamian authorities.

George Chalmers, the London-based colonial agent responsible for the Bahamas (including the Turks and Caicos Islands) disputed the Bermudan territorial claims in a series of memorandums to the colonial secretary. Chalmers claimed that disorder existed and would continue in the islands as long as the Bermudan government was allowed to interfere. He stated that the Bermudan intrigue was "unneighbourly, unofficial and . . . undutiful to His Majesty" [GB/COR, Bahamas. CSOP, folio 23. no. 37. Chalmers to Dundas, July 4, 1793. The Chalmers Papers, 1792–1803 (Bahamas/PRO. 1971), 44]. Chalmers went on to complain that the rebellious agent incited a reactionary spirit in the inhabitants by "holding up to their ignorant eyes" the prospect of independence from the Bahamas. He accused the Turks and Caicos Island Board of Trade of mischief and warned that its attempts to exert its powers were illegal, because an "agent cannot act as Agent without acting illegally, because the Law does not recognize his authority."

Initially, Bahamian legislators, reluctant to expend funds for the development of the Turks and Caicos Islands, yet unwilling to jeopardize financial investments there, supported the Bermudan territorial claims. In 1770, for example, Bahamian assemblymen deliberately frustrated plans by the imperial government to introduce taxes on salt production in the Turks and Caicos Islands. Governor Shirley, enraged by the political insubordination, dissolved the House of Assembly and accused the members of "carrying on the Business of this session in an unconstitutional manner and in open defiance of the King's instructions" (Williams 1989:13). By 1780, however, Bahamian politicians began to demonstrate an appreciation for the growing success of the salt industry and a realization that the Bahamas (and ultimately they) could profit from revenue generated from taxes. Craton (1992:209) noted that in 1827 the tax on salt accounted for approximately 25 percent of the entire revenue generated in the Bahamas. He claimed less than one-eighth directly benefited the Turks and Caicos Islands. Most had become convinced by then that the islands were indeed valuable, because of the "immense quantity of salt which [was purportedly] . . . capable of supplying all of North America with that important article, proper for every branch of trade" [GB/COR. Bahamas. CSOP. folio 23. no. 26. Symmer to Germaine. September 1, 1780. (Bahamas/PRO, 1971), 1–2]. Eventually, most Bahamian legislators decided that the islands should remain politically (and more important, economically) a part of the Bahamas.

In the late 1700s, the Turks Islands were a major salt producer. They were reportedly the principal salt-producing islands in the region, surpassing in economic importance production from other Bahamian salt-producing communities at Inagua, Ragged Island, Rum Cay, Long Island, and Crooked Island. By 1843, the islands exported 706,467 bushels of salt valued at £12,532. In comparison, the combined export from the other salt-producing islands in the Bahamas during the same period amounted to 231,513 bushels valued at £4,126. An export tax of 1/2 penny was levied on each bushel, and an additional tonnage duty of one shilling per ton was imposed on ships loading salt. By 1895, the Turks Islands exported more than one million bushels, while that of the entire Bahamas was less than 300,000 bushels [F. H. Watkins. Turks & Caicos Islands: Report on the Salt Industry. 1802–1827. (Bahamas/PRO. 1971), 7–18].

The Bermudan immigrants especially resented the official use of the revenue generated from taxes on salt production. Between 1802 and 1827, salt producers earned an estimated £88,600. (Watkins 1971:10). Most of this revenue, however, was reportedly expended in the development and maintenance of roads and buildings in Nassau and other areas of the Bahamas. In particular, the immigrants protested the use of the revenue to maintain the police force, whose duties focused on Nassau and did not include their protection (Williams 1989:13). Thus, taxation without representation became "a source of grave discontent as the inhabitants felt that any revenue received from salt should be used for the upkeep of the [salt] ponds and for any infrastructure needed in the islands."

In 1799, the Turks and Caicos Islands were officially incorporated into the Bahamas by a series of imperial acts. Bahamian colonial authorities thereupon established in the islands a customs house, staffed by a collector, a comptroller, and two weighers and searchers of customs "answerable [only] to the Bahamas Government." The islands were, however, only theoretically represented in the Bahamas House of Assembly. Craton (1992:209) noted that the Turks and Caicos Islands representative encountered many difficulties in the execution of his legislative duties. He rarely sat in Parliament because communication between the islands and Nassau was poor and irregular. Furthermore, the representative who sat in Parliament was made to feel like "an alien in an unfriendly land." Craton went on to explain that in the early 1800s, the channels of communication between the Turks and Caicos Islands and Jamaica were kept open by ships from England that stopped there on the route to Kingston and that the Turks and Caicos Islanders were then "more akin to Kingston than with Nassau."

Twenty years later, in 1819, Turks and Caicos Islanders, led by Bermudan immigrants, petitioned the crown for permission to establish a local government in those islands [GB/COR. Bahamas. CSOP, folio 23. no. 74. Petition from Turks & Caicos Islanders for Secession from the Bahamas. 1819. (Bahamas/PRO. 1971), 235–40]. The petition noted that:

> The Turks & Caicos Islands [are] situated 70 miles from San Domingo, 160 miles from Cuba, 350 miles from Jamaica, but 500 miles from New Providence, the seat of Government. Because of this distance, communication between the out station and the capital [is] difficult, since it [takes] three to four weeks to complete the entire trip. . . . Consequently if an emergency occurred, prompt assistance would not be forthcoming from the capital.

The petitioners protested the lack of adequate representation in the Bahamian House of Assembly which, they argued, made it impossible for Turks and Caicos Islands representatives to obtain favorable resolutions or laws in Parliament. Additionally, they argued that laws unfavorable to the economic and social interest of the islanders were repeatedly passed.

The islands were allowed three representatives in the Bahamian Legislative Assembly of thirty members. The assemblymen were predominantly Bermudan immigrants who had acquired wealth and property from profits earned in the salt industry. The representatives were reportedly forced to bear the cost of travel to attend the usually lengthy sessions of parliament, often in neglect of their economic interests at home (Williams 1989:13). Occasionally, the islands were without representation because their assemblymen were reluctant to pay the high cost of travel to Nassau and to endure extensive periods of absence from their businesses. Those who maintained a residence in Nassau were faced with the disadvantage of poor communication between the islands, and the inevitability of losing meaningful political, social, and economic connection with their constituents. As a result, some representatives suffered serious economic losses and family crises while attempting to meet their political obligations.

One such case was that of Henshall Stubbs, a representative for the Caicos Islands who maintained a residence in Nassau because "membership in the Legislative Assembly kept him [there] over considerable periods," according to an article by Lewis W. Beater in the *Nassau Daily Tribune*, (1957:1–2). Beater wrote what he called "an intimate and revealing account of relations between the Turks and Caicos Islands and the Bahamas in the nineteenth century." His information was based on research of the "Stubbs Papers Collection," a collection of intimately revealing documents covering over fifty years and many aspects of the life experiences of the Horatio Stubbs family. Stubbs left the management of the 800-acre family plantation to the care of Horatio, his teenage son. Horatio, "while his father was in Nassau . . . reported frequently on his own stewardship of the family business." The younger Stubbs, in correspondences with his father, complained of a number of problems, including slave escapes and revolts, and the fact that his father and brothers were not there to assist him in the management of the estate. Evidently, the weight of responsibility eventually became unbearable for Horatio. In 1831, he attempted to escape aboard a ship sailing from Puerta Plata (now in the Dominican Republic). His escape was unsuccessful, however, because the ship sailed just hours before he arrived. In a lengthy letter to his younger brother, Richard, who with another brother, Alfred, was at school in New York, Horatio commented on his attempted escape: "It gave me time for reflection and I finally began to think it my duty to return again, solely on yours and Alfred's account. [Our] father has threatened in case I do not behave myself . . . to order you both home."

Most prominent Turks and Caicos Islanders, as a demonstration of their resistance to Bahamian authority, refused to serve as representatives in the Bahamas Legislative Assembly. In 1833, when C. J. Anderson (Bahamas receiver general) suggested that Horatio Stubbs become a representative in the Bahamas Legislative Assembly, Stubbs reportedly replied:

> You ask me why I do not get myself elected as a member to represent
> this place—the fact is, that had I no private reason to decline this
> honour, the apparent and evident unkindness manifested by many
> humans here and these, too, the most influential—would almost de-
> bar me. . . . They actually ridicule the very existence of a Legislature
> as far as our interest is concerned, and because we (the Turks) are
> not generously dealth [*sic*] with, they would give up all claim on you
> and annihilate all future hopes.

Turks and Caicos Islanders continued to avoid elected office in the Bahamas Legislative Assembly until the islands were politically separated from
the Bahamas.

In 1848, the British government acquiesced to the continuous petitions
for separation and granted the Turks and Caicos Islands self-government.
Under the charter, the islands were administered by an elective legislative
council headed by a president. Self-government, however, proved too expensive, and in 1873 the islanders petitioned the crown for an abrogation
of the charter. In 1873, the islands were politically reassigned to Jamaica as
a dependency. In July 1959, a new constitution was introduced, providing
for an executive council to advise the Jamaica-appointed administrator.
The governor of Jamaica, by virtue of his office, remained the governor of
the Turks and Caicos Islands.

In 1961, after Jamaica withdrew its support, the Turks and Caicos Islands were unsuccessful in negotiations to become an associated territory
of the Federation of the West Indies. Negotiations to become an associated territory of Jamaica also failed when most Turks Islanders voted to
remain a British colony. On August 6, 1962, two days before Jamaica's
independence, a new constitution was introduced, which transferred the
powers held by the governor to the administrator. Coincidentally, this
was a return to the system of government introduced in 1848, but later
abandoned in 1873. On November 5, 1965, the constitution was further
amended to allow the governor of the Bahamas to also act as governor
of the Turks and Caicos Islands, thus establishing the islands once again
as a part of the Bahamas. The social, political, and economic relationship
between the islands endured until political separation came in 1973 when
the Bahamas became an independent nation. Today, the Turks and Caicos
Islands remain a British colony.

Migration under Colonial Jamaican Political Authority, 1848–1890

Migration from the Turks and Caicos Islands to the Bahamas was insignificant during the early decades of colonial Jamaican political administration, largely because most islanders were comfortably employed in the lucrative salt industry or in trade with the neighboring islands. The Jamaican colonial government generally regarded the islands as an insignificant dependency, and instituted marginal public administration. Visits by Jamaican officials were infrequent and little attention was devoted to the economic development of the islands. Islanders, therefore, fostered social and economic links with Bermuda, Haiti, and the Dominican Republic. On February 16, 1998, the author interviewed 102-year-old Helen, who recalled that her father and some of the older Turks Islanders living in Inagua often complained about the "lack of concern and commitment" the Jamaican authorities demonstrated toward Turks and Caicos Islanders. She remembered most complaints specifically focused on the disrepair of docks, public buildings, and roads. Helen said the most frequent complaint, however, concerned the absence of employment opportunity in the islands.

During the 1820s, contact with Española increased when political refugees from Santo Domingo fled to the Turks and Caicos Islands to escape the carnage resulting from the struggle for independence from Haiti (Grasmuck 1982:368). In 1821, a group of Dominigans led by two high-ranking Spanish officials reportedly sought exile on Grand Turks (Smith 1968:5–10); and in 1822, Haitian General Boyer, after uniting the island of Española under his presidency, encouraged Turks and Caicos Islands trade and migration. Smith claimed that in 1866, after a hurricane devastated the Turks and Caicos Islands, churches in Port-au-Prince, Haiti, collected funds to assist the unfortunate victims. By the early 1870s, a significant number of islanders had apparently migrated to Española so that by 1871, the registrar general for the islands reported: "The population of the Turks & Caicos Islands shows a considerable increase not withstanding a good deal of emigration to San Domingo" (Pusey 1989:56–57). Some Turks and Caicos Islanders migrated to Bermuda where relatives lived, while a small number migrated to Jamaica and the United States. In the late 1890s, however, significant numbers began to migrate to the Bahamas in search of employment.

The Recruitment of Turks and Caicos Islanders as Stevedores and Deck Hands, 1890s–1950s

In the 1890s, scores of Turks and Caicos Islanders began to migrate to the southern Bahamas in search of employment as laborers on passing steam vessels. At the turn of the twentieth century, Mayaguana, Inagua, Fortune Island, and Long Cay were important destinations from which laborers (including Turks and Caicos Islanders) were contracted to work as stevedores and deck hands on mostly American ships transporting cargo to and from ports in the Caribbean and Central and South America (Albuquerque and McElroy 1986:178–180). The islands mentioned are located in the southeastern Bahamas along the primary shipping lanes connecting the east coast of North America with ports in the Caribbean and the Atlantic shores of Central and South America. In their strategic maritime locations, they offered an easily accessible source of cheap labor. The governor's official report for 1899 stated that the ships sailed to ports in Jamaica; the principal ports of Haiti; Greytown and Bluefields in Nicaragua; Livingston in Guatemala; Tampico in Mexico; Santa Marta in Colombia; Colon in Panama; Puerto Cortez and Cape Gracias in Honduras; and Havana, Santiago, Daiquiri, Cienfuegos, and Nuevitas in Cuba [GB/COR. Bahamas. Colonial Annual Report, 1889. no. 277. (Bahamas/ PRO, 1971), 50].

Laborers signed short-term contracts made under the supervision of the resident justices and the resident American consular agent. They traveled on the ships to unload and load cargo, whereupon they were returned to the Bahamas as the ships carried cargoes of fruit, lumber, and other products to destinations along the Atlantic coast of the United States. In 1899, sixty-nine ships, mostly of the United Fruit Company and Hamburg-American lines, recruited an estimated 3,000 laborers from Inagua as stevedores. Laborers were employed, according to this report, to work on the construction of railroads in Panama and Mexico and the Panama Canal, in the lumber industry, on banana and coffee plantations, and clearing land and building roads in Nicaragua, Guatemala, Colombia, and British and Spanish Honduras.

Turks and Caicos Islanders were attracted to the southern Bahamas by comparatively higher wages and more consistent employment opportunities than were available at home. In 1899, the resident justice at Long Cay reported that 111 steamers recruited 2,234 laborers from that island.

According to the report, combined wages that year were offered at "2s. a day for ordinary hands, 2s. 6d. for carpenters, and 2s 11d. for foremen, with overtime per hour at the rate of 5d." This amounted to an average wage of US$1,378 for each of the 2,234 laborers [GB/COR. Bahamas. Colonial Annual Report, 1889. no. 277 (Bahamas/PRO, 1971), 50]. In 1912, 160 laborers recruited as stevedores earned an average of US$87.50 a month [GB/COR. Bahamas. Colonial Annual Report, 1912. no. 789 (Bahamas/ PRO, 1971), 29]. By 1929 the total payroll for stevedores recruited in Inagua was estimated at US$32,174 [GB/COR. Bahamas. Colonial Annual Report, 1929. no. 1477 (Bahamas/PRO, 1971), 43].

Turks and Caicos Islanders, like many other West Indians, migrated to escape the economic depression that gripped their islands. The following statement in the colonial annual reports on the Turks and Caicos Islands for the years 1900 through 1930 illustrates the prevailing economic conditions:

> The manufacture and export of salt, which is the Dependency's principal export, remained at a low level. The difficulties of this industry, on which the Dependency's economy rests, were accentuated by the continuing low price of salt. . . . The standard of living remains low. Then difficulties of the Dependency are aggravated by the increasing cost of imports, especially food. Full employment and an appreciable improvement in the standard of living are not in sight. . . . Unemployment is severe and there is the tendency for the best men to leave the Dependency whenever a chance of employment elsewhere occurs. . . . Many seek employment on steamers and in the salt industry in the Bahamas [GB/COR, Financial and Economic Position: Turks & Caicos Islands, 1900–1930, Report[s] of the Commissioner appointed by the Governor of Jamaica (Bahamas/PRO, 1987)].

After 1929, the recruitment of stevedores and deck hands from the southern Bahamas dwindled to an average of just sixty men each month and ceased altogether by 1950. The decrease in employment opportunity in the shipping industry caused some Turks and Caicos Islanders to migrate to the United States or return to their homeland. An undetermined, but apparently significant number, however, remained and became assimilated into southern Bahamian communities. The number of immigrants was increased by scores of other islanders recruited to work in the expanding salt industry at Inagua. Helen noted in an interview on

February 16, 1998, that during the 1890s her grandparents migrated from Grand Turks to Inagua to work in the salt industry. She remembered that as a young girl growing up in Inagua at the turn of the century, many of her neighbors were Turks and Caicos immigrants. Helen recalled that the number of immigrants to Inagua continued to increase until the 1970s.

Roosevelt, a prominent Bahamian entrepreneur, proudly noted in a February 14, 1998, interview that in the early 1930s, his Turks Island forebear, William Alexander, was recruited to manage the salt industry at Inagua "because no suitably knowledgeable Bahamian could be found." William reportedly recruited many veteran salt rakers from the Turks and Caicos Islanders to work the ponds. James, a native of Inagua and rector of one of the largest Anglican churches in the Bahamas at the time of his interview on February 14, 1998, argued that the majority of Inaguans today can trace at least one branch of their family tree to Turks and Caicos immigrants to that island.

In the late 1920s, the predominant type of Turks and Caicos immigrant to the Bahamas began to shift from young, single men seeking employment in the shipping industry to an increasing number of older immigrants with families. Most heads of immigrant families (generally men) established themselves with a job and home an average of two years before their families arrived [GB/COR. Bahamas CSOP, List of Registered Aliens in the Bahamas, 1930 (Bahamas/PRO. 1931)]. The destination of most immigrants began to shift from the southern Bahamas to New Providence and the northern islands. Many immigrants in Nassau migrated from the southern islands in a continued search for employment. Most found jobs in the expanding tourism industry and development of public works projects. Many, reportedly lured by tales of high salaried jobs in a developing cosmopolitan environment, were disappointed by their initial experiences.

Paul, an immigrant and age 86 at the time of the interview, recalled in December 17, 1997, accepting an invitation by a friend to immigrate to the Bahamas in 1928, "only to be shocked at the level of hard-times Turks [and Caicos] Islanders suffered in Nassau." According to Paul, some male immigrants, desperate to leave home, but unable to immediately find jobs and adequate means of financial support in Nassau, reportedly slept under the floors of houses and in abandoned sheds, awakening and moving from the properties just before dawn to avoid detection. Paul, a victim of similar circumstances, explained that during the 1920s, most Turks and

Caicos immigrants were young men exposed to life in the metropolitan cities of Central and South America and the Caribbean. Many, therefore, were disappointed that Nassau did not meet their expectations of similar economic development and opportunity. For some immigrants, the Bahamas served as a migration conduit to the United States. Many, however, remained and found employment in the lumber industry being developed in the northern Bahamas.

Employment in the Logging Industry

Shortly after the turn of the century, groups of Turks and Caicos Islanders were recruited to work in the American-owned and operated pine lumber industry in the northern Bahamian islands of Abaco, Grand Bahama, and Andros. The initial lumber enterprise was operated by the Bahamas Timber Company, which was incorporated in 1906 and had a concession to produce lumber in those islands. Little is known of the operation, except that it was headquartered in Abaco and exported most of the lumber to Cuba (Moseley 1926:67). The company built a community called Wilson City (after one of the developers), that consisted of rows of barracks to accommodate the laborers.

The number of Turks and Caicos Islanders recruited, estimated at several hundred, is difficult to precisely determine because of the lack of company records and the complication due to the number of recruits who came via Nassau and Inagua. Additionally, official records on the recruitment methods have been difficult to find. The influx of islanders temporarily shifted the demography of Abaco. In 1901, for instance, the population of the island was approximately 3,600—the same as it was (with fluctuations) during the 1880s [GB/COR, Bahamas. Report on the Census of the Bahama Islands Taken the 25 March 1902: Abaco Island, schedule 39, 1902. (Bahamas/PRO, 1902), 2–3]. The population reached a peak estimated at 4,500 in 1911, however, when Wilson City was in full operation [GB/COR, Bahamas, Report on the Census of the Bahama Islands Taken the 18 February 1911 (Bahamas/PRO, 1911), 2]. After 1916, when Wilson City shut down, the population fell to the level it was at before the recruitment of the loggers.

The assumption that most laborers at Wilson City were Turks and Caicos Islanders is based on the fact that, at the time, most Bahamian laborers were more interested in securing employment at higher wages as stevedores and deck hands on passing ships and in Miami, than in engaging in the backbreaking work required in the logging industry according to an article in the *Miami Metropolis* on June 12, 1909. According to the paper, more than 1,400 Bahamians migrated to Miami after July 1908. The large number of Bahamians who migrated to Miami during the period is suggested by the fact that, after 1911, the Bahamian population decreased by over 5 percent, from 55,944 in 1911, to 53,031 in 1921 [GB/COR. Bahamas. Report on the Census of the Bahama Islands Taken on the 24 April 1921. (Bahamas/PRO. 1921), 1–2]. The exodus of Bahamian labor to south Florida is further evident in the 1915 census taken by the State of Florida, which reported 3,743 foreign-born blacks in Dade County, 1,870 in Monroe County, 615 in Palm Beach County, and 490 in Broward County (McRae 1915:66). Turks and Caicos Islanders, evidently, filled the labor void that Bahamian immigrants to south Florida created.

In the 1940s, Turks and Caicos Islanders were again recruited for labor in the Bahamas when the Abaco Lumber Company expanded its operation to the island of Grand Bahama. The immigrants were joined by hundreds of Bahamians from Andros and Cat islands. The operation covered large acres of pine forests and appears to have been highly organized. According to one eyewitness account: "A path was first cleared for the saw-team. The two-man team then cut all the trees in this area of over 8-inch girth at waist height. If any trees were felled outside the allotted area the tally man would not count them. The saw-men would lop the branches of the felled tree and move on. After the saw-men, a team of about eight men on the skidding units would fasten a cable and pull three or more trees to the railway track where they were stored in piles and from where they were loaded onto a flat car and taken to the sawmill" (Barratt 1972:80). The machinery used, which was mostly diesel powered, included steam-powered locomotives that traveled along miles of tracks which led to the coast.

A new community called Pine Ridge, consisting of a series of wooden barracks, was established to accommodate the hundreds of laborers employed. Paul said in a December 17, 1997, interview that a rental charge of 3 shillings each week was subtracted from his weekly salary of 18 shillings.

Dr. Evans Cottman (1979:81), an American general medical practitioner, was temporarily employed as the camp physician. He established a small medical clinic on the waterfront in a building previously used as a

missionary hospital. According to his accounts, the Bahamians and immigrant laborers were constantly embroiled in verbal and physical confron-
tations that required his medical skills. He also reported that romantic
clashes and alcohol were the main causes of conflict between the groups
of laborers. He reminisced (with obvious exaggeration) that at times it
seemed as if he was in a race with the laborers to see if he could patch up
the wounds as fast as they could inflict them upon each other (Cottman
1979:81).

Barratt (1982:83) opined that the influx of predominantly Bahamian
women to the settlement created an atmosphere of heated rivalry for their
affections. He also noted that Bahamians resented the presence of the
immigrants who they accused of taking away their jobs and women. According to one of the laborers, frequent fights erupted between groups
of Bahamian and immigrant laborers that usually left victims with knife
and club wounds. He did not recall, however, any fatal encounters. The
rivalry between the groups was so intense during the postwar years that
the laborers were housed in separate sections of the community according
to their island of origin.

In 1953, Turks and Caicos immigrants made up the largest percentage of the population of Pine Ridge. Barratt noted (1979:84) that, by 1953
when the lumber company was at peak operation, it was the "single largest employer in the Bahamas with about 1,800 people on the payroll, and
in fact . . . the community of Pine Ridge comprised 1,668 inhabitants,
or more than three times the population of the next largest settlement
at West End." Statistics from the 1953 census confirm that more than 75
percent of the population of Pine Ridge was immigrants from the Turks
and Caicos Islands. The report classified most male residents as unskilled
laborers and females as domestic servants, suggesting that very few artisans migrated to the area. The 1953 census revealed that most skilled Turks
and Caicos migrated to Nassau where the labor market was better able to
accommodate their particular skills. Most unskilled immigrants migrated
to the lumber camps in the northern Bahama Islands.

More immigrants came to Abaco (Table 7.1) from the Caicos Islands
than from the Turks Islands [Bahamas/PRO, 1953)]. The administrator of
the dependency partially explained the reason: "The number of females
exceed the number of males by 19.9 percent. This excess has, if anything,
increased during the intervening years and it is estimated that at any given
time up to 50 percent of the adult male population are absent seeking their

livelihood abroad. This is particularly noticeable in the Caicos Islands where the ratio of women to men at any public function is frequently more than three to one" [GB/COR, Report on The Turks & Caicos Islands (Dependency of Jamaica) for the years 1953–1954 (Bahamas/PRO, 1987), 5]. The administrator noted that, although lobster and conch (shellfish) fishing "provided the chief source of income in the Caicos Islands . . . a large number of adult males [were] absent working in the salt industry at Inagua and the lumber industry on Grand Bahama Island" [GB/COR, Report on The Turks & Caicos Islands (Dependency of Jamaica) for the years 1953–1954 (Bahamas/PRO, 1987), 7].

In the 1950s, the influx of Turks and Caicos Islanders to Pine Ridge established that community as the economic capital of Abaco. The immigrants saved substantially more money at the local post offices than residents of the predominantly Bahamian neighboring communities. In 1951, for example, the commissioner for Abaco reported that residents of the political capital of West End collectively deposited approximately £1,651 in the local post office. Residents of Pine Ridge, in comparison, deposited approximately £5,857, causing the commissioner to report that "an unusual amount of business was done by [the Pine Ridge sub-post] office" [GB/COR, Bahamas, CSOP. folio 23. no. 130. Annual Reports of The Bahama Islands: Abaco Island: the Districts of West End and Pine Ridge, 1951–1952 (Bahamas/PRO, 1953), 13–15]. Until the establishment of Freeport in the 1960s, West End was the principal community in Abaco, and the seat of colonial administration. In 1953, as the number of immigrants at Pine Ridge increased, they collectively saved more than £10,600 at the local post office and forwarded approximately £24,600 in remittances to their home islands [GB/COR, Bahamas. CSOP, folio 23. no. 130. Annual Reports of The Bahama Islands: Abaco Island: the Districts of West End and Pine Ridge, 1951–1952 (Bahamas/PRO, 1953), 15–16]. Remittances were forwarded as United States and Canadian postal money orders. The economic importance of Pine Ridge was reflected in the fact that, along with the office at West End, only the Pine Ridge sub-post office was authorized to sell telegraph messages and money orders, and transact withdrawals on account of the Nassau-based Post Office Savings Bank. Operations at the other sub-post offices were limited to the handling of letters and parcels.

In 1953, the commissioner for Abaco noted the improvements in housing that the immigrants at Pine Ridge implemented. According to the

Table 7. 1. Population of Abaco Island, 1948–1953

Community	1948	1949	1950	1951	1952	1953
West End	643	590	746	627	652	624
Eight Mile Rock	300	360	318	220	265	272
Pine Ridge	1050	900	1600	1061	1457	1688
Pinder's Rock	117	141	75	102	134	127
Holme's Rock	170	165	140	121	113	106
Brady Point	125	134	65	55	51	47
High Rock	165	190	192	212	228	243
Water Cay	255	248	250	230	234	218
Sweeting's Cay	148	160	183	209	187	196

Source: Commissioner's Annual Report, Abaco Island, 1948–1953.

government official, the mostly Turks and Caicos Islands immigrants se-cured the financial assistance of the lumber company to construct new homes, which were "improvements on previous buildings constructed as they are spaced 100 feet apart and built up on concrete blocks. . . . This method should also decrease the fire hazard in this location" [GB/COR, Bahamas. CSOP, folio 23. no. 130. Annual Reports of The Bahama Islands: Abaco Island: the Districts of West End and Pine Ridge, 1951–1952 (Ba-hamas/PRO, 1953), 20]. The new homes boasted two bedrooms, living room, dining room, pantry, kitchen, and a pit latrine. The immigrants, despite improvements in housing, generally lived in overcrowded condi-tions that accommodated a combination of family members, friends, and boarders.

Typically, the recruited laborer rented or built a house with money saved from wages and borrowed from the company. He invited rela-tives and friends to live with him while they, in turn, secured a job with which to financially establish themselves. Often, he would accommodate Bahamian and immigrant boarders for a negotiable weekly fee. Under such conditions, it was common to find the owner, his wife and children, other relatives, and boarders residing in a house only suitable for a fam-ily of four [Report on the Census of the Bahama Islands Taken on the 12 April. 1953. Grand Bahama. Schedule 210 (Bahamas/PRO. 1953), 10–15]. A typical case was that of John Delancy, a recruit from Turks Island, who while living with his wife Daisy and six children, simultaneously rented accommodations to Simon Rigby (his wife's brother), Charlotte Williams (a niece), and Agnes Rigby (a family friend) [Report on the Census of the

Bahama Islands Taken on the 12 April. 1953. Grand Bahama. Schedule 210 (Bahamas/PRO. 1953), 13]. After 1955, residents of Pine Ridge established a new community called Seagrape, just north of the main highway. According to Barratt (1982:179), some of the houses in the new community were literally moved there from Pine Ridge. By 1969, the population of Seagrape was estimated at 2,000, "about 95 percent of whom were originally Turks [and Caicos] Islanders either formerly engaged, or descended from people formerly engaged, in lumbering."

In the late 1950s, the Owens-Illinois Corporation acquired the National Container Corporation and gained access to a 100-year timber lease. Beginning in 1959, the company invested large sums of money to establish a pulpwood operation that involved the cutting of lumber for shipment to Jacksonville, Florida. Owens-Illinois built a container terminal at Snake Cay (six miles south of Marsh Harbour). The company brought an old Hudson River side-wheeler, the *Robert Fulton,* to Snake Cay to provide administrative offices, a clinic, a school, and housing for administrators. Workers' accommodations were established and a highway system connecting all major settlements was constructed. The Bahamas government relocated the commissioner's office from Hope Town to Marsh Harbour to accommodate the new investors with easier access to government services.

In 1960, Owens-Illinois employed more than 1,000 laborers, including Turks and Caicos Islanders and Haitians. Most of the Turks and Caicos Islanders worked for the company on Grand Bahama before moving to Abaco. The Bahamians and Turks and Caicos Islanders were accommodated in housing separate from the Haitian laborers, who were subsequently relegated to the lowest rung of the economic and social ladder. Little else is known about the Turks and Caicos Islanders living in Abaco during the 1960s, except the sketchy reminiscence of some laborers, government officials, and Abaconians. According to Henry, in an interview conducted September 13, 1997, he worked with mostly Turks and Caicos immigrants, who after a short time in Abaco moved to the higher paying jobs available as a result of the development of Freeport in Grand Bahama.

During the mid-1960s, the administration of the Turks and Caicos as a part of the Bahamas encouraged migration. The islands, beginning in November 1965, were administered by a common governor, and officers from the Royal Bahamas Police Force were attached to the small force in Grand Turk to assist with law and order. Prisoners sentenced to terms longer than twelve months were incarcerated in Nassau, according to Cornish. In 1965–1966, a judge was dispatched from Nassau to adjudicate cases, but appeals were heard at the court of appeals in Nassau. Bahamian authorities allowed Turks and Caicos Islanders easy travel, employment, and citizenship in the Bahamas. In the previous year, after the local salt industry temporarily ceased operations, many Islanders migrated to the Bahamas. Many others migrated because, "owing to the low salaries paid by Government, it [had] become impossible to encourage any school leavers to join the Public Service" [Turks & Caicos Islands. Report for the Years 1965 and 1966, p. 8]. Bahamians began to invest extensively in the Turks and Caicos Islands. In 1965, for example, Bahamian investors constructed a general provision and food store and an open-air theater in Grand Turks [Turks & Caicos Islands. Report for the Years 1965 and 1966, p. 7]. The Nassau-based Bahamas Airways offered a twice weekly service to Grand Turks to accommodate the growing human traffic between the islands and regular airmail service was maintained between the territories.

In the late 1960s, migration from the Turks and Caicos Islands to the Bahamas was significantly affected when the PLP assumed political control of the host country. In 1964, colonial authorities initiated discussions between the two territories to determine how the Turks and Caicos Islands could best be absorbed into the Bahamas. Some members of the predominantly white, then-ruling UBP favored territorial absorption, primarily because they had considerable financial investments in the Turks and Caicos Islands they wished to protect. The predominantly black Progressive Bahamian Party, however, had no vested economic interest in the islands, which many considered a potential financial burden. In a December 12, 1997, interview with the author, an anonymous Bahamian, who is a former high-ranking officer of the Progressive Liberal Party, said the PLP government was uninterested in the annexation of the Turks and Caicos Islands because those islands were generally less developed than the most undeveloped island in the Bahamas, and offered "nothing to the development of the archipelago, except a bunch of unskilled immigrants." According to the interviewee, annexation of the islands would have "opened an uncontrollable floodgate for the migration of Turks and Caicos Islanders, Haitians, and Jamaicans using the islands as a port of entry into the Bahamas labor market." In 1968, the new government discontinued annexation negotiations and enacted laws against unrestricted migration from the Turks and Caicos Islands.

Beginning in 1968, illegal Turks and Caicos Islanders were arrested and deported from the Bahamas. The action against the immigrants was perhaps most pronounced in Inagua, where illegal salt workers were arrested and summarily deported. Gwendolyn, a resident of Inagua since 1949, insisted that the deportations were politically motivated. She recalled that the large and influential Turks and Caicos immigrant population of Inagua traditionally supported the UBP. According to Gwendolyn, in a February 1998 interview, the PLP "victimized the Turks Islanders because they did not vote for their candidate in the [1968 general] elections." Gwendolyn's accusations, though discounted as untrue by some Bahamians, are widely accepted in Turks and Caicos Islands communities in the Bahamas. The incident divided the island of Inagua along political lines and threatened the destruction of many old friendships, according to Helen in an interview of February 16, 1998. Helen's nephew was the PLP candidate defeated in the 1968 elections. The motive for the untraditional arrests and deportations remains the subject of continued speculation. The events of the late 1960s, however, marked the resumption of a strained political relationship between the Bahamas and the Turks and Caicos Islands that was reminiscent of the political separation of 1848. Interestingly, the situation was confined primarily to Inagua, generally because most Bahamians were ignorant of, or otherwise unconcerned with local affairs in Inagua. After Bahamian Independence in 1973, however, the relationship between the Bahamas and the Turks and Caicos Islands has become increasingly more cordial.

Summary

The Turks and Caicos Islands, consisting of ten islands and cays, lie between latitude 21° and 22° north and longitude 71° and 72° west, to the southeast of the Bahamas. They are situated about 90 miles to the north of the Dominican Republic, 720 miles to the southwest of Bermuda and 450 miles northeast of Jamaica. The islands were visited by Spanish and later English explorers in the 1500s. Bermudan salt producers who initially visited the islands seasonally to harvest salt for export effected the first

European occupation. In 1799, the Turks and Caicos Islands were placed under the jurisdiction of the Bahamas government. In 1848, however, in answer to petitions from the inhabitants, a separate charter was granted, under which the islands were allowed a form of local government. The system proved too expensive, however, and in 1873 the islands were annexed to Jamaica as one of its dependencies. The islands remained under Jamaican jurisdiction until 1962, when Jamaica became an independent country. The islands, thereupon, were again politically connected to the Bahamas. This political relationship was severed in 1973, when the Bahamas gained independence.

Beginning in the 1890s, Turks and Caicos Islanders migrated to the Bahamas in search of employment opportunities. Initially, migration was confined to the southern Bahamas, where immigrants sought employment first as stevedores and deck hands on passing ships, and later in the salt ponds of Inagua. After 1930, however, greater numbers of Turks and Caicos immigrants found employment in the lumber industry in the northern Bahamas. Some immigrants used employment in the Bahamas as a conduit to the United States. Most, however, settled in the Bahamas where, as in the cases of Pine Ridge and Seagrape in Grand Bahama, they developed communities dominated by Turks and Caicos Islanders.

Beginning at the turn of the century, hundreds of Turks and Caicos Islanders migrated to the southern Bahamas to work as stevedores and deck hands, and to the northern Bahamas to work in the lumber industries. The information available on the number of immigrants to the Bahamas is limited, and there is even less information available on their contribution to the social, economic, and political development of the Bahamas. Some fragmentary information, however, has been gleaned from colonial dispatches and consular reports. Other sketchy details were gathered through interviews with immigrants and their descendents.

Generally, Bahamians have exhibited ambivalence toward migration from the Turks and Caicos Islands. The high level of social and economic acceptance accorded Turks and Caicos Island immigrants is uncharacteristic in a Bahamian society which has traditionally demonstrated intolerance toward West Indian immigrants. Factors for this acceptance include the traditional social, economic, and political ties that have existed between the Bahamas and the Turks and Caicos Islands, as well as the fact that the islands are generally recognized by both Bahamians and Turks and Caicos Islanders as geographically connected. In addition, both share close similarities in Loyalist descent, English accent and grammatical pronunciation, cuisine, cultural heritage, and family lines. Finally, although Turks and Caicos Islanders constitute the second largest West Indian immigrant group in the Bahamas, their assimilation is so complete as to make them virtually indistinguishable (except, perhaps, by name) from the average Bahamian. This latter distinction cannot be attributed to any other West Indian immigrant group in the Bahamas.

8

Post-Independence West Indian Migration, 1973–1992

West Indian migration to the Bahamas was selectively controlled after the Bahamas became independent in 1973. The method of control used was embodied in the government program locally referred to as "Bahamianization" and "The Bahamas for Bahamians." The program was primarily designed to control the immigration of non-Bahamian whites to the Bahamas. In general, the black-majority government attempted to ensure that control of the economic and social destiny of the Bahamas was in the hands of Bahamians. In the process of its implementation, however, the program selected some West Indians for migration into the country, and denied entry to others. Most Haitians, for example, were systematically denied entry, while Guyanese immigrants were officially welcomed.

Bahamianization

In 1967, the newly elected PLP government, in preparation for nationhood, redefined its immigration policy for the Bahamas. The new Immigration Act, which replaced the 1963 act, introduced the work permit and allowed the Bahamas government control over the employment of non-Bahamians. Previously, the entry permit regulated the recruitment of non-Bahamian labor, and the type of employment an immigrant to the Bahamas could engage in. The PLP government was victorious in the general elections that year, gaining a majority with twenty-nine of the thirty-eight seats in Parliament. In September 1968, in preparation for independence, a constitution was produced as the basis of the law of the Commonwealth of the Bahamas. The constitution, among other things, detailed the rights of a citizen to protection from arbitrary arrest or detention. Interestingly, it made allowances for exceptions in cases where officials attempted to prevent unlawful entry into, and expulsion and extradition from, the Bahamas. In effect, the constitution allowed the government full control over matters relating to immigration in the country.

After 1968, the attitude of the Bahamian government toward West Indian migration was inseparable from the much larger issue of sovereignty and perceived infringements on Bahamian autonomy surrounding the establishment of the city of Freeport in Grand Bahama Island. In 1955, the predominantly white United Bahamian Party government signed the Hawksbill Creek Agreement, which initially granted 50,000 acres of land to the foreign-owned Grand Bahama Port Authority. By 1970, however, the Port Authority controlled more than 230 square miles of land, almost three times larger than the island of New Providence. The new city recorded significant population growth, due largely to immigration, from 3,012 in 1963 to 15,298 in 1970. Ironically, Bahamians were a minority in Freeport. Generally, most held service-related jobs despite being qualified for better jobs. Large groups of foreign laborers were recruited, instead, to perform duties Bahamians were qualified for. One observer [GB/COR, Bahamas/ CO, Hugh Wooding, Report of the Royal Commission appointed in the Recommendation of the Bahamas Government to Review the Hawksbill Creek Agreement (Bahamas/PRO. 1969), 117, para.156] noted that after the public announcements made following the constitutional conference of September 1968, there should not have been any doubt that the PLP government was "gearing itself to . . . integrate Freeport into the Bahamian Community and to plug the immigration loophole."

In November 1968, the government and the Port Authority engaged in a series of discussions on the regulation of immigration to Freeport. The Port Authority insisted that it had the legal right to recruit the personnel it required without the approval of the Department of Immigration. The government responded that it had the right to withhold such privileges. In 1969, Prime Minister Pindling argued that work permits were necessary, and stated in the *Nassau Daily Tribune* of November 7, 1969, that his government had determined that the agreement should be interpreted "in the light of the laws of the land." The Pindling government was severely criticized in the *Nassau Gazette* on November 12, 1969, by the predominantly white Bahamian elite, who charged that the new immigration regulations jeopardized the economy by restricting available manpower. On March 6, 1970, a compromise was arrived at in the form of the Immigration (Special Provisions) Bill. In effect, the bill nullified any part of the Hawksbill Creek Agreement "which constituted, or purported to constitute, any undertaking on behalf of the government to allow . . . any person or class of persons into the Bahama Islands for any purpose" [GB/COR, Bahamas/CO, Hugh Wooding, Report of the Royal Commission appointed in the Recommendation of the Bahamas Government to Review the Hawksbill Creek Agreement (Bahamas/PRO. 1969), 117, para.173].

The Immigration (Special Provisions) Bill had serious implications for future West Indian migration to the Bahamas, despite the conclusion of the commission appointed to investigate the situation, which determined that no serious problem seemed to have arisen, or was likely to arise with regard to unskilled laborers [GB/COR, Bahamas/ CO, Hugh Wooding, Report of the Royal Commission appointed in the Recommendation of the Bahamas Government to Review the Hawksbill Creek Agreement (Bahamas/PRO. 1969), 117, para.155]. The procedure of the new immigration bill, covered in paragraph 37, made it mandatory for the government to be informed of all requirements for unskilled laborers and allowed thirty days to fill the requirement with Bahamians. Failure to satisfy the requirements allowed the Port Authority to recruit laborers with their families from outside the Bahamas for an initial maximum period of three years. The statement of the commission—perhaps made on the assumption that the procedure would be properly implemented—proved erroneous. The expansive development of Freeport created many job opportunities and attracted thousands of Bahamian and West Indian unskilled laborers.

On November 21, 1969, immigration officials launched a campaign against illegal laborers, with the main offenders being Haitians and Jamaicans who, "unlike the Haitians, entered the Bahamas legally as visitors, then overstayed their time and sought employment without work permits" (Marshall 1979:126). The *Nassau Daily Tribune* reported on November 21, 1969, that: "more than two hundred Haitian and Jamaican men and women were taken from their beds or caught on the roads in Grand Bahama in a series of immigration and police raids. . . . The raids began about 3 A.M. on Friday when the Haitians and Jamaicans were sleeping in their beds." The raids were repeated in December, when approximately 300 Haitians and Jamaicans were arrested. According to the *Nassau Daily Tribune* on January 3, 1970, one of the arresting officers complained that the immigration officers were determined to "clean out Freeport. A Bahamian can't get a job here, but we are going to clean it up"

By 1971, the "Bahamas for Bahamians" policy was completely formalized. The Bahamian government, through the permanent secretary in the ministry of home affairs, announced its intention to restrict the employment of expatriates, which is the immigration classification of non-Bahamian whites employed and living in the Bahamas. The statement noted that no foreigner would be permitted to stay in the Bahamas over five years. If, after five years, the employer justified the need for foreign labor, non-Bahamians other than the one previously employed had to be recruited. The government, reported a *Nassau Daily Tribune* article dated August 11, 1971, in an effort to implement a successful program, upgraded the resources of the Immigration Department "through expansion, training, reorganization and updating of procedures." In essence, it attempted to address national manpower requirements, as well as the aspirations and demands of Bahamians. After Independence, groups of West Indians continued to migrate to the Bahamas, despite the "finishing touches on the Bahamas for Bahamians movement" the independence order reportedly produced (Marshall 1979:127). Guyanese, for example, were recruited for work as public defenders, surveyors, and teachers. Many married Bahamians and became assimilated into Bahamian society. Haitians represented the group most frequently denied entry and least likely to become assimilated, and continued to constitute the largest group of post-Independence immigrants to the Bahamas.

Guyanese Immigrants

The history of Guyanese migration to the Bahamas, particularly during the post-Independence years, is inextricably linked to the history of economic and political instability in Guyana. At the end of the fifteenth century, Spanish sailors traced the coastline of Guyana. During the sixteenth and seventeenth centuries, the search for the fabulous city of Eldorado—historically linked to the exploits of Sir Walter Raleigh—stimulated further European exploration and the establishment of several Dutch settlements. In 1612, the Dutch West India Company was granted a charter giving it control over Essequibo. In 1615, additional holdings in Berbice were annexed, and by 1773 the Dutch had constituted Essequibo, Demerara, and Berbice as independent colonies. During the next four decades, there was constant rivalry between the Dutch, British, Spanish, and French for possession. The territory was eventually ceded to Britain in the peace settlement that followed the Napoleonic Wars. In 1831, they were unified as British Guiana, which remained a British colony until 1966, when it gained its independence and became a member of the British Commonwealth of Nations and of the United Nations and some of its principal agencies. On February 23, 1970, British Guiana became the Republic of Guyana (Smith 1962).

Guyana, the "Land of Six Peoples" as it is sometimes called locally, is inhabited by peoples of African, East Indian, Portuguese, Chinese, and European extraction, as well as by Amerindian peoples who live mainly in the forests and savannas. The total land is estimated at 83,000 square miles. It comprises areas of cultivatable land in the coastal belt and river valleys, pasture-bearing lands of varying quality on the plains and savannas, vast forest tracts in the central areas which cover nearly four-fifths of the total, and mountains. The economy of the country is primarily agriculture, with sugar and rice as the main crops. Other important industries include mineral products—gold, diamonds, and bauxite—and timber. Combined, minerals and forest products account for approximately 80 percent of the total industrial production. According to the *West Indian and Caribbean Yearbook* (1987), the monetary unit is the Guyana dollar (G$), comprising 100 cents, and Georgetown is the largest city, the seat of government, the main commercial center, and the principal port.

Guyana is rich in vast natural resources and possesses the technical capability of supplying most of the needs of its people internally or through trade. According to Guyanese-Bahamian economist Winston Headley, interviewed February 4, 1998, in the decade following independence, the country was able to accomplish this goal and produce balanced budgets through strict adherence to feasible fiscal programs and prudent expenditures. Headley reckoned that most Guyanese were sufficiently secure financially to remain at home and concluded that during the presidency of Forbes Burnham, the increasing fragility of the economy and fear of political victimization motivated him and many other Guyanese to immigrate.

Beginning in the 1970s—primarily because of poor fiscal management, stagnant agricultural production, and lower industrial output—the Guyanese economy (Table 8.1) became progressively more fragile. In the 1990s, the country was regarded as one of the poorest in the Western

Table 8.1. Guyanese Financial Status, 1953–1973

Year	Revenue (G$)	Expenditure (G$)
1953	26,224,086	25,777,465
1963	67,500,580	67,700,000
1973	225,791,600	145,854,386

Source: West Indian and Caribbean Year Book (1987)

Hemisphere and in need of economic aid. The Guyanese dollar, which in 1970 was valued at 2.5 to one U.S. dollar, was systematically devalued until in 1990 it was estimated at G$140 = US$1. In 1992, the rate of inflation in the country was estimated at 14 percent. In 1996, the external debt was estimated in excess of US$2 billion. Two-thirds of the government revenue was committed to debt servicing. National expenditures on structural and financial constraints intended to stabilize the economy had become the major obstacle to social and economic progress (*Guyana Fact Sheet* 1996). Guyanese, like many other West Indians, planned to migrate to North America, where more stable political environments and economies, and better employment opportunities existed. The Bahamas, for many, provides a migration conduit to this ultimate goal.

The Guyanese are the latest of the West Indian groups to migrate to the Bahamas during the post-Independence era. Their numbers increased significantly during the 1980s when hundreds of Guyanese were recruited by the Bahamas government to work as teachers. The recruits, like their Jamaican predecessors during the 1970s, were generally employed as science, mathematics, and technical arts teachers. They filled the vocational void left by Jamaican and Bahamian teachers who had either secured higher paying jobs at private schools or left the profession. During the 1980s, the Bahamas was faced with a severe shortage of teachers. This shortage was partially because most Jamaican teachers recruited during the 1970s for service in the Bahamas left for North America during the 1980s after their contracts expired. Simultaneously, many Bahamian teachers trained during the post-Independence years on government scholarships left the profession to become professionals in the private sector. Additionally, the Guyanese became a temporary buffer between the government and the militantly antigovernment public school teachers. During the 1980s, the Bahamas government encountered considerable political opposition from the Bahamas Union of Teachers, which represented the mostly public school teachers who were demanding higher wages and improved working conditions. The protestors staged a series of public demonstrations that resulted in serious challenges to the political leadership of the prime minister and encouraged political opposition to his government.

Guyanese migration to the Bahamas began in 1946 when a squad of twenty-one Guyanese ex-soldiers were recruited as policemen. The men, ranging in ages from twenty to thirty-six, served in the Commonwealth Forces during World War II before returning to their country, where they were recruited for employment in the Bahamas. According to Wilson in a February 4, 1988, interview with the author, most of the ex-servicemen came to the Bahamas for adventure. Wilson, one of the 1946 recruits, stated that he and the other Guyanese were recruited through the Ex-Servicemen's Association of Guyana. He explained that the men were young, "fresh from the excitement of the war," and not ready then to settle down. Service in the Bahamas offered the opportunity for a "paid adventure" in another country. These early Guyanese policemen were different from other West Indian police recruits in several areas. They had the advantages of military experience and exposure to European culture outside the region. Perhaps more significant, their experiences in combat against white men and of racial discrimination in the armed forces and in England made them more resentful of—and less intimidated by— white colonial authority. Occasionally, this resentment was manifested in the execution of their duties, which at times challenged the social status quo in the islands. Wilson reported that when a young recruit arrested a white Bahamian girl for riding her bicycle after dark without proper lights, an angry mob of local whites reportedly surrounded the small jail and threatened to forcibly release the girl and "discipline the impudent policeman." Subsequently, superior officers ordered the girl released on a misdemeanor charge, whereupon the crowd dispersed. Wilson, the recruit, was required to defend his actions before a tribunal of superior officers, and eventually acquitted with a warning to "be more discretionary" in the execution of his duties. Wilson stated that "the warning was subtle, yet abundantly clear that we [black policemen] were not to arrest whites for minor offences." After the 1946 squad, the recruitment of policemen from Guyana ceased.

During the 1950s, most of the Guyanese police recruits migrated to North America and England. The few who remained, however, made significant contributions to the social and economic development of the

Bahamas. Wilson, for example, became a highly respected recruit and training officer in the Royal Bahamas Police Force, and Reginal Dumont, another recruit and spouse to Senator, the Honourable Dame Ivy Dumont who at the time of this writing was the minister of education, helped to develop the traffic department within the force. Perhaps the most influential of the squad was Rudolph Burdzorg. According to an article in the *Pepperpot*—the official newsletter of the Guyanese-Bahamian Association and named for a traditional Guyanese food—"Burdzorg joined the Royal Bahamas Police force after some hesitation as he had already refused to join the police in his native Guyana" (Pluck 1997:1–6). In the 1950s, he resigned from the force and secured an appointment with the Bahamas Electricity Corporation (BEC) as superintendent of meter testing. At BEC, Burdzorg designed six electronic meter reading and disconnection systems and established the first trade union. He became vice-president of the National Trade Union Congress that for many years was the umbrella organization for all trade unions in the Bahamas. During the 1960s, he established the first cooperative credit union and cooperative food store in the colony. The cooperative organizations, based on the Rochdale (France) principles, served as models for the future development of the cooperative movement in the Bahamas.

During the 1950s and 1960s, Guyanese were recruited as the principal surveyors of crown lands in the Bahamas. The surveyors, numbering less than two dozen, were recruited directly from Guyana where a surplus of surveyors existed. During the postwar years, the colonial government in Guyana encouraged many young Guyanese to train as surveyors and cartographers in England. A program was developed to train a cadre of professionals to properly map the extensive forests and frontier in that country. These surveyors are largely responsible for charting much of the Bahamas, but during the 1970s, many migrated to North America. The remaining surveyors established private practices that are today the most prestigious in the Bahamas, and reportedly include a monopoly on the survey of prime local real estate. Some Bahamian surveyors, interviewed anonymously on August 14, 1997, claimed that for many years the Guyanese used their positions as senior surveyors to suppress the upward mobility of Bahamians in the field and to secure large acres of crown land in previously underdeveloped areas of the Bahamas at prices far below the market value. The lands, said to be worth considerable amounts of money today, have reportedly enriched the investors. Interestingly, in early 1997, after the landslide reelection of the Free National Party government, the Office of the Prime Minister assumed responsibility for crown lands and allowed more Bahamians direct responsibility for the distribution of and access to crown lands. In late 1997, the transition of responsibility for administration of public lands from Guyanese to Bahamian was completed when a Bahamian was named to head the Department of Lands and Survey.

In the 1980s, Guyanese were recruited to work in the Department of Legal Affairs. The recruits, mostly draftsmen, included veteran lawyers who became prominent in Bahamian legal circles. For several years, Guyanese headed the legal department and served as stipendiary and circuit magistrates. The recruitment of Guyanese resulted partially because most Bahamian lawyers spurned employment in the public service as lacking prestige and immediate rewards. Most, instead, favored employment in or the establishment of the more lucrative private practice, where a lawyer could become a millionaire within a few years (Cash et al. 1991:331–333). During the 1970s and 1980s, the Bahamian economy was relatively healthy, largely because of expansions in the tourism and banking industries, and an infusion of U.S. dollars derived from the use of the Bahamas as an entrepôt for the transshipment of drugs into the United States. Lawyers subsequently earned large sums of money representing the interests of drug smugglers and associates.

Guyanese legal professionals reportedly favored employment in the Bahamas because of a glut in the legal profession in Guyana. A Guyanese-Bahamian economist, Winston Headley, opined in his February 4, 1998, interview, that some Guyanese professionals migrated because of political differences with former Guyanese president Forbes Burnam. He said many became fearful for their lives and those of their families after the "mysterious death" of noted Guyanese historian and political activist Walter Rodney. Most professionals, he noted, fled the economic deterioration of the Guyanese economy. The economist said economic factors motivated the mass migration of Guyanese teachers to England, North America, and the Bahamas. Dr. Headley, the Guyanese son of Barbadian immigrants, is a retired professor of economics at the College of the Bahamas. Prior to immigration to the Bahamas, Dr. Headley lived in London and later served in various capacities in the Burnam government in Guyana.

In 1997, an estimated 250 Guyanese were included among the approximately 3,000 teachers employed in public and private schools in the

Bahamas. Michael, a Guyanese immigrant living in the Bahamas since the 1980s, is a teacher at a private school in Nassau, and when interviewed on January 29, 1998, reported that most were contracted to work in the public schools in the rural islands. The teachers, mostly males of African and Indian extraction, generally avoid involvement in local politics. Their contribution to the advancement of education in the Bahamas is measurable by the frequency of the commendations for commitment to excellence in the classroom many have received. This list is, perhaps, led by Dr. Chandra Baccus, who during the 1970s served with distinction as the first president of the College of the Bahamas. Some teachers—especially those with families—admit that their ultimate goal is to migrate to the United States. A small number have married Bahamians and become totally assimilated into Bahamian society.

Haitian Immigrants

Haitian migration to the Bahamas increased significantly after Bahamian Independence in 1973. In 1974, for example, the number of Haitians in the Bahamas was conservatively estimated at over 40,000, out of a total official population of just under 200,000, indicating a significant increase from approximately 1,000 in 1957, and representing an average annual migration increase of 3,624 (Marshall 1979:205–206). Most Haitians in the Bahamas live on the islands of New Providence, Grand Bahama, Abaco, and Eleuthera. The exact percentages of Haitians living on the various islands are difficult to determine, because of the unavailability of statistics and the inability of officials to control illegal entry into the country. Brief insights, however, into the Haitian presence on the mentioned islands can be gleaned from interviews, fragments of official documents, and general research.

Haitians in New Providence

The largest concentration of Haitians in the Bahamas can be found in New Providence. Most arrived in the late 1960s and 1970s in hopes of participating in the Bahamian employment surge created by renewed expansions of the tourist industry that resulted from the American economic embargo against Cuba and resulting decline of the Cuban tourist industry. Marshall (1979) provides invaluable knowledge on the Haitian immigrants to the Bahamas and notes that thousands of Haitians live in shanty communities in the more rural parts of the island. Her comments on the Haitian community in the Carmichael district were fully explored in chapter 6.

Arguably, more Haitian immigrants live in the "Over-the-Hill" district than anywhere else in the Bahamas. Little is documented about their presence, however, because their uncertain immigration status has made most wary of researchers and reluctant to discuss their existence in the islands. In the 1970s, the Ministry of Immigration recognized the presence of large numbers of Haitians living in Over-the-Hill. This was noted in an interview with Carl on August 15, 1997, who was, at the time of interview, the deputy permanent secretary in the Ministry of Public Safety and Immigration, with direct responsibility for matters relating to immigration. Carl said that some Haitian emigrants chose to live in Over-the-Hill because the communities offered them anonymity (and thus security from deportation), affordable accommodations, and clandestine (albeit low-paying) jobs.

Historically, the district called Over-the-Hill was deeded to freed slaves in 1836 and 1838 either through crown grants or token purchases. Over-the-Hill, an adjunct to Nassau, was intentionally designed by colonial authorities as a community for slaves and indentured servants. For many years, the majority of black Bahamians sought employment in affluent Nassau. Traditionally, Over-the-Hill, in many respects, is the major ghetto to which much of the laboring class returned at the end of each day. Property owners living in Over-the-Hill have progressively relocated to communities in the suburbs. At the time of Independence, a government study revealed that 53 percent of occupants of Over-the-Hill were tenants. Additionally, approximately 47 percent of the houses in the district were rented from landlords who owned more than one building in the area, but who were no longer residents [The Bahamas: Department of Physical Planning. Report on Preliminary Survey of Existing Housing Conditions. August 1973. (Bahamas/PRO. 1973), 13]. Haitian immigrants living in Over-the-Hill are predominantly tenants, who in turn rent rooms to other Haitians—a common experience for most Haitian immigrants.

The growing number of Haitian immigrants living in Over-the-Hill is evident in the increasing number of *kweyole* (Creole)-speaking churches with Haitian pastors that have been established in the district. Most of the churches are humble buildings that cater to small congregations of less than fifty. Additionally, the arrival in the area of large numbers of Roman Catholic Haitians has resulted in the recruitment of French-speaking priests to address the spiritual (and at times, social) needs of immigrants. Voodoo worship is not openly practiced or encouraged by Bahamians living in Over-the-Hill. Ironically, the Haitians living in Over-the-Hill, through renting old, often dilapidated houses, provide their predominantly Bahamian landlords with a source of income to rise to a higher economic level. Invariably, the Haitian tenants replace these Bahamians at the bottom of the social and economic ladder.

Haitians in Grand Bahama

In October 1992, the Grand Bahama Human Rights Association, in conjunction with the New York-based Haitian Refugee Mission, sponsored a conference on the "Haitian Problem" in the Bahamas. A number of local human rights, government, and non-government organizations participated. The conference determined, among other things, that the second largest concentration of Haitians in the Bahamas lives in Grand Bahama. It recognized the fact that there was no public register of Haitian residents in the Bahamas maintained by the Bahamas government or any other organization. The conference acknowledged that, although many Haitians attend, churches refuse to allow public access to their records to protect the identity of members. The conference also noted that there is difficulty in obtaining numbers or locations of Haitian immigrants because many fear reprisals—which could include renewed immigration raids, loss of employment, and alienation from and the possibility of physical harm by, other Haitians (Bethel 1992:7).

Generally, Haitians occupy the lowest rung of the social ladder in Grand Bahama. Most work in Freeport in the service industry, performing the more menial tasks, and the great majority—being illegal aliens and, therefore, uncertain of their future—are diligent and efficient in their work. Haitians in Grand Bahama, in the absence of communities similar to Over-the-Hill, live in more comfortable conditions than those living on most other islands. This phenomenon is partially explained by the large numbers of illegal immigrants from other ethnic groups living on the island, who are more concerned with self-preservation than the cultivation of prejudices against Haitians.

Most Bahamians in Grand Bahama relocated to that island from other areas of the Bahamas within the past two decades, seeking employment in the development of Freeport. Many secured jobs that paid sufficiently well to allow them to hire their "own Haitian" on a full-time basis to care for their yards, homes, children, and businesses. For many, the Haitian laborer—whether illegal or documented—is considered a necessity to be protected and, if necessary, harbored. Rarely, if ever, would the immigrant be required to show proof of eligibility to live in the Bahamas. More frequently, Bahamians hire illegal Haitians because most work diligently for a nominal fee and without protest. Most evident in Grand Bahama, together with Haitians, are a large number of illegal Jamaicans and Turks and Caicos Islanders.

Many Haitians in Grand Bahama have become assimilated and live in relative harmony with Bahamians and other West Indian immigrants. This is especially evident in the poorer communities where most Haitians live. This situation, uncommon throughout the rest of the Bahamas, is partially explained by the fact that Haitians and Bahamians arrived in Grand Bahama almost simultaneously. Many unskilled Bahamians were relegated to almost the same social level as the Haitians. Also, many of the Haitian residents who have lived on Grand Bahama since the 1960s and 1970s married Bahamians and had children there, and were thus permanently integrated into local society. Many of the Haitians falling into this category are allowed to conduct normal lives, regardless of their questionable immigration status.

Some Haitians reportedly went to Grand Bahama to secure forged documents, which may have included U.S. visas, U.S. and Bahamian passports, and Bahamian work permits. An anonymous informant, interviewed April 2, 1997, is a Bahamian "entrepreneur" who operates between Nassau and Freeport and has close associations with the Haitian communities in both cities. He stated that U.S. visas may cost as much as US$10,000 on the black market and that a U.S. passport, which is reportedly more difficult to secure, can cost as much as US$15,000-$20,000, while Bahamian passports cost B$5,000-$7,000 on average. The interviewee boasted that Bahamian work permits are relatively easy to secure and cost an average of B$1,500-$3,000. Forged documents reportedly proliferated at an increasing rate during the 1980s. Equally interesting is the fact that, in the 1990s, several senior and subordinate Bahamian employees of the passport office were discharged from their duties, with one sentenced to prison for a series of offenses. The United States Embassy also reportedly dismissed some members of its staff for alleged misconduct.

Haitians in Abaco

Haitian immigration to Abaco presents an interesting case of social and economic "catch 22." In the 1960s, Haitian laborers were brought to Abaco by the Owens-Illinois Consortium to work in their lumber and agricultural industries. Haitian laborers were favored because "they were willing to work for minimal wages" (Dodge 1983:155). In the 1970s, many others were recruited for work on the Key-Sawyer Farms. The laborers were grossly exploited and subjected to intolerable living conditions. The Haitians protested by temporarily refusing to work. Their protests were largely ignored and some were swiftly replaced with other Haitians. Some Haitians established squalid squatter communities in vacant sections of Marsh Harbour, two of which were disparagingly called Pigeon Peas and the Mud because of their wretched appearance and unsanitary conditions.

On January 16, 1990, it was reported in the *Tribune* that Haitians constituted 45 percent of the population of Marsh Harbour (Damianos 1990:1:16). Residents complained that the immigrants posed a threat to sanitation in the community, with some arguing that the Haitians living in unsanitary conditions would eventually contaminate the water supply and possibly create outbreaks of disease. In 1991, the Abaconian fears were heightened by news of a report from the Ministry of Health, which noted that between 1977 and 1981, Haitians accounted for as much as 53 percent of all pulmonary tuberculosis cases reported in the Bahamas.

Paradoxically, some Abaconians who vehemently protested the presence of large numbers of Haitians on the island included those who employed Haitians for agricultural and domestic duties, the latter at times involving the preparation of meals and the care of children. In 1992, Abaconians were shocked by the report that the parliamentary representative for Marsh Harbour proposed to extend electrical supply to the shanty towns at the Mud and Pigeon Peas. The plan was proposed, despite the fact that most of the shanties were fire hazards and ill-suited to receive electrical supply, according to informant Andrew, who, at the time of the April 1992 interviews, was manager of the Bahamas Electricity Corporation operations in Abaco. It was later revealed that the proposal was based on political and not humanitarian motives.

During the 1980s, Haitians were pressured to relocate to more remote areas of Abaco. Predominantly black communities like Murphy and Dundas Towns refused to allow Haitians to settle there. Few Haitians—perhaps less than forty—settled in the northern communities of Treasure Cay and Cooper's Town because jobs were scarce there and residents were hostile (Dodge 1983:158). Fewer were allowed to settle in such affluent residential areas as Pelican Point or outlying cays like at Hope Town. Those who worked in these areas were ferried to the destinations each morning and returned to the mainland before dark. Elbow Cay was an exception, as Haitians were allowed to squat in the woods off the Centerline Road, or rent land from Bahamian owners to build shacks and develop small farms. Generally, most Haitian immigrants to Abaco settled in Pigeon Peas and the Mud communities of the Marsh Harbour district.

Today, second and third generation families continue to live in communities where, regrettably, conditions have only modestly improved. Buildings continue to be built on crown and private lands without building permits and proper authority. Most buildings lack the basic essential amenities of electricity, water, and sanitary facilities. Garbage and abandoned vehicles litter the yards where barefoot children play and emaciated dogs forage. Generally, cooking is done outside with the use of small kerosene stoves and charcoal. The houses which can afford electricity extend the service to neighbors by way of extension cords for undetermined fees. "Landlords," despite the fact that the houses were illegally built, appear each weekend to collect cash payments for use of the properties. According to Emile, interviewed on April 15, 1992, "we [Haitians] have to pay $50 a week to live here." Emile, at the time of interview, was a laborer on a nearby farm. He refused to confirm the identity of his "landlord," even after the name of the suspected person, who is well known in the area, was mentioned. Such "ground renters" sub-rent rooms to other immigrants at the rate of $5 or $10 each week.

One of the most recent Haitian communities in Abaco is a shantytown of small, crude, but neat wooden shacks called "The Camp." Located north of Marsh Harbour, it is home to approximately 1,000 Haitians, including women and children. Most residents of the community provide labor for the 3,000-acre farm on which the community is located. The conditions at the community are improved in comparison with those at the Mud and

Pigeon Peas. The absence of abandoned vehicles and piles of garbage indicate progress in the improvement of conditions for Haitians in Abaco.

Haitians in Eleuthera

During the 1960s, Haitians generally performed the menial jobs in Eleuthera. Their presence was most noticeable in Spanish Wells, an island community off northern Eleuthera. Spanish Wells is a picturesque community that has become one of the most exclusive and prosperous in the Bahamas. Its exclusivity is based on the successful determination to work cooperatively and to maintain a predominantly white population. Its prosperity is based on a successful fishing industry and—although the reports are unconfirmed—on drug running. In an interview with an anonymous subject on February 28, 1997, who was born and raised in Spanish Wells, the interviewee said the average young man in Spanish Wells has a high school education and is employed as a fisherman. He stated that the young men, by the age of twenty-five, owned a home worth over $150,000, shares in a multimillion-dollar cooperative fishing or consumer products company, and had a net worth in excess of $500,000. According to the informant, the wealth came from a combination of fishing and drug running. An unwritten decree, which stated that no blacks be allowed to live on Spanish Wells or remain after dark, was vigilantly enforced. Traditionally, black laborers on Spanish Wells were ferried to the island each morning and returned before nightfall.

In the 1960s, Haitian immigrants became the first group of blacks allowed to settle in Spanish Wells. In actuality, the Haitians were allowed to squat among the extensive citrus groves on Russell Island, a small cay separated by a narrow, shallow channel from St. George's Island, where most residents of Spanish Wells lived. During the 1970s, profits from fishing and other endeavors, combined with population growth, resulted in a proliferation of new homes and commercial expansion. Inevitably, the expansion spilled over into Russell Island, which was connected to St. George's Island by a narrow bridge. The Haitian community on Russell Island, in the meanwhile, expanded simultaneously with that on neighboring St. George's Island until the availability of land for future expansion became an issue and a matter of contention between the immigrants and residents of Spanish Wells.

In the 1980s, the contention between the Haitians and residents of Spanish Wells reached a critical point when twenty-five white children were withdrawn from the public school by their parents who did not wish them to share the same facilities with Haitian children. The parents complained that Haitian students—who reportedly spoke only *kweyole*, were unkempt, and said to be carriers of contagious diseases—outnumbered their children. Haitians were emboldened and unofficially encouraged by the presence and advice of government nurses and teachers and their families living in Spanish Wells to enroll their children in the traditionally white public school. In 1993, the crisis was temporarily averted when the government announced renewed efforts to control illegal Haitian migration, as the *Nassau Guardian* reported in May. The Haitian community at Russell Island was eventually raided. Hundreds of legal and illegal aliens were apprehended and either expelled from the island or processed for deportation from the Bahamas. In the aftermath of the raid, most shanties were destroyed on the official basis that they were unregulated, unauthorized, and unsanitary. Many of the remaining Haitians relocated to other communities on the mainland and to other islands.

Haitians allowed to remain on Russell Island were provided with assistance to build better houses equipped with electricity, water, and sanitation facilities. Their situation is comparable to the South African townships in which laborers for the Afrikaners were traditionally confined. They were not, however, granted titles to the properties. Instead, they were charged rent and thus made inextricably dependent upon the paternalism of the residents of Spanish Wells, where most were employed. In contrast, most of the 300 Haitians expelled from the island settled in new shanty communities at Blackwood and Gene's Bay. There, they were subjected to harassment from black Bahamian neighbors on whose land many had squatted. The majority are now compelled to eke out a miserable living as subsistence farmers and laborers in the neighboring black communities.

Summary

In the post-Independence decades, Haitians and Guyanese made up the most significant West Indian groups to migrate to the Bahamas. In the aftermath of Independence, an official immigration program called "Bahamianization" influenced immigration to the Bahamas. Essentially,

"Bahamianization" was an attempt by the new government to control the recruitment of non-Bahamian labor into the country. Especially targeted under this program were white foreigners recruited by the Grand Bahama Port Authority and, to a lesser extent, Haitians and Jamaicans. West Indians, despite immigration restrictions, continued to migrate to the Bahamas.

In 1946, Guyanese were first recruited for employment in the colony as policemen. The recruits, ex-servicemen from the last world war, displayed antipathy toward the social values of whites in the islands. Perhaps because of this antipathy, no other Guyanese policemen were recruited. Later, in the 1960s and 1970s, Guyanese were recruited to work as surveyors and in public legal agencies. The early surveyors were responsible for charting much of the islands. Many, however, eventually emigrated to North America. Those remaining established private practices that today represent some of the most prestigious in the Bahamas. The Guyanese legal professionals recruited included draftsmen and judges, and the former chief justice of the Bahamas.

During the 1980s, hundreds of Guyanese were recruited to teach in the Bahamas. The teachers represented the largest category of Guyanese immigrants to the Bahamas. Most were recruited during the 1980s when the Guyanese economy was unstable and when the government of the Bahamas was involved in a protracted dispute with public school teachers. Many Bahamian and Jamaican public school teachers left the public service for employment in other professions or at private schools. The resignation of large numbers of Bahamian and foreign teachers from the public service created a vacuum which the recruitment of Guyanese teachers was designed to fill. Simultaneously, the new recruits formed a buffer between the government and the disgruntled teachers.

After Independence, Haitians continued to migrate to the Bahamas. In 1974, it was estimated that over 40,000 Haitians lived in the country, which had a population then of just under 200,000. Generally, most Haitian immigrants lived in communities on the islands of New Providence, Grand Bahama, Abaco, and Eleuthera. The immigrants were subjected to different experiences on each island. In New Providence, for example, many Haitians lived in communities isolated from the center of town, where they built shanties and existed at substandard levels. Others rented miserable accommodations in predominantly poor black communities, where they were forced to constantly avoid official detection, but where they had easier access to employment as laborers in the service industries and gardeners on private properties.

Haitians in Grand Bahama were generally able to assimilate into the local society more rapidly than Haitians living on other islands, including New Providence. This phenomenon is partially explained by the fact that Haitian migration to Grand Bahama was simultaneous with that of their Bahamian and non-Bahamian neighbors. Many Haitians in Grand Bahama who have married Bahamians, raised children there, and live in low-income communities, are generally accepted as social equals by their neighbors. Some have established businesses and relocated to more affluent neighborhoods. Second and third generation Haitian-Bahamians have anglicized their names and are indistinguishable from other Bahamians.

Haitians in Abaco are mostly agricultural laborers employed on large farms. Most live in squalid shanty communities, such as the Mud and Pigeon Peas located on the fringes of the city of Marsh Harbour. The communities are not equipped with basic amenities such as water, electricity, and proper sanitation facilities. The immigrants are relegated to a subservient social role and constantly reminded of their place in society. Some live in the woods in small makeshift communities and subsist largely on the sale and use of produce grown on small farms. Their white employers protect the Abaconian Haitians from raids by immigration authorities.

Most Haitians in Eleuthera live on Russell Island located at the northern end of the island. Essentially, they are employed by their white "neighbors" on Spanish Wells, to whom perhaps most, if not all, are indebted. Their physical environment, however, is considerably more improved than in other Haitian enclaves throughout the archipelago. Generally, their houses are neatly maintained and equipped with basic amenities such as water, electricity, and indoor plumbing. Haitians living on the mainland of Eleuthera, in contrast, squat in unauthorized shanties built on public and private lands. Their existence is uncertain, largely because they are compelled to eke out a living among predominantly hostile neighbors who generally resent their presence.

Afterword

Migration processes are complicated human dramas. The actors include po-litical exiles and refugees, people fleeing violence and terror, displaced per-sons who have lost home and occupation, economic migrants who are valued for their skills or for willingness to do bottom-of-the-ladder work, and finally, an enormous army of illegal aliens who are in search of ways to better their lives even in the face of obstacles put before them. The actors come smack up against impersonal bureaucracies, racial and ethnic prejudice, and oc-cupational discrimination. And yet for all their agony and difficulty, these dramas are ultimately stories of hope and enormous courage, the source of many productive human experiences (Levine 1987:vii).

It is an established fact that migration is an essential and widely accepted aspect of West Indian life. It is equally established that all West Indians—including Bahamians—are descendants of immigrants. Bahamians, like other West Indians, are dramatis personae who include descendants of European colonists, African slaves, indentured Asian laborers, Catholics, Protestants, Hindus, Muslims, Rastafarians and "Voodoo" adherents, planters and merchants, felons and pirates, all fashioned into a fasci-nating, restless tropical mélange. Historically, West Indian migration is rooted in the immediate post-Columbian period. During the first century of European colonization, groups of economic and political refugees and adventurers—mostly from the overpopulated seaports of Portugal, Spain, Holland, France, England, and Denmark—migrated to the West Indies.

Beginning in the post-Emancipation period, the West Indian Diaspora, fueled primarily by economic motives, expanded both interregionally and internationally. West Indian laborers went to newly developing neigh-boring territories such as Trinidad, Guyana, Cuba, and the Dominican Republic, and from these destinations to more distant destinations such as Panama and south Florida. After the world wars, many West Indian immigrants settled in Europe and North America. Traditionally, young men seasonally recruited as contract laborers dominated the movements. Since the 1960s, women have emerged as a significant immigrant labor group. Most West Indian migration focused on movements to major metropoles. Small groups, however, went to the Bahamas, where they significantly impacted politics, economics, and society.

The history of West Indian migration to the Bahamas is, in many instances, illustrated in the introductory statement excerpted from Barry B. Levine's *The Caribbean Exodus* (1987). The movement, although numerically small in comparison to migration to other destinations, is nonetheless vitally important to achieving a fuller appreciation for the history of the Bahamas. The Bahamian experience, when viewed as a microcosm of larger migration movements, demonstrates the social, economic, and political impact West Indian immigrants have had on receiving destinations. One experience, heretofore overlooked, is the impact that West Indian teachers had on the development of education in the outer islands during the 1950s and 1960s. The importance of their contribution to the development of the Bahamas is, perhaps, best demonstrated by the fact that, during the 1960s and 1970s, a number of mid-level and senior managers of public service and private sector institutions were once impressionable students of these pioneer educators.

In many instances, the West Indian educator was largely responsible for challenging his or her young charges to aspire to their highest goals. It is significant to note that this happened during a period in Bahamian history when many Bahamian parents were relatively uneducated and ignorant of the full importance of education. During the 1950s through the 1960s, most Bahamian parents placed more emphasis on the acquisition of technical skills than on formal education. Then, young men were prepared for manual and young women for domestic labor. The colonial government, on the other hand, was reluctant to overstimulate or fully satisfy the young inquiring minds for fear of cultivating aspirations that might challenge the political and social status quo.

Records of Bahamian history often understate or omit the important role immigrants play in the development of communities and industries. One example of this omission is that of Turks and Caicos Islanders in the development of the salt industry in the southern Bahamas and forestry in the northern islands. Regrettably, little is known (even by Bahamians) of Turks and Caicos Islanders' pioneering efforts in the development of communities in Grand Bahama and New Providence. Hopefully, further research in the near future will record the contribution of these immigrants to the development of such successful communities as Coconut Grove and Englerston in the south of New Providence. These suburbs were important avenues of upward social mobility for thousands of blacks wishing to escape from the old ghettos such as Over-the-Hill.

Arguably, no West Indian immigrant group in the Bahamas is larger, yet traditionally more maligned and socially castigated than Haitians. Paradoxically, no West Indian group is more highly valued in the Bahamas (albeit grudgingly) than Haitians. Theories have been offered to explain this phenomenon. Gordon K. Lewis, for example, in the foreword to Palmer (1990), stated rather simplistically that, "Haitians in the Bahamas are disliked because they do not speak English." Lewis attributed this attitude to cultural prejudice. It is probably more correct to state that among West Indian groups, Bahamians typically dislike Jamaicans. Generally, Bahamians (and most other West Indians) dislike (and perhaps fear) the assertiveness of the typical Jamaican they encounter. The antipathy exists largely because of a general unfamiliarity with, and ignorance of, the Jamaican psyche and history and the social and economic factors that compel people to cultivate assertive natures to survive in dynamic and overcrowded societies (Palmer 1990:xi). In reality, Bahamian intolerance toward Haitians transcends language differences. It should be emphasized, however, that it is erroneous to categorically state that Bahamians dislike Haitians. Bahamian discrimination against Haitians is primarily an expression of fear that overwhelming numbers of Haitian immigrants will eventually supplant Bahamian culture. The Haitian immigrant, in this respect, is perceived as an invading element who threatens to unravel the very fabric of Bahamian society through the introduction of infectious diseases, an unfamiliar language, foods, and strange customs. Equally threatening to the average Bahamian are the increasing demands that Haitians place on social institutions, such as medical facilities and schools. Most Bahamians complain (in some cases with justification) that access to these services is severely constrained by increased Haitian demands. Officials of the Ministry of Education complain about pressures on their limited resources created in part by the demands of Haitian immigrants. The officials praise Haitian parents for their response to the

educational needs of their children and faithful attention to school matters. They note, however, that some schools are becoming "saturated" with
Haitian students. Unofficially, some administrators claimed that Haitian
attendance at a few schools in Abaco Island was as high as 75 percent of
total enrollment.

An understanding of the Bahamian identity is key to understanding
Bahamian-West Indian relations. Bahamian society, culture, and identity
are constantly evolving. Although many Bahamians fear change and the
loss of "traditional culture," what is now "tradition" was once novel, as is
evident in the replacement of "white" standards and leadership by "black"
ones and "things British" with "things American." Bahamian identity, to a
large extent, is a complex concept that varies according to the social and
cultural values of the interpreter. Generally, Bahamian identity is shaped
by historical experiences. The various migrant groups that settled in those
islands, therefore, shaped those historical experiences. Understandably,
the more dominant (which were not necessarily the numerically superior)
groups influenced the perception of that identity more than others. The
migration of groups of Loyalists to the Bahamas during the 1700s, for example, typically characterized "the transformation of the islands by a new
and more progressive type of white colonist" (Craton 1992:179). Members
of this group rapidly assumed dominance over society, politics, and commerce in the country. Their values contributed significantly to the shaping
of a uniquely Bahamian identity.

Haitians migrate from a larger island, topographically, physically,
socially, politically, and economically different from the Bahamas. The
migrants, primarily French-patois speaking peasants from the impoverished northern sections of Haiti, are inheritors of a proud history of Black
Nationalism incubated in revolution, and possessors of an independence
sustained by a fervently proud will to remain socially and politically free.
Predominantly black, as opposed to mulatto, Haitians are socially, economically, and politically stratified by divisions of skin color and wide
disparities in the accumulation of and access to wealth. Since the 1790s,
Haitian history has demonstrated a continuous process of oppressive dictatorships, foreign intervention, and general political instability. Invariably, because many Haitian experiences have no parallels in the Bahamas, the immigrants generally experience difficulties adapting to their
new home. Ironically, unbeknown to most Bahamians and ignored by

many enlightened others, Haitian cultural heritage is inherently richer and enviably more diverse than the Bahamian cultural experience.

The beginnings of a Bahamian perception of Haitians may have been initiated in the late 1790s and early 1800s after groups of Haitian refugees fled to the Bahamas before the fury of the Haitian Revolution. Initially, the Bahamian elite were concerned by the possible political, social, and economic effects of the Haitian exodus. In 1797, after an alleged plot by the Haitians to capture Nassau and free the local slaves was discovered, Bahamians enforced restrictions on Haitian migration and deportations. Black Bahamians were taught to view black Haitians as inherently dangerous and bloodthirsty savages to be avoided and feared. Bahamian blacks were encouraged by rewards to spy on Haitians and report suspicions of social misconduct [GB/COR, Bahamas, CSOP. Hunt to Portland, 7 November 1797. no.35 (Bahamas/PRO, 1971), 97–99]. After 1804, anti-Haitian sentiment was further ingrained in the Bahamian psyche. The Bahamian elite feared that the colored Haitians would influence the growing local colored middle class with revolutionary ideas. They were equally concerned that the enterprising Haitians would challenge their monopoly as merchants and craftsmen [GB/COR, Bahamas, CSOP. Hunt to Portland, 7 November 1797. no.35 (Bahamas/PRO, 1971), 99]. Subsequently, most Haitians allowed to remain in the Bahamas were relocated from Nassau to islands on the fringes of the Bahamian archipelago and society.

Bahamians are an English-speaking people living in an archipelago that is geographically and topographically an extension of the southern section of the Florida peninsula. The people, in the absence of mountains, rivers, and large areas of arable land, have become largely dependent upon the resources of the sea and their geographical location to survive. Geographical proximity to the United States has largely influenced the Bahamian identity and made many Bahamians feel a cultural affinity to their neighbor to the north. In many respects, the Bahamian ideal of civilization is to become closely integrated into the North American value system. The process of "Americanization" is perpetuated by a huge, almost insatiable appetite for "things American" that causes Bahamians to spend millions of dollars in south Florida annually. Currently, the Bahamian lust for American consumer goods is sufficiently high to motivate some businesses in south Florida to accept Bahamian currency and to advertise in Bahamian newspapers and periodicals. Approximately 10 percent of the advertisements in the Bahamas telephone book are for businesses in Miami and Fort Lauderdale.

Since the 1770s, Bahamians have maintained a consistent level of economic and social contact with the southern United States that has never existed between the islands and the rest of the Caribbean. In the late 1880s, the islands were drawn closer into the United States' social, economic, and political hegemony by the emergence of tourism as a viable economic alternative to large-scale agriculture. Today, tourism and banking are the major industries in the Bahamas, affecting approximately 80 percent of all employment in the country. Natives play host to almost four million tourists (mostly from the United States) annually. With the advent and growth of tourism, the Bahamas is being slowly transformed into the southernmost of American suburbs. At the end of 1997, there were an estimated 15,000 hotel rooms and more than 400 financial institutions in the Bahamas [Bahamas Chamber of Commerce: Country Profile, 1997]. An advertisement in a Bahamian magazine demonstrates the gradual "Americanization" of the islands:

> English is spoken everywhere in the Bahamas; it is the principal language of the islands. Electricity is the North American standard 120 volt, 60 Herz alternating current (AC). . . . AT&T offers its USA Direct service for collect and credit card calls. . . . The Bahamian dollar (B$) is equal in value to the United States dollar and both are acceptable for cash payment. . . . Banks are open Monday through Thursday from 9:30 am until 3 pm and on Friday until 5 pm. . . . Should you run out of cash, Bahamian banks are interconnected with major U.S. systems that accept ATM cards and major credit cards that provide cash advances. (Hopkins 1998:8)

"Americanism" has produced a pseudo-identity of "West Indian elitism" in many Bahamians, an attitude of economic and, perhaps, social superiority exhibited toward other West Indians. Many Bahamians, ignorant of the history of their own labor migration, look with near contempt upon the traditional West Indian immigrants as labor journeymen persuaded to live in the Bahamas because life is supposedly better there. The Bahamas Ministry of Tourism advertisement slogans for the past decade have been "It's Better in the Bahamas" and "The Bahamas: It Keeps Getting Better." Few Bahamians realize that the average West Indian prefers to remain in his own familial environment, where he is surrounded by friends, relatives, and a familiar culture that allow him more control over his destiny than as an immigrant in a foreign land. Few realize that most West Indian immigrants, including Haitians, are economic and (to a lesser extent) political refugees who, if the economic and political environment in their respective countries became sufficiently stable, would probably return to their homes (Palmer 1990:7–9).

Regrettably, few West Indian immigrants to the Bahamas ever return to their native countries to live out their retirement years. One reason for this is that, generally, their children are also living in the Bahamas and have become fully assimilated. Also, many of their immediate relatives and friends in the homelands have either migrated to other countries or died. Ellen, a Barbadian immigrant living in the Bahamas with her family since the 1950s, noted in a May 28, 1997 interview with the author that only her father remains in Barbados. She stated that she is content to live in the Bahamas because her immediate family lives there and because during a recent and rare visit to Barbados, she discovered that her home village seemed distantly foreign. According to Ellen, "it had changed so much that I hardly knew anybody living there. Even the landmarks and landscape seems to have changed."

Bahamians complain that Haitian immigrants, through the continuous outflow of remittances, "drain" the country of valuable "hard currency" and encourage other Haitians to migrate to the Bahamas (Marshall 1979:116–117). Marshall said in 1979 that remittances were estimated at over three million dollars. She noted, however, that "the reliability of this estimate is low." Most consider this an unfair drain on the economic resources of the country. Admittedly, remittances strengthen perceptions about economic opportunities in the Bahamas and encourage migration. Few supposedly humanitarian Bahamians, however, consider (or apparently care about) the fact that most immigrants in a sending country are workers. Generally, most of the very young and old remain at home and rely heavily on remittances for basic sustenance. Few Bahamians realize (and some choose to forget) that, until the 1960s, they, their relatives, or friends were included in the tens of thousands of Bahamians who migrated mostly to destinations in south Florida as a part of the wider Caribbean migration movement. Few realize (or choose to admit) that remittances sent home during those years sustained many families and often formed the financial foundation of many Bahamian economic successes. Undoubtedly, remittances allowed many Bahamian families to relocate from rented, often dilapidated wooden houses in the ghettos such as Over-the Hill to newly built stone-framed homes in the suburbs south of Nassau.

Received information influences migration from the West Indies to the Bahamas as do life experiences and calculations about the economic future. It has already been established that the gravitational "pull" of a more economically stable environment—particularly when in close proximity to less progressive and stable economies—will draw a flow of workers. The evidence is overwhelming that the great majority of West Indians voluntarily migrate to the Bahamas for economic reasons. Information, however, has played a crucial role in the decision to migrate and the choice of destination. The typical sources of information have included friends and relatives already living in the considered destination, television, magazines, newspapers, and in some cases, potential employers. The early Guyanese policemen, for example, responded to recruitment advertisements placed on bulletin boards in ex-servicemen's entertainment centers. West Indian teachers responded to advertisements in local newspapers in their respective countries offering positions for teachers in the Bahamas. Some immigrants, like Jamaican-Bahamian Steve, responded to invitations from friends to seek employment in the islands. In a February 1998 interview with the author, Steve, a Jamaican-born departmental manager at one of the major newspapers in the Bahamas at the time of interview, stated that he came to Nassau during the late 1960s on the invitation of a friend. Others overheard stories recounted in barber shops, beauty salons, marketplaces, and other public gathering forums, of gilded opportunities for employment in the Bahamas and the relatively easy access to North America achievable from that country.

The future of Caribbean migration to the Bahamas, particularly Haitian immigration, is widely regarded in the Bahamas as an uncontrollable problem. The continuous influx of large groups of indigent people presents serious questions about public policies in the Bahamas, that may significantly affect the politics, society, and economy of the Commonwealth. Instead of fostering national assimilation into a pluralistic cultural mélange, immigration policies in the Bahamas have produced a multicultural society of socially, economically, and politically separate and unequal ethnic groups. The degree of inequality between different ethnic groups is demonstrated by the social inclusion of Turks and Caicos Island immigrants, and the social exclusion of Haitians. Regrettably, many Bahamian policymakers are not alert to the possible future ramifications of ethnic stratification, and the probability that the balance of the minority-majority status quo may eventually and, perhaps, irrevocably, shift toward economic, social, and political dominance by present-day minorities.

Hopefully, within the near future, Bahamian lawmakers will demonstrate a greater awareness of, and positive response to, the need to assimilate equally all West Indians, including Haitians, into every aspect of local political, cultural, and economic development. There is encouraging evidence that steps toward a more complete assimilation are underway. This is particularly noticeable in the growing public recognition of and appreciation for the contribution Haitians and other West Indians have made and continue to make to the development of the country. This is perhaps best demonstrated in the increasing number of Bahamians from the private and public sectors enrolled in *kweyole* language classes. Another positive sign is evident in the publication in a major local newspaper of a weekly *kweyole* column of news and current events in Haiti, written by an employee of the Haitian Embassy in the Bahamas and published each Monday in the *Nassau Daily Tribune*. The level of social acceptance of Haitians is again demonstrated in the integration of Haitian-Bahamians in local sports leagues and associations. Many Haitian-Bahamians have enhanced the assimilation process through marriage to Bahamians and the Anglicization of their names.

Today, large crowds of Bahamians of all ethnic backgrounds, without any apparent social distinction, gather shoulder-to-shoulder to see predominantly Haitian-Bahamian soccer teams compete against Bahamian and European expatriate teams in Sunday matches. Thousands of Haitian-Bahamians attend public and private schools or are employed in the public and private sectors and are totally unidentifiable from any other ethnic group. Haitian entrepreneurs, like florist Claude Fowler, photographer Antoine Ferriere, Mitch-the-Tailor, building contractor Rolland Lamour, lawyer Eliezer Regnier, and heavy equipment owner and operator Max Julian demonstrate the successful integration that some Haitian immigrants have achieved and will probably continue to achieve.

Almost imperceptibly, the identification of West Indian–Bahamians—including those of Haitian descent—is slowly shifting from a predominant emphasis on ethnic heritage to include social and economic acculturation and accomplishments. Perhaps this is a tangible, measurable indication that the balance of the minority-majority status quo is, indeed, shifting, and that the "Bahamian identity" jealously guarded for so many generations is being redefined by immigrant groups which include those West Indians traditionally excluded, isolated, and socially ignored.

Bibliography

Documentary Collections

The Bahamas

Annual Reports on Prisons, 1930–1973.

Annual Reports, Royal Bahamas Police Force, 1890, 1893, and 1908–1973.

Annual (Governor's) Reports for the Years 1965–1968.

Blue Books, 1892–1939.

Commissioner's Annual Reports for 1943–1953. Double General Index, 1927–1930.

Executive Council Minutes, 1760–1930.

Government Dispatches, 1890–1940.

Government High School Records, Special Collections, Department of Archives, Nassau, the Bahamas.

Governor-in-Council Records, 1750–1890.

House of Assembly Minutes, 1760–1970.

Moseley-Cuevas Collection, Special Collections, Department of Archives, Nassau, the Bahamas.

Nassau Quarterly Mission Papers, Special Collections, Department of Archives, Nassau, the Bahamas.

Report on Preliminary Survey of Existing Housing Conditions (August 1973).

Report of the Royal Commission appointed on the Recommendation of the Bahamas Government to Review the Hawksbill Creek Agreement, 1971 [also referred to as the "Wooding Report"].

Reports of the Vice-Admiralty Court, 1790–1810.

Society for the Propagation of the Gospel Papers, Special Collection, Department of Archives, Nassau, the Bahamas.

Summary of Manpower Utilization Survey in the Bahama Islands [also referred to as the "Clappe/Mayne Report"] 1968.

Votes of the House of Assembly, 1830–1860, and 1930–1973.

Wesleyan Methodist Mission Society Papers, Special Collections, Department of Archives, Nassau, the Bahamas.

Turks and Caicos Islands

Financial and Economic Position: Turks and Caicos Islands, 1900–1930. Report on the Salt Industry, 1802–1827.

Reports for the Years 1965–1967.

United States

Dispatches from the United States Consuls in Nassau, New Providence Island, 1821–1906.

Record group 59, microfilm edition, reel 24. National Archives, Washington, DC: US Government Printing Office.

Newspapers

Bahama Gazette, September 1793; January 1794; November 1796; August–September 1797; January and July 1799; January 1786.

Bahamian Times, January 1958; August 1967.

Miami Daily News and Metropolis, May 1907; June 12, 1909; June 24, 1924.

Miami Herald, April 13, 1909; June 24, 1924; July 6, 1926.

Nassau Guardian, September 1888; April-December 1926; August 1961; May 1961; January 1964; January-August 1967; June 1968; February 1969; May 1993.

Nassau Herald, July 1961; January-July 1966; July-August 1967.

Nassau (Daily) Tribune, November 1923; April and December 1924; April 1925; January-August 1927; July 1929; November 1930; January 1955; May-June 1957; May 1958; January 1959; May-June 1960; April-July 1967; July 1968; November 1969; January-July 1970; August 1971; January 1990; November 1992.

Palm Beach Post, July 29, 1921.

Royal Gazette, July 1804; July-August 1805; August-October 1828.

Interviews by the Author
(All interviewees have been granted pseudonyms)

Alfred. September 21, 1997.

Alma. July 2, 1997; September 23, 1997.

Andrew. April 14 and 18, 1992.

Anne. September 21, 1997.

Anton. September 13, 1997.

Archer. September 17, 1996.

Browns. September 13, 1996.

Carl. August 15; September 15, 1997.

Chester. September 13, 1997.

Dale. May 18, 1997.

Davis. September 20, 1996.

Dolton. May 18, 1997.
Edna. July 18, 1997.
Eliza. September 18, 1996.
Ellen. May 28, 1997.
Emile. April 15, 1992.
Francina. August 10, 1997.
Frank. August 15, 1997.
George. July 3, 1997.
Gwendolyn. February 16, 1998.
Harold. September 6, 1996.
Helen. February 16, 1998.
Henry. September 13, 1997.
James. February 14, 1998.
Jason. January 17, 1997.
Joan. September 17, 1996.
John. September 18, 1997.
Joseph. November 2, 1996.
Karen. December 11, 1996.
Kendrick. May 23, 1997.
Maxie. December 25, 1997.
Michael. January 29, 1998.
Miriam. September 18, 1996.
Neil. May 23, 1997.
Paul. December 17, 1997.
Pearl. August 13, 1997.
Perry. October 6, 1996.
Robert. October 24, 1996.
Roosevelt. February 14, 1998.
Rose. November 4, 1996.
Samuel. September 17, 1997.
Sandra. April 22, 1995.
Steve. February 7, 1998.
William. September 30, 1996.
Wilson. February 4, 1998.

Secondary Sources

Aarons, George Anthony. "Reconstructing the Canaye: An Exercise in Experimental Archaeology." *Journal of the Bahamas Historical Society*. (October 1991):20–25.
Abbott, Elizabeth. *Haiti: The Duvaliers and their Legacy*. New York: McGraw-Hill, 1988.
Albuquerque, Klaus de, and Jerome L. McElroy. "Bahamian Labour Migration." *New West Indian Guide* 60 (1986):167–203.
Albury, Paul. *Story of the Bahamas*. New York: St. Martin's Press, 1976.

Augier, F. R. *The Making of the West Indies*. London: Longmans, 1960.

Barratt, P.J.H. *Grand Bahama*. London: Macmillan Caribbean, 1982.

Beater, Lewis W. in the *Nassau Daily Tribune*, published on June 16, 1957 (1957:1–2).

Bethel, Ed. "The Bajan Connection." *Caribah* (Spring 1997):38–41.

Bethel, Patrick. "The Condition of Haitian Refugees as Illegal Immigrants in the Bahamas." Unpublished report, Grand Bahama, the Bahamas: Island Printers. 1992.

Bonacich, Edna. "A Theory of Middlemen." *American Sociological Review* 38 (1973):583–594.

Burns, Sir Alan. *Colonial Civil Servant*. London: G. Allen and Unwin, 1948.

Byron, Margaret. *Post War Caribbean Migration to Britain: The Unfinished Cycle*. London: Ashgate, 1994.

Caribbean Basin Databook. Washington, D.C: Caribbean/Latin American Action 1991.

Cash, Philip. *The Making of the Bahamas*. Kingston, Jamaica: Collins-Longman, 1992.

Cash, Philip, Shirley Gordon, and Gail Saunders. *The Sources of Bahamian History*. London and Basingstoke: Macmillan, 1991.

Chandler, A.A. "The Experience of Barbados." *Journal of the Barbadian Museum and Historical Society* 13 (1946):8–14.

Conniff, Michael. *Black Labor on a White Canal: Panama, 1904–1981*. Pittsburgh: University of Pennsylvania Press, 1985.

Cottman, Evans. *Out Island Doctor*. London: Haider and Stroughton. 1979.

Craton, Michael. *A History of the Bahamas*. New York, New York: Collins, 1962.

Craton, Michael, and Gail Saunders. *Islanders in the Stream: A History of The Bahamian People: From Aboriginal Times to the End of Slavery*. Athens: University of Georgia Press, 1992.

Cronon, E. David. *Black Moses: The Story of Marcus Garvey and the Universal Negro Improvement Association*. Madison: University of Wisconsin Press, 1969.

Diederich, Bernard. *Papa Doc: The Truth about Haiti Today*. New York: McGraw-Hill, 1987.

Diederich, Bernard, and Al Burt. *Papa Doc: Haiti and its Dictator*. London: Bodley Head, 1970.

Dodge, Steve. *Abaco: The Story of an Out Island and Its Cays*. Decatur, Illinois: White Sound Press, 1983.

Dunn, Richard S. *Sugar and Slaves: The Rise of the Planter Class in the English West Indies, 1624–1713*. New York and London: W. W. Norton, 1973.

Dupuch, Alfred. *The Tribune Handbook*. Nassau: Tribune, 1926.

Durrell, Zoe C. *The Innocent: Abaco in the Bahamas*. Battleboro: Durrell. 1972.

Eaton, George E., *Alexander Bustamante and Modern Jamaica*. Kingston, Jamaica: University of the West Indies Press, 1975.

Eneas, Cleveland W. *Baintown*. Nassau: Tripaul, 1976.

Ferguson, James. *Papa Doc, Baby Doc: Haiti and the Duvaliers*. New York: B. Blackwell, 1987.

Ferguson, Robert. "Too Loyal to Forsake Their Flag." *The Bahamas Handbook and Businessman's Journal*. Nassau: Etienne Dupuch, Jr. Publications, 1966, pp. 17–25.

Ferguson, Vincent. "The Impact of Non-Bahamian Teachers on Bahamian Education and a Process of Assimilation." Master's Thesis. Mankato College, 1974.

Fraser, Peter D. "British West Indians in Haiti in the late Nineteenth and Twentieth Centuries." *Immigrants and Minorities* 7, no.1 (March 1988):79–94.

Geggus, David. *Slavery, War, and Revolution: The British Occupation of Saint Domingue, 1793–1798.* Oxford, England: Oxford University Press, 1982.

Gmelch, George. *Double Passage: The Lives of Caribbean Migrants Abroad and Back Home.* Ann Arbor: University of Michigan Press, 1992.

Goode's World Atlas. Chicago: Rand McNally, 1996.

Granberry, Julian. "The Lucayans: Our First Residents." *The Bahamas Handbook and Businessman's Journal.* Nassau: Etienne Dupuch, Jr. Publications, (1973):22–30.

Grasmuck, Shem. "Migration within the Periphery: Haitian Labor in Dominican Sugar Cane and Coffee Industries." *International Migration Review* 16 (Summer 1982):368–79.

Guyana Fact Sheet, Department of Foreign Affairs and International Trade. Cooperative Republic of Guyana. December 1996. Embassy of Guyana, Washington, D.C.

Hall, Douglas. "The Flight from the Estates Reconsidered: The British West Indies, 1838–1942." *Journal of Caribbean History* 10, no. 11 (November 1978):7–22.

Hall, Douglas, Elsa Goveia, and Roy Augeir, eds. "Immigration into the West Indies." In *Chapters in Caribbean History.* Bridgetown, Barbados: Caribbean Universities Press. 1971.

Harvey, Stefano. *Nationalism and Identity: Culture and Imagination in a Caribbean Diaspora.* New York: St. Martins Press, 1996.

Henderson, Julie J. "Foreign Labor in the United States, 1942–1945." Ph.D. diss., University of Minnesota, 1945.

Higman, Barry W. *Slave Populations of the British Caribbean, 1807–1834.* Baltimore: The Johns Hopkins University Press, 1976.

Hill, Robert A., ed. *The Marcus Garvey and Universal Negro Improvement Association Papers.* 7 vols. Berkeley: University of California Press, 1983.

Holmes, C. *John Bull's Island: Immigration and British Society, 1871–1971.* London: Macmillan, 1988.

Hope, K. R. *Economic Developments in the Caribbean.* New York: Praeger, 1982.

Hopkins, Tom. "Getting to Know Paradise." *Paradise Islander* (Winter 1998):3–12.

Hunt, Alfred. *Haiti's Influence on Antebellum America: Slumbering Volcano in the Caribbean.* Baton Rouge: University of Louisiana Press, 1988.

Iglesias, Ramon. *Columbus, Cortes and Other Essays.* Translated and edited by Lesley B. Simpson. Berkeley: University of California Press, 1969.

Ireland, Jenny. "The Growing Respectability of the Bahamas" *The Banker* (December 1986):55–61.

James, Mike. "Uniting a Rainbow of Cultures." *Latin America Press* 28 no. 25 (July 1996):4–16.

James, Winston, and Clive Harris, eds. *Inside Babylon: The Caribbean Diaspora in Britain.* London: W.W. Norton, 1994.

Johnson, Doris. *The Quiet Revolution in the Bahamas.* Nassau: Family Island Press. 1972.

Johnson, Howard. "Barbadian Immigrants in Trinidad, 1870–1897." *Caribbean Studies* 13, (1973):5–20.

———. "Labor on the Move: West Indian Migration to the Bahamas, 1922–1930." Paper presented at the Conference on Dimensions of Latin American and Caribbean Migration. Chicago: University of Illinois, 15–17 November 1984.

———. *The Bahamas in Slavery and Freedom.* Kingston, Jamaica: Ian Randle, 1992.

Johnson, James Weldon. *Along the Way: The Autobiography.* New York: The Viking Press. 1933.

Jones-Henderson, S. B. "Movement of Caribbean Peoples." *Caribbean Affairs* 9 no. 3 (1989):34–37.

Keegan, William F. *The People Who Discovered Columbus: The Pre-History of the Bahamas.* Gainesville: University Press of Florida, 1992.

Kelly, M. Patricia Fernandez, and Al Portes. "Continent on the Move: Immigrants and Refugees in America." In *Americas: New Interpretive Essays.* Alfred Stepan, ed. New York and London: Oxford University Press, 1992.

Knox, Stephen. "The Men who Dug the Canal." *Caribbean and West Indies Chronicles* 100 (February/March 1985):23–26.

La Guerre, John. "The Moyne Commission and the West Indian Intelligentsia, 1938–39." *Journal of Commonwealth Political Studies* 13, no. 1 (1972): 134–57.

Laurence, K. O. "Immigration into Trinidad and British Guiana, 1834–1871." Unpublished Ph.D. diss., Cambridge University, 1958.

Levi, Darrell E. "Perspectives on Caribbean Migration." Unpublished manuscript in possession of author, 1980.

———. *The Poverty of Nations: Reflections on Underdevelopment and the World Economy.* Concord, MA: Pluto, 1991.

Levine, Barry B., ed. *The Caribbean Exodus.* New York: Praeger, 1987.

Lewis, Arthur W. *Labor in the West Indies: The Birth of a Workers's Movement.* London: New Beacon Books, 1938.

Lewis, Gordon K. *The Growth of the Modern West Indies.* New York: Monthly Review Press, 1968.

Malcolm, Harcourt. *Historical Documents Relating to the Bahama Islands.* Nassau: Nassau Guardian, 1910.

Marshall, Dawn. *The Haitian Problem: Illegal Migration to the Bahamas.* Kingston, Jamaica: University of the West Indies, 1979.

———. "The History of Caribbean Migrations: The Case of the West Indies." *Caribbean Review* 11 (Winter 1982):52–57.

———. "Emigration as an Aspect of the Barbadian Social Environment." *Caribbean Review* 16 (Summer 1986):6–14.

Martin, Tony. *The Pan-African Connection: From Slavery to Garvey and Beyond.* Cambridge: Harvard University Press. 1983

Masud-Piloto, Felix. *From Welcomed Exiles to Illegal Immigrants: Caribbean Migration to the United States. 1969–1995.* Boston and London: Rowman and Littlefield, 1996.

McRae, W. A. "The Fourth Census of the State of Florida Taken in the Year 1915." *Acts of the Legislature of 1915.* Tallahassee: Florida Department of Agriculture.

McWeeny, Sean. "The Haitian Problem in the Bahamas at the Close of the Eighteenth Century." *Journal of the Bahamas Historical Society* 16, no. 1 (October 1994): 2–10.

Miller, Herbert W. "The Colonization of the Bahamas, 1647–1670." *William and Mary Quarterly,* Third Series, 2 (1945):33–46.

Mintz, Sidney. *Caribbean Transformations.* New York: Columbia University Press, 1989.

Mohl, Raymond. "Black Immigrants: Bahamians in Early Twentieth-century Miami." *The Florida Historical Quarterly* (January 1986):271–97.

Moseley, Mary. *The Bahamas Handbook.* Nassau: Nassau Guardian, 1926.

Lord Moyne, Chair, Report of the West Indies Royal Commission. 1938–1939. London: Colonial Office Records, microfilm edition, 1945:10–11.

Murphy, Martin. *Dominican Sugar Plantations.* New York: Praeger, 1991.

Nash, Gary. "Forging Freedom: The Formation of Philadelphia's Black Community, 1720–1837." Master's thesis. Cambridge University, 1988.

Newton, Velma. "Aspects of British West Indian Emigration to the Isthmus of Panama." Unpublished paper presented at the Ninth Conference of Caribbean Historians, University of the West Indies, Bridgetown, Barbados, 1977.

Nicholls, David. *From Dessalines to Duvalier: Race, Colour, and National Independence in Haiti.* New Jersey, Rutgers University Press, 1996.

Ottley, C. R. *East and West Rescue Trinidad.* Port of Spain: Crusoe, 1975.

Pactor, Sidney Howard. "Communication in an Island Setting: A History of the Mass Media of the Bahama Islands, 1784–1956." Ph.D. diss., University of Tennessee, 1985.

Palmer, Ransford W. *The Jamaican Economy,* New York: Praeger, 1968.

———. *In Search of a Better Life: Perspectives on Migration from the Caribbean.* New York: Greenwood Publishing Group, 1990.

———. *Contemporary Caribbean Migration to the United States: The Economics of West Indian Migration to America.* New York: Praeger, 1995.

Pastor, R. A. *Migration and Development in the Caribbean.* Boulder, Colo.: Westview Press, 1985.

Patterson, S. *Dark Strangers: A Study of West Indians in London.* Harmondsworth, England: Penguin. 1965.

Peach, Ceri. *West Indian Migration To Britain.* New York and Cambridge: Cambridge University Press, 1990.

Perez, Jr., Louis. *Cuba : Between Reform and Revolution.* New York and London: Oxford University Press, 1988.

Peters, Thelma. "The American Loyalists and the Plantation Period in the Bahama Islands." Ph.D. diss., University of Florida, 1960.

Petras, Elizabeth, M. *Jamaican Labor Migration: White Capital and Black Labor.* Boulder, Colorado: Westview Press, 1988.

Phillips, Carol. *The Final Passage.* New York: Random House, 1995.

Pluck, Will. "Life Members of the Association." *Pepperpot* (April 1997):1–6.

Pratt, C. G., and Morris Simmons. *History of the Royal Bahamas Police Force, 1840–1990.* Nassau: Gold Coast Graphics, 1990.

Pusey, J. H. *Handbook of the Turks and Caicos Islands*. Kingston, Jamaica: Colonial Publishing, 1989.

Powells, L. D. *Land of the Pink Pearl or Recollections of Life in the Bahamas*. London: St. Dunston's House, 1888.

Richardson, Bonham C. *Caribbean Migrants: Environment and Human Survival on St. Kitts and Nevis*. Knoxville: University of Tennessee Press, 1983.

Roberts, George. *The Population of Jamaica*. Cambridge: Cambridge University Press, 1975.

Rumbold, Angela. "Britain's Ethnic Minority Community." *The Courier* No. 129 (September–October 1991):52–55.

Saunders, Gail. *Bahamian Society After Emancipation*. Kingston: Ian Randle Publishers, 1994.

Saunders, Hartley. *The Other Bahamas*. Nassau: Bodab Publishers, 1991.

Sharer, C. "The Population Growth of the Bahama Islands." Ph.D. diss., University of Michigan, 1960.

Shattuck, G. B. *The Bahama Islands*. Baltimore: Johns Hopkins Press, 1905.

Singham, A. W. *The Hero and the Crowd in a Colonial Polity*. New Haven: Yale University Press, 1968.

Smith, Hosay. *A History of the Turks and Caicos Islands*. Hamilton. Bermuda: Island Press, 1968.

Smith, R. T. *British Guiana*. London and Oxford: Oxford University Press, 1962.

Smith, Whitney. *Bahamian Symbols: The First Five Centuries*. Nassau: Government Printing Department. 1986.

Soest, Jan Van. "The World on an Island: The International Labour Force of Shell in Curacao, 1915–1960." Unpublished Paper presented at the Ninth Conference of Caribbean Historians, University of the West Indies, Bridgetown, Barbados. 1977.

Stark, James H. *Stark's History and Guide to the Bahama Islands*. Boston: Plimpton Press. 1891.

Stephens, Evelyn Huber, and John D. Stephens. *Democratic Socialism in Jamaica*. Princeton: Princeton University Press, 1986.

Stone, Carl, and Aggrey Brown, eds. *Perspectives on Jamaica in the Seventies*. Kingston, Jamaica: Jamaica Publishing House, 1981.

Thomas-Hope, Elizabeth. "The Establishment of a Migration Tradition: British West Indian Movements to the Hispanic Caribbean in the Century after Emancipation." In *Caribbean Social Relations*. Colin G. Clark, ed. Liverpool: University of Liverpool, 1978.

Tinker, Keith L. "Nassau and Blockade Running." Master's thesis. Boca Raton: Florida Atlantic University, 1982.

Trouillot, Michel-Rolph. *Haiti, State Against Nation: Origins and Legacy of Duvalierism* New York, Monthly Review Press, 1990.

Watkins, F. H. "Turks & Caicos Islands: Report on the Salt Industry, 1802–1827." (Bahamas/PRO. 1971), 10.

West Indian and Caribbean Yearbook. London: Thomas Skinner, 1987.

Wickham, John. "The Thing about Barbados." *Journal of the Barbados Museum and Historical Society* 35 (1975):223–30.

Williams, Patrice. "The Separation of the Turks and Caicos Islands from the Bahamas, 1848." *Journal of the Bahamas Historical Society* 11, no. 1 (October 1989):10–16.

Wood, Peter H. *Black Majority; Negroes in Colonial South Carolina from 1670 through the Stono Rebellion.* New York: Knopf, 1974.

Wylly, William. *A Short Account of the Bahama Islands.* London, 1789.

Index

Keith L. Tinker is director of the National Museum of the Bahamas and adjunct professor of Caribbean history at the College of the Bahamas.